7 <u>95</u>

D1236651

MICROECONOMIC ANALYSIS

MICROECONOMIC ANALYSIS

ALLAN J. BRAFF

University of New Hampshire

JOHN WILEY & SONS, INC.

NEW YORK · LONDON · SYDNEY · TORONTO

Library of Congress Catalog Card Number: 68-54910
SBN 471 09540 0
Printed in the United States of America

To Carol and Peter

Preface

This book was written to make the reader aware of the intellectual substance and excitement of microeconomic analysis. I have tried to avoid overemphasizing mechanics and terminology, to point out possibilities for extension and application of theory, and to keep very clear the distinction between normative economic theories, which indicate "what might be if" and positivistic economic theories, which attempt description and prediction.

I explain in the text the limitations of this type of analysis, and claim no more than is warranted. The conventional subject matter of microeconomic theory has been peculiarly insensitive to changes in the "real" world, but slowly the theory has been modified and extended. The central problems of microeconomics—valuation, allocation of resources, and distribution of income—remain relevant and important.

Microeconomic Analysis is not for everyone, but I hope it will be useful to: (1) any educated person who is willing to make an effort to obtain more than a superficial knowledge of the operation of a market economy; (2) undergraduates, particularly those preparing for graduate studies in economics, business administration, or industrial engineering; and (3) first-year graduate students whose primary undergraduate discipline was not economics.

The material is self-contained, but it will be less difficult for those who have done some introductory reading in economics. Any mathematics more difficult than high school algebra is relegated to footnotes. Certain more advanced sections, as indicated in the text, may be omitted without any interruption in the development of the main argument. The bibliographical material is extensive and should be helpful to students wishing to go beyond the necessarily limited horizons of a textbook.

The text contains extended discussions of imperfect markets, the problem of identification, stability conditions, the process of adjustment to equilibrium, the integration of classical utility theory with indifference curve analysis, behavioral theories of the firm, general equilibrium, and welfare economics. Topics such as futures markets, learning theory, bilateral monopoly, game theory, input-output, cost-of-capital, social welfare function, and linear programming are discussed in the contex of their relationship to microeconomic analysis.

* * *

For their very helpful comments during the writing of this book, I wish to thank Professor R. W. Pfouts, who read critically the early drafts; Professors J. H. Keith, Jr., Trout Rader, and T. J. Whalen, who read and commented on later drafts; and my colleagues at the University of New Hampshire Lawrence Cole, John Donovan, James Horrigan, John Korbel, Sam Rosen, and Kenneth Rothwell, who gave freely of their time and advice.

My special thanks to Gilbert R. Whitaker, Jr., and Dwayne Wrightsman for their scholarly and friendly suggestions and encouragement, and to Gerald T. Papke, who provided most able assistance as editor.

I have a long-standing debt to Professor Martin Bronfenbrenner, who kindly offered to read the manuscript of the chapter on Income Distribution, and who first aroused my interest in this subject and many others.

My students at Northwestern University and the University of New Hampshire have used early drafts of this book, and have offered much helpful criticism. Jacques Artus and Wolfgang Berger provided capable research assistance.

And since even an economic man is not a completely rational and efficient animal, I owe an extraordinary debt to the secretarial services of Florence M. Byrne and others who helped me work and rework early drafts of the manuscript.

Allan J. Braff

Dublin, Ireland
1968

Contents

MICROECONOMIC ANALYSIS

1

Introduction

It is unlikely that man would have survived if each individual or even each family unit had remained self-sufficient. Instead of undertaking all tasks, man devised methods of organizing production whereby the various tasks were divided among the community. As the production process became more complex and people began to specialize in certain skills and to divide their labor among a great many products, a system of distribution more elaborate than simple barter or exchange of goods was needed. Before a man prepared himself to become a maker of pin heads, he needed some assurance he would be able to secure food, clothing, and shelter. Money provided a basis for supporting more complex ways of organizing production and distributing consumer goods to households.

In a complex industrial economy, services are rendered not in exchange for some consumable commodity but for money income, distributed to the owners of resources—labor, raw materials, land, and capital. The money income earned in the production process is exchanged for "real" income—the goods and services produced. The proceeds from the sale of these products is distributed to owners of the resources that contributed to production.

Today's complex industrial economy appears quite remote from the simpler, self-sufficient societies of the past. Specialization of task and division of labor have greatly increased our capacity to provide goods and services, but the complex, ever-changing production processes drastically alter the fabric of society and challenge our ability to master what we create.

Functions Common to All Economic Systems

There is great variety and ingenuity in the systems people have devised to perform the primary economic functions of producing and distributing

1

economic goods. Each economic system in its own way tries to solve the central economic problem of allocating scarce resources among alternative ends. The ends are the goods and services the economy can produce. Resources are scarce because people's wants are not easily satisfied, if not insatiable. Consumers desire more purchasing power for private goods, and citizens desire more and better public goods. Amidst the myriad of institutional mechanisms, we can identify three extreme forms of control: decision by central authority, by tradition, and by an automatic control mechanism. Most contemporary societies utilize some combination of the three forms of control.

All economic systems, whatever the method of control, must resolve the central economic problem and perform the necessary functions related to the production and distribution of goods and services.

Production encompasses certain central questions. What goods are to be produced? How are resources to be employed in producing "what goods"? When? How rapidly? Even to begin to answer these questions requires some understanding of how goods are chosen and how resources are allocated and organized in the particular society.

Production, abstractly defined, is the transformation of basic resources to create value. Production must be broadly interpreted to include a great range of tasks and processes which are of value to someone. For example, production includes mining and processing iron to make the steel parts in an automobile, training the people involved, financing the various operations, transporting the intermediate and final products, marketing and insuring the automobile. These tasks and many more are value-adding, and part of the process of producing an automobile. Most production processes utilize capital: building, machines, tools, even accumulated stocks of goods. Capital is the result of a time-consuming embodiment of labor and natural resources intended to improve the productiveness of more primary resources. Educating people and building factories are examples of investment in human and nonhuman capital. Ultimately, if the investment is worthwhile, the roundabout capital-using method of production will be more productive than the simpler, more direct method.

The question of when to produce, now or at some future time, is of considerable importance to a world growing in population and constantly striving to improve its capacity to fulfill peoples' wants. Investment in capital usually involves some sacrifice, some deployment of resources away from the production of consumer goods and toward the production of capital goods, in order to increase future capacity to produce consumer goods. This is always true if all resources are currently fully employed. Resources must then be released from present tasks to produce new capital goods. This is a time-consuming process where the gain is not immediate. It is undertaken because there is a prospect of net gain. The rewards are future rewards.

Distribution is another common function of economic systems. How are the end products of the production process distributed? For whom is the "real income" produced? In theory the distribution process could be independent of the production process. There could conceivably be some random device, or an egalitarian system, or a hierarchical system based on tradition or authority to distribute the goods produced. In a market economy, distribution is based principally on the incomes earned in the production process. The incomes reflect the contribution of the resources to production and provide the principal incentive to produce.

Economy

The goods and services desired by consumers are the ends toward which the private economy is directed. The resources are allocated according to the dictates of "consumer sovereignty," where the consumer guides the determination of what goods are to be produced, as contrasted to "citizens sovereignty," where political decisions are in the public sector. If resources were available in abundance, many of the tasks of economists would disappear; the function of "economy"—the efficient allocation of scarce resources—would become superfluous.[1] Also, if the ends—public or private—are not "well" chosen, efficiency and economy in achieving these ends cannot be very important. But who is to decide whether an end is "well" chosen? Obviously the procedure through which decisions are made is of great significance. The importance of economics derives from the process by which the ends are chosen, and the scarcity of resources relative to these "well chosen" ends.[2]

Whereas our major concern is with the private sector and with the way decisions by "micro" units (households and businesses) are made and transmitted, it is evident that a great many of the decisions concerning the production and distribution of goods and the allocation of re-

---

[1] There have been times in recent history when the problem of the employment of unemployed resources has taken priority over the problem of how to allocate scarce resources efficiently.

[2] Economists are aware of a certain "dependence effect," where the process of satisfying wants creates wants; some have used this lack of independence as an argument for rejecting consumer preferences as an ultimate criterion for community welfare.

sources are not private decisions. Public goods, including schools, roads, parks, hospitals, and missiles, often vie with private goods for the scarce resources. Most often in the American economy, governmental decisions to provide public goods involve purchases from private producers, as in the federal government's road construction and urban renewal programs.

On the other hand the provision of goods by private producers in response to consumer preferences is not free from the influence and regulation by governmental bodies. Examples are commonplace: prohibition of the sale of commodities judged to be harmful, special excise taxes on selected commodities considered to be relatively undesirable, price regulation, licensing, blue laws, public standards.

Although there are many qualifications to be made, the American economy is primarily market oriented. The composition of goods and services provided is principally the result of private decisions transmitted through a network of private markets. The consumer is sovereign and free choice is permitted within limits.

In this book we are primarily concerned with the impersonal control mechanism: the price system, and how it works under a variety of conditions. We begin with an examination of the microeconomic behavior of particular households and firms in a private enterprise economy, and then consider the results of goal-directed individual activities coordinated by a price system that transmits information through interconnecting markets.

On Theory and Methodology

A theoretical argument is always hypothetical. It involves a conditional statement. Certain conclusions can be deduced *if* certain premises (postulates or behavioral assumptions) hold true. Often there are implicit assumptions regarding the institutional environment. The theoretical argument contains parameters or data which are taken as fixed; it contains exogenous variables whose values are determined outside the particular model; and it contains endogenous variables, whose values are implied by the premises of the model.

Theory implies abstractions selected from the complexity of economic phenomena. Theory simplifies and sacrifices descriptive realism to gain understanding. The goals of theory are explanation and prediction. Some have argued that the ability to predict is the only goal, and the ultimate test of a theory is how well it fits the facts—the empirical verification of its conclusions and implications.[3]

Others have taken a more moderate position and worry over the realism of assumptions. To interpret the conclusions and assess the applicability and relevance of the theory with some confidence, they require that the assumptions be "reasonably" realistic.

A theory to be tested and found dependable must be somewhat general. It must apply to more than one unique set of events. Its assumptions must sacrifice some detail and concentrate on relevant aspects of reality if the implications of the theory are to be generally useful.

A normative theory has another purpose beyond predictability. A normative theory is prescriptive, indicating what ought to be if certain goals are to be met. A normative theory examines what facts and postulates are implied by the objectives of the theory. Then, if the existing facts do not "fit," we must alter the facts or conditions to achieve the objectives.

A positive theory must be refutable empirically. If without sacrificing generality, a better theory is found that corresponds more closely to the facts, the old theory should be modified or replaced.

There is also a place for hypothetical models that abstract so much from reality that they are not easily tested. They explain specific phenomena without being of direct predictive help. Such theories explain economic phenomena under idealized conditions and provide standards for judging. They may be of considerable prescriptive value.

The economist's methodological predilections explain to a considerable extent his assessment of the theory of perfect competition and other market models we shall examine. The model of a perfectly competitive economy can be considered in the light of any of the three methodological categories.

---

[3] Milton Friedman has emphasized this positivist position by asserting that the assumptions of a theory are never descriptively realistic (the realism of assumptions is irrelevant) and the only test of hypotheses (assumptions) is an indirect one: Do the assumptions imply predictions which are sufficiently good approximations for the purpose at hand? Milton Friedman, "The Methodology of Positive Economics," *Essays in Positive Economics, University of Chicago Press,* Chicago, 1953, pp. 1–43.

2

Demand Analysis

Of primary importance in a market economy is the role of the tastes and preferences of consumers (households) in determining what goods are to be produced and in what amounts. Final demand for goods by households and costs of supplying goods by profit-seeking producers jointly determine market prices. Let us begin by devising means of describing the individual consumer's behavioral response to changes in prices and money income.

A certain primacy is often attached to tastes as the cornerstone of the analysis of resource allocation in a market economy. And yet only rarely does the economist focus his attention on the determinants of taste, or on the possibilities of influencing and evaluating individuals' tastes and preferences. He is of course aware that the tastes and preferences of people change with changes in demographic factors, education, information, and experience. He is aware too of product innovations and selling activities directed toward the manipulation and modification of consumer preferences and behavior. As a starting point, however, we assume consumer preferences are stable and independent of price changes, and that consumers attempt to satisfy their preferences.

Individual Consumer Behavior

With tastes fixed, and independent of prices in a given time period, the individual's rate of purchase of commodity $X(x)$ can be expressed as a function of the price of $X(p_x)$, the price of all other commodities (p_y), and money income (m). Using these symbols we can write the consumer's demand function for X:

$$x = f(p_x, p_y, m) \tag{2.1}$$

6

This equation means that the consumer, given the values of the independent variables $(p_x,\ p_y,$ and $m)$ will purchase a certain quantity of X in a given period of time. The x is a flow or rate of purchase per specified time period. The x/t is used in the diagrams as a reminder that the time period must be specified before x is meaningful.

In analyzing the consumer's response to changes in price and income, we look first at the partial relationship between the consumer's rate of purchase of X and each of the independent variables taken individually, with the values of all other variables assumed constant. This condition—that the values of all related variables are taken as constant while we examine the effects of a particular variable on the dependent variable (x in Eq. 2.1) is often referred to as the *ceteris paribus* condition.

Demand Curve

The relationship between the rate of purchase of X and the price of X illustrated in Fig. 2.1 is called a demand curve. It depicts the partial relationship:

$$x = f(p_x) \tag{2.2}$$

at a certain point in time, with other prices, income, and taste assumed constant.

The demand curve for the individual consumer simply describes his willingness to make certain rates of purchase at a particular time as

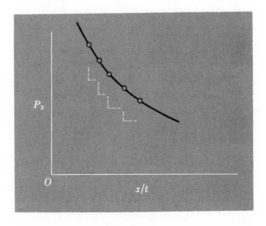

Fig. 2.1

a function of price.[1] So often has this inverse relationship been observed that the negative slope of the demand curve is referred to as the *law of demand*. Although the relationship is often drawn as if it were continuous (a smooth curve), the response to changes in price for a given individual is more likely to proceed in lumps or steps (the dashed line in Fig. 2.1).

Market Demand

The discontinuities in individual demand curves will tend to be smoothed away when the market demand curve for the commodity is considered. The market demand curve is the sum of individual rates of purchase at various market prices: $\Sigma x = f(p_x)$. While the negative slope of the market demand curve has been verified empirically, we shall discover later that there are exceptional situations where the demand curve relationship need not be inverse. For operational purposes—notably forecasting—demand analysis begins with the statistical specification of market demand.

The individual or the market demand curve may shift as a result of changes in other prices, income, or taste. A change in the rate of purchase of X as a response to a change in the price of X is a movement along a demand curve. It does not mean that "demand" has changed or shifted. The distinction is illustrated in Fig. 2.2. The move from A to B in response to a change in p_x is not considered a change in demand, only in the quantity demanded. The change from A to C is a change in demand. It represents a shift in the demand function resulting from a change in one or more of the underlying variables: prices of other commodities, income, or taste.

Market Demand: Qualifications

In aggregating individual demand functions to derive the market demand function, it is plausible to argue that the whole is not merely the sum of the parts. Another way of expressing this is to point out that individual demand functions are not always independent of each other. The satisfaction an individual derives from a particular purchase may not be solely related to the functional aspects of the product. There may

[1] Contrary to mathematical convention, price—the independent variable—is measured on the vertical (ordinate) scale in economic literature.

be elements of conspicuous consumption or "keeping ahead of the Smiths" or "keeping up with the Joneses." The dependence effect may be thought of as an external economy or diseconomy of consumption, which is to say: If others buy precisely the same car you buy, your satisfaction may be more or less than if they had not. In the analysis that follows, we shall suppose that individual demand functions are independent of each other. The market demand is, then, simply the sum of individual rates of purchase at various prices.

We shall assume, too, that the consumers respond to each price or price change as if it were final—the elasticity of expectation is zero. A price change does not set up expectations of further change.

Cross-Demand: Rate of Purchase as a Function of the Price of Other Commodities

The shift in demand from A to C in Fig. 2.2 might have been due to a change in the price of some other commodity with the price of X fixed. This cross-demand relationship, $x = f(p_y)$, illustrated by a shift in the demand curve in Fig. 2.2, can be represented directly, as in Fig. 2.3.

A positively sloping cross-demand relationship indicates that commodities X and Y are economic substitutes. For example, beef and pork are economic substitutes if, as pork prices increase, more beef (but less pork) is purchased. If the commodities are substitutes in consumption,

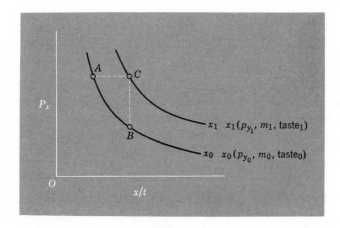

Fig. 2.2

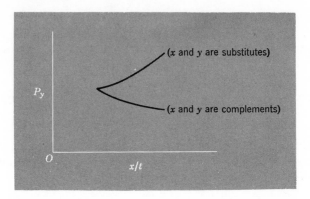

Fig. 2.3

the price of Y and the rate of purchase of X move in the same direction—the slope of the cross-demand curve is positive.

Two commodities are said to be economic complements if an increase in the price of Y induces a decrease in the rate of purchase of X. An example of this inverse relationship might be gasoline and automobile tires, or bread and butter. Where a change in the price of Y induces no behavioral response with respect to the rate of purchase of X, the commodities may be assumed to be neutral or unrelated to each other. Given sufficient time and careful scrutiny, an initial judgment of neutrality may turn out to be premature in an economy where all commodities, however remotely related, compete for consumers' income.

Money Income

The income curve relationship is sketched in Fig. 2.4. When the slope is positive the commodity is identified as a "normal" good; the slope is negative for "inferior" goods. The same commodity may be "normal" and "inferior" at different values of income, as illustrated in Fig. 2.4. As an example, let us take wine of inferior quality. As income increases slightly, the rate of purchase increases, but as income increases to still higher levels, the rate of purchase begins to decrease in favor of better quality wine.

This relationship between money income and rate of purchase is often referred to as an Engel curve after Ernst Engel, who investigated empirically the incomes and food purchases of Belgian workers. On the basis of family budget studies, Engel concluded that the proportion of income spent on food decreases as the household's income increases. This result is sometimes called Engel's law.

Two points should be clarified. First, although the proportion spent on food was found to decrease as income increased, food was not an inferior good. To be an inferior good, the rate of purchase must bear an inverse relationship to income. Particular kinds of food—lower grades of meat or potatoes—are more likely to qualify as inferior goods than the broader category including all food.

Second, real income varies inversely with the prices of commodities purchased. Later we shall analyze the income effect of price changes on the rate of purchase. Even where the income effect on the rate of purchase is negative, as is the case with inferior goods, the income effect of a price change is unlikely to dominate the substitution effect, which refers to the tendency to substitute relatively lower-priced goods for higher-priced substitutes. The expected inverse relationship between price and the rate of purchase can, as we shall see, be viewed as the result of two components—the substitution and income effects of a price change.

Elasticity

The shapes of the relationships just discussed are typically described by elasticities. Elasticity is a measure of the responsiveness of one variable to changes in another. We define elasticity generally as the ratio of the relative change in one variable to the relative change in the

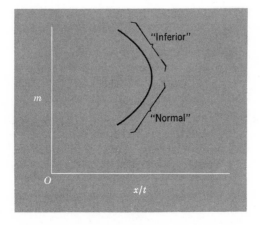

Fig. 24

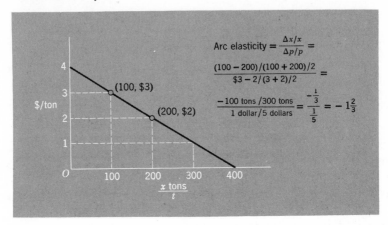

Fig. 2.5

other variable. Two points on a demand curve give us a basis for measuring arc elasticity, which is the measure of average price elasticity between two points. In Fig. 2.5, suppose the two points (100,$3) and (200,$2) are estimates of rates of purchase of commodity X (in tons) at the two prices of X (in $'s).

Elasticity is a measure of response independent of the units of measure. The units (in the above example: dollars and tons) cancel, since we measure the *relative* changes in the two variables.[2] To calculate arc elasticity, we compute the "change in" (Δ) each variable and divide the Δ by the arithmetic mean of each variable ($\bar{x}$ and $\bar{p}$) to find the relative changes.

Price elasticity of demand gives us a convenient basis for comparing consumer responsiveness to price changes in different product markets, even though the units of measure may vary between products.

In the extreme case where consumers made no adjustment in their rate of purchase in response to a change in price, demand would be zero elastic with respect to price. Given sufficient time to respond, this

---

[2] In terms of calculus, if the function $x = f(p_x)$ is given, point elasticity (e) can be defined as

$$e = \frac{dx/x}{dp/p} = \frac{p}{x} \cdot \frac{dx}{dp}$$

where dx/dp is the reciprocal of the slope of the conventional demand curve with price on the vertical axis and quantity on the horizontal axis. Price and quantity are both positive, and elasticity takes the same sign as does the slope. If the slope is negative (law of demand), the price elasticity of demand will be negative.

extreme value would be unlikely for an individual's demand and very unlikely indeed for a market composed of many individual demands. At the other extreme we have an infinitely elastic demand, where the slightest price change triggers an infinitely large change in the rate of purchase.

We would expect larger numerical values of price elasticity, the closer are available substitutes. Copper and aluminum are both reasonably good conductors of electricity. The demand for copper tends to be elastic, because aluminum is a good substitute for copper in most uses.

Reasoning from the principle that demand will be more elastic the closer are available substitutes, we would expect demand to be more elastic the greater the variety of uses for the product. Besides being a good conductor of electricity, aluminum is a rather light metal that is used in the construction of airplanes, automobiles, boats, and buildings. A decrease in the price of aluminum makes it relatively more attractive with respect to substitutes in each of its uses.

Less reliable, since they depend so much on the particular situation, are the following frequently mentioned rules: first, demand tends to be more elastic, the smaller the importance of the product in the consumer's budget—salt and mustard are examples; second, the more dispensable the product, the greater the elasticity—an often used example is the indispensability of insulin to a diabetic. Both of these rules are derived from the primary principle relating to the availability of substitutes or alternatives in the particular situation.

There is a time dimension to elasticity that must not be overlooked. The long-run demand curve assumes that adjustment to a price change is complete, that sufficient time has elapsed for the information to be generally known. Time is necessary to overcome habit and familiarity of old buying patterns. In cases where a product is used in conjunction with some more durable product, the long-run demand will depend on the adjustment of the stock of the more durable complementary product—for example, the response to a change in the price of oil for home heating will depend on the adjustment of the stock of oil burners.

Of particular importance is the direct relationship between price elasticity of demand and total revenue (or total expenditure). Total revenue TR equals unit price p times quantity purchased q. As price decreases and quantity increases along a negatively sloping demand curve, total revenue will increase, remain constant, or decrease, depending on elasticity. Marginal revenue MR is by definition the change in total revenue per unit change in quantity: $MR = \Delta TR / \Delta q$. Average revenue AR is total revenue divided by quantity: $AR = TR/q$. If a uniform price is charged, $p = AR$.

Table 2.1

Units Sold (tons)	Unit Price ($s)	Total Revenue ($s)	Average Revenue ($s)	Marginal Revenue ($)	Arc Elasticity
0	4	0	—	—	—
100	3	300	3	3	−7
200	2	400	2	1	−5⁄3
300	1	300	1	−1	−3⁄5
400	0	0	0	−3	−1⁄7

If price elasticity is greater than 1,[3] then the relative increase in quantity sold is by definition greater than the relative decrease in price. Total revenue increases as quantity increases and price decreases, if the price change occurs in the elastic region of the demand curve. If the price decrease takes place in the inelastic portion of the demand curve (when $|e| < 1$), the total revenue will decrease (MR will be negative). In this case the relative response of quantity sold is not sufficient to offset the relative decrease in price, so total revenue declines.

The exact relationship between price elasticity of demand, price, and marginal revenue is

$$MR = p\left(1 + \frac{1}{e}\right) \tag{2.3}[4]$$

Marginal revenue here applies to changes in total revenue for positive changes in quantity.

---

[3] We refer here to the absolute numerical value of elasticity $|e|$. We noticed previously that elasticity takes the sign of the slope of the function. Since all known demand curves are negatively sloping, we shall assume elasticity e is negative (or that $−e$ is positive).

[4] This relationship is easily derived for infinitesimal changes in quantity. Take the derivative of the total revenue function with respect to q (which is by definition marginal revenue):

$$MR = \frac{d\,(TR)}{dq} = \frac{d\,(pq)}{dq} = p + q\frac{dp}{dq}$$

Marginal revenue equals price (average revenue) plus quantity times the slope of the demand curve. Since point elasticity is by definition $e = p/q \cdot dq/dp$, by multiplying numerator and denominator of the last term by p, we obtain the result that

$$MR = p + p\left(\frac{q}{p}\frac{dp}{dq}\right) = p\left(1 + \frac{1}{e}\right)$$

In Fig. 2.6a, we see that MR = 0 if $e = -1$ (unitary elasticity). Equation 2.3 confirms our suspicion that if the relative decrease in price is counterbalanced exactly by the relative increase in quantity, there will be no change in total revenue. If total revenue (total expenditure) were unchanged at all prices, unitary elasticity would prevail throughout the demand curve.[5]

If an inelastic portion of the demand curve applies, say $e = -0.5$, MR $= p[1 + 1/-0.5] = p(-1)$, we see that total revenue will decrease. When demand is elastic, say $e = -2.0$, marginal revenue would be positive.

---

[5] A demand curve with constant elasticity would be a hyperbole of the general form $q = c/p^a \ (= cp^{-a})$, where a and c are constants and the exponent a is the price elasticity.

Proof. Taking the derivative of this function $q = cp^{-a}$ with respect to p, multiplying by p/q and substituting cp^{-a} for q, we get an expression for price elasticity in terms of p:

$$q = xp^{-a}$$

$$\frac{dq}{dp} = -acp^{-a-1}$$

$$e = \frac{p}{q}\frac{dq}{dp} = \left(\frac{p}{cp^{-a}}\right)(-acp^{-a-1}) = -a$$

If $a = 1$, this function reduces to $dp = c$, a rectangular hyperbole with total revenue = constant (c).

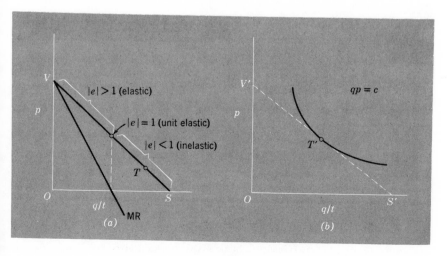

Fig. 2.6

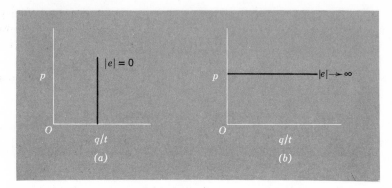

Fig. 2.7

Since $e = p/q \times 1/\text{slope}$, it follows that a linear demand curve ($p = a + bq$) with constant slope b does not yield constant elasticity throughout, since p/q varies. (See Fig. 2.6a and notice that p/q varies along the linear demand curve.)

A graphic measure of point elasticity at, say, point T in Fig. 2.6a can be obtained by dividing TS by TV. If TS is $\frac{1}{5}$ of TV, $|e| = 0.2$ at point T. (The simple geometric proof is not given.) This method applies as well to nonlinear functions by drawing a straight line tangent to the curve at a particular point (see the dashed line tangent to point T' in Fig. 2.6b, which depicts a rectangular hyperbole, $p = TR/q$ with $e = -1$ at any point on the curve, so if the curve is accurately sketched, $T'S' = T'V'$.[6]

The extremes of absolute inelasticity ($e = 0$) and infinite elasticity ($|e| \to \infty$) are illustrated in Figs. 2.7a and 2.7b. Zero elasticity over a very large price range is unlikely, even for the most urgently desired commodity. The infinitely elastic demand curve is the perfectly competitive firm's demand curve (as we shall see later).

Cross-Elasticity of Demand

Cross-elasticity of demand (e_{xp_y}) measures the shape of the cross-demand relationship: $q_x = f(p_y)$. It is defined as the relative change in the rate

---

[6] The logarithm of both sides of $p = TR/q^a$ yields $\log p = \log TR - a \log q$, whose logarithmic form is linear. If such a function with constant elasticity a were plotted on a rectangular coordinate system with logarithmic spacing on both axes, it would appear linear.

of purchase of one good divided by the relative change in the price of another good:

$$e_{xp_y} = \frac{\Delta q_x/q_x}{\Delta p_y/p_y}$$

Cross-elasticity serves as a behavioral measure of the degree of substitution between commodities. When e_{xp_y} is positive, commodities X and Y are substitutes; an increase in p_y results in an increase in q_x. When cross-elasticity is negative, commodities X and Y are complements; an increase in the price of Y leads consumers to purchase less of X. The existence of close substitutes for commodity X is the primary reason for high price elasticity of demand for X.

Cross-elasticities of demand are used (but not without difficulties) to define industry boundaries. They provide a quantitative measure of gaps in the chain of substitute commodities. The gaps (small size of e_{xp_y}) tend to increase, the more broadly we define the commodity groups (industries).

Income Elasticity

Income elasticity e_{xm} measures the responsiveness of the rate of purchase of commodity X to rate of change in income m. Again our elasticity measure overcomes the units problem and makes possible comparison among commodities with dissimilar units by considering the relative changes. Income elasticity measures the shape of the income or Engel curve:

$$e_{xm} = \frac{\Delta x/x}{\Delta m/m}$$

If e_{xm} is positive, the commodity in question is a normal good. If e_{xm} is negative, the commodity in question is an inferior good, meaning that a relative increase in income induces a relative decrease in the rate of purchase of the commodity, or vice versa. The more broadly the commodity group is defined, the less likely is e_{xm} to be negative; for example, a poor grade of beef may be an inferior good, but if we look at all meat products, the income relationship is likely to be positive (without violating Engel's law). A category of superior goods is sometimes reserved for those commodities with income elasticity greater than unity.

Permanent Income Hypothesis

A notable attempt to add precision to our knowledge of the consumer's behavioral response to changes in income is the permanent income hypothesis.[7] The hypothesis is advanced that observed income has a transitory and a permanent component (as does consumption), that the transitory components of income and consumption are uncorrelated, and that consumption in a given period is functionally related to the permanent component of income. Consumption, it is argued, does not systematically vary with observed income, which may fluctuate from year to year due to transitory factors such as unexpected bonuses, accidental windfalls, or losses. Over an individual's lifetime, observed income will most certainly vary more than an individual's expected permanent income.

The usefulness of the hypothesis is to some degree diminished by the difficulties in measuring and defining permanent income, as anticipated by an individual. Permanent income depends on the individual's anticipated lifetime income. It is a function of such basic (but difficult to measure) factors as nonhuman wealth (all forms of property that earn income or can be converted into income-earning assets or money), training, and ability. Estimates of permanent income have usually been based on a weighted average of past incomes over a period of several years, giving more weight to most recent income.

Friedman hypothesized that the ratio of permanent consumption to permanent income would be a constant, if tastes, interest rates, and the proportion of nonhuman wealth to income remained constant.

[7] Milton Friedman, *A Theory of the Consumption Function,* National Bureau of Economic Research, New York, 1957.

3

Utility and Consumer Choice

In Chapter 2 we did not explain *why* consumers respond as they do. The demand function—$x = f(p_x, P_y, m)$—describes the consumer's response to changes in prices or income. It describes the economist's estimate of a consumer's reactions, assuming tastes and preferences are known and independent of price changes. We noticed that at certain values of p_x, p_y, and m, the consumer would choose to purchase certain quantities of X or of some other good, Y, in a given period of time. We now develop a theory, based on reasonable postulates and behavioral assumptions, to explain the consumer's reaction—why the consumer chooses x and y rather than some other rates of purchase of commodities X and Y. In deriving the demand curve, we try to bridge the gulf between consumer preferences and market behavior.

Indifference Curves

Indifference curves are well-suited to the task of representing consumer preferences and of explaining the relationship between the preferences and the market behavior of a rational consumer.

All combinations (x, y) on a given indifference curve (Fig. 3.1) yield the same level of satisfaction, or conversely all equally satisfying combinations lie on the same indifference curve. Rationality is a basic postulate of our theory. A rational consumer is one who tries to maximize his level of satisfaction (utility) and is consistent in his preferences.

The Meaning and Measurement of Utility

Utility is pleasure or satisfaction. A good may possess a great variety of characteristics that afford utility. An automobile may be safe, fast,

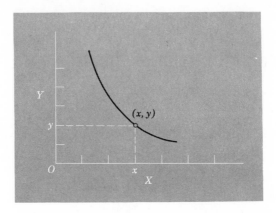

Fig. 3.1

good looking, and convenient. We assume that when the consumer considers a purchase he judges the pleasure-satisfying capability of the good as a combination of all of its characteristics. A burden is placed on an individual if he must decide which of several goods affords the most total utility; an even greater burden exists if he must decide whether the extra satisfaction from the marginal unit of one good is greater than the extra satisfaction from the marginal unit of some other good. The analysis of consumer choice using indifference curves does *not* require that the consumer place a meaningful cardinal measure[1] of utility on the last unit of a certain commodity. He need not decide that the marginal utility (addition to total utility) from a sixth bottle of beer is 17 utils, from a seventh bottle is 3 utils, from an eighth bottle is —9 utils (implying the eighth bottle is not desirable, and that total utility would be greater from seven bottles than from eight).

Diminishing Marginal Utility

We define marginal utility as the change in total utility per unit change in consumption of commodity X (*not* as the change in utility *of* the last unit consumed).

[1] A cardinal measure has a well defined unit of measure and base for measurements. A temperature of 33 degrees Fahrenheit is one degree above freezing. If t_1, t_2, and t_3 are various temperatures measured cardinally, it is possible to say that the difference between t_1 and t_2 is greater than, equal to, or less than the difference between t_2 and t_3 $[(t_1) — (t_2)] \lesseqgtr [(t_2) — (t_3)]$.

As more units of a certain commodity are consumed *in a given period of time, other things equal (ceteris paribus)*, the inflection point of the total utility function is reached—N in Fig. 3.2—and marginal utility begins to decline.

Whether marginal utility begins to diminish initially (as the second unit of X is consumed) or after some arbitrary number of units (six in Fig. 3.2), diminishing marginal utility has its basis in the psychological make-up of most human beings. Various qualifications of this behavioral proposition should cover even the most perverse among us. Because of its generality it is dignified by being referred to as the Law of Diminishing Marginal Utility. The direct implication of diminishing marginal utility is that if a consumer increases his rate of purchase of a particular good, its marginal utility will eventually diminish, and conversely by decreasing the rate of purchase, marginal utility will increase.

The concept of marginal utility requires that a cardinal measure of utility be assignable to total utility so that we can know the change in total utility per additional unit of a commodity. Since indifference curve analysis was introduced to avoid the necessity of applying the stronger cardinal measure of utility, numbers of utils are not usually applied to indifference curves. However, in Fig. 3.3 we illustrate the diminishing marginal utility of X (holding Y constant). The marginal utility function in Fig. 3.3b, indicating the change in total utility per unit change in X, is derived directly from the indifference curves in Fig. 3.3a. (The uncharacteristic feature of these indifference curves is the assignment to them of cardinal measures of utility.)

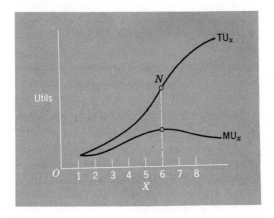

Fig. 3.2

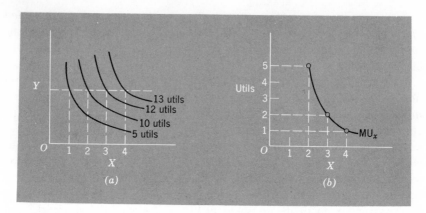

Fig. 3.3

Indifference curves require only that the consumer be able to distinguish between and rank various combinations of commodities. He need not say that combinations *A*, *B*, and *C* are each worth so many utils, but only that he prefers *A* to *B* and *B* to *C*.[2]

The Rational Consumer

If we agree that the preferences of the rational consumer can be described adequately by indifference curves, we can proceed to develop the theory of choice based on the postulate of the rational consumer. The rational consumer maximizes utility and makes consistent choices. Consistency means that the ranking of preferences is transitive: if *A* is preferred to *B* and *B* is preferred to *C*, then (if transitivity holds) *A* will be preferred to *C*.[3]

Consistency of choice implies that indifference curves will not intersect.

[2] Note that this ordinal measure of utility, which requires only a ranking of preferences, precludes an answer to the question: By how much do you prefer *A* to *B*? The spacing between the indifference curves is of no significance if there is no cardinal measure of utility. By how much *A* exceeds *B* is never considered in ordinal measurement.

[3] The transitivity of ordinal measurement does not allow interpersonal comparisons. If I prefer combination *A* to *B* and you prefer *B* to *A*, we cannot say which of us derives the greater satisfaction from *B*. See Kenneth Arrow, *Social Choice and Individual Values*, Wiley, New York, 1951.

By definition all combinations of goods yielding the same level of utility must lie on the same indifference curve. So it would be a logical contradiction to have equivalence of utility at the point of intersection, C (see Fig. 3.4), and at some other points, such as A and B, on different indifference curves.

Negatively Sloping Indifference Curves

Let us agree at this stage of our analysis of consumer behavior to consider only desirable goods, and let us assume nonsatiety. With these provisos, it follows that consuming additional units of any commodity adds something to total utility. More of commodity X is always preferred to less of X. In Fig. 3.4 combination A is preferred to B since A contains more units of X than does combination B, whereas both A and B contain the same number of units, y_1 of Y. (Again note the inconsistency in intersecting indifference curves—combination A is preferred to combination B but at the same time the consumer exhibits no preference between combinations A and C.)

This nonsatiety assumption—that both X and Y are desirable and extra consumption of each provides additional satisfaction—implies negatively sloping indifference curves. Moving along a given indifference curve, the consumer remains indifferent only if by giving up some of Y he receives additional units of X; i.e., along a given indifference curve the slope $(\Delta y / \Delta x)$, which is called the marginal rate of substitution, is negative.

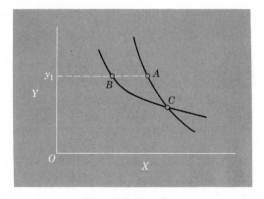

Fig. 3.4

Diminishing Marginal Rate of Substitution (MRS) and the Law of Diminishing Marginal Utility

The slope of an indifference curve—MRS_{yx}—is equal to the ratio of the marginal utility of X to the marginal utility of Y ($\Delta y/\Delta x = -\text{MU}_x/\text{MU}_y$).[4] MRS_{yx} is the rate at which the consumer is willing to substitute Y for X. Although the slope is the ratio of marginal utilities, the cardinal measurement of utility can be dispensed with, since the marginal utility of Y can be measured in terms of the number of units of X that yields equal satisfaction. The convexity or diminishing MRS_{yx} of indifference curves is an empirical proposition about behavior. Moving upward and to the left along an indifference curve (substituting more units of Y for units of X), it takes more and more units of Y to offset the loss in utility as each additional unit of X is traded off for additional units of Y—the MU_x increases with fewer units of X while the MU_y decreases with more units of Y, so that MU_x/MU_y takes on a larger numerical value as X is exchanged for more Y.

If we move in the opposite direction the slope of the indifference curve (MRS_{yx}) becomes more horizontal as Y is exchanged for more X, and for the same reason, which is closely related to the law of diminishing marginal utility. Careful scrutiny will reveal, however, that diminishing MU_x and diminishing MU_y are not sufficient conditions for diminishing MRS_{yx}; the law of diminishing marginal utility by itself does not imply convexity. We need the further requirement that X is independent of Y—a neutrality condition. Otherwise, although the MU_x may tend to rise as less of X is consumed, more of Y may offset this rise in MU_x by inducing a negative shift in MU_x, assuming X and Y are economic substitutes, as in Fig. 3.5a.

Indifference Curves and Consumer Preferences

We have established that where goods are desirable the marginal rate of substitution will be negative, and where nonsatiety holds, a utility

---

[4] Since utility is constant at every point on an indifference curve, the disutility of small negative changes in y (dy) must be exactly offset by the utility of small increases in x (dx), or satisfaction gained must equal satisfaction lost. If MU_x is additional or marginal utility for small changes in x (dx) and MU_y is marginal utility or loss in total utility for small negative changes in y (dy), at any point on the indifference curve $\text{MU}_x\,dx + \text{MU}_y\,dy = 0$. The slope of an indifference curve is dy/dx, and $dy/dx = \text{MU}_x/\text{MU}_y = (\text{MRS}_{yx})$, or the marginal rate of substitution of Y for X.

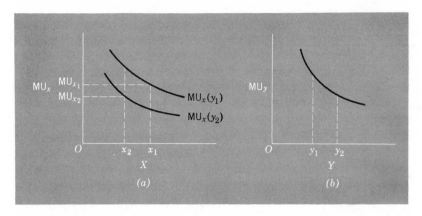

Fig. 3.5

surface representing the total utility of any combination of goods would continually rise moving outward in any direction from the origin.[5]

In addition, our typical indifference curve was convex to the origin, based on the empirical proposition of diminishing marginal rate of substitution. There are special cases, however, that deserve our attention. Where commodities are perfect technical substitutes, the marginal rate of substitution between X and Y is constant and the indifference curve is linear, as in Fig. 3.6. Where X and Y are perfect complements and must always be consumed in fixed proportions, the indifference curves appear as in Fig. 3.7.

If we relax our assumption of two desirable commodities and suppose that X is a discommodity or nuisance good, the indifference curves appear positively sloping as in Fig. 3.8. For example, money income Y is a desirable commodity and hours of work X, a discommodity. The curvature indicates that the greater the number of hours of work, the greater the number of dollars required in exchange for an hour of work to maintain the same utility level. The initial negative slope in the highest indifference curve indicates that at some levels of income, some work may be desirable. We can view most discommodities as commodities (desirable goods). In the preceding example, we could have considered hours not-worked or leisure time instead of hours worked (assumed a discommodity).

---

[5] Note that indifference curves can be formed from equal contours on a utility surface; however, since our ordinal measure of utility places no absolute value on the various indifference curves, a utility surface cannot be formed on the basis of an indifference map or group of indifference curves.

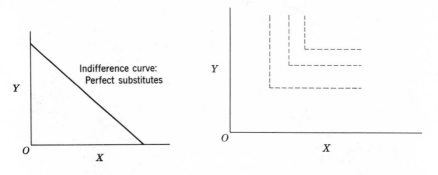

Fig. 3.6. Indifference curve: perfect substitutes.

Fig. 3.7

The Income Constraint

On the same set of coordinates, units of commodity Y on one axis and units of X on the other, we can draw the budget line for a given income. Any point along a budget line is a combination of Y and X that can be purchased with a given money income. The budget line is, in fact, a line of attainable combinations. Let us assume all money income I is spent on Y or on X, and the price of $Y(p_y)$ and the price of $X(p_x)$ are given. Since all income is spent,

$$I = p_x x + p_y y$$

which means that with a given income, x units of X and y units of Y can be purchased at existing prices, p_x and p_y. The equation of the

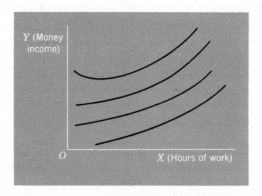

Fig. 3.8

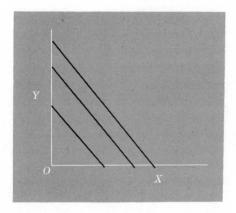

Fig. 3.9

budget line can be written

$$Y = \frac{I}{p_y} - \left(\frac{p_x}{p_y}\right) x$$

The slope of the budget line is the ratio of the prices $(-p_x/p_y)$. As long as the price ratio remains the same, various levels of income can be represented by parallel budget lines as in Fig. 3.9.

The linearity of the budget line reflects a constant unit price independent of the number of units of either commodity the buyer decides to purchase. (This linearity condition holds if there are no quantity discounts and, as under perfectly competitive conditions, there are many buyers acting independently so that no single buyer can affect price.)

At this point we find it convenient to let our Y commodity be all other goods or money income, so that, retaining our definitional requirement that all income be spent in the period involved, money income is either spent on commodity X or on all other goods Y.

Let us take an example. Suppose the consumer earns $200 per week; $p_y = \$1.00$, the price of money income; the price of X is given as $100 per unit; and the X-axis represents units of commodity X purchased per week. The budget line under these assumptions connects the two extreme points $(x = 0, y = \$200)$ and $(x = 2, y = 0)$. Both points, and all other points on the budget line connecting the two extreme points, can be purchased with $200. (The equation of the budget line, B_1, here is $y = \$200 - \$100x$.) This is shown in Fig. 3.10.

The rational consumer will choose that combination where the budget line, B_1, touches the highest indifference curve at E_1. If the budget line is linear and the indifference curve is convex, the budget line will touch

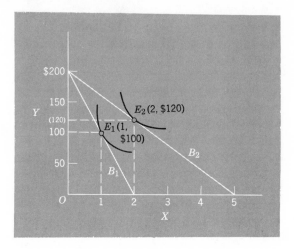

Fig. 3.10

the highest attainable indifference curve at one unique point. This will be the point of tangency,[6] where the slope of the indifference curve—$MRS_{yx} = MU_x/MU_y$—equals the slope of the budget line p_x/p_y.

In equilibrium the rational consumer will find the rate at which he can exchange Y for X (p_x/p_y) equals the rate at which he is willing to substitute Y for X (MU_x/MU_y):

$$\frac{MU_x}{MU_y} = \frac{p_x}{p_y}$$

This equilibrium condition can be written

$$\frac{MU_x}{p_x} = \frac{MU_y}{p_y}$$

which means the rational consumer maximizes his utility by allocating his income between X and Y in such a manner that the marginal utility per dollar spent on X equals the marginal utility per dollar spent on Y. Any other allocation of income, where the marginal utilities per dollar's worth of purchasable commodities are not equal, will fail to maximize utility. Some reallocation of income, from the commodity whose

[6] The exception is where the budget line touches the highest indifference curve at one of the axes, in which case the income will be spent entirely on X or entirely on Y (if the indifference curve were concave, the point of tangency would be a point of minimum satisfaction).

marginal utility per dollar is smaller to the commodity whose marginal utility per dollar is larger, would bring the consumer closer to maximizing his total utility.

Suppose now that there is no change in p_y, but a new market price is established for product X—a lower price of $40 per unit instead of the former price of $100 per unit. This new price, with tastes and money income unchanged, is represented by a new budget line (B_2 in Fig. 3.10) still cutting the y-axis at $200 but with a slope representing the new relative price ($40/$1) and cutting the x-axis at $x = 5$ ($200/$40). A new equilibrium point, E_2, can now be identified at the point of tangency between the new budget (price) line and a higher indifference curve. At $p_x = $100, the rational consumer will purchase 1 unit of X (point E_1); at $p_x = $40, he will purchase 2 units of X (point E_2). From the points of tangency of the indifference curves and budget lines, we have derived two points on this consumer's demand curve (see Fig. 3.11).

Income and Substitution Effects of a Price Change

The typical demand curve derived above is based on the assumption that money income and the prices of other goods remain constant. It becomes apparent that real income or purchasing power (money income/consumer price index) does not remain constant as we move along a demand curve. When p_x changes, so does the consumer price index

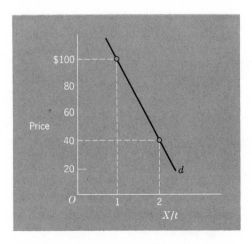

Fig. 3.11. Demand curve.

(to the extent of the weight attached to product X in the price index). If the price of commodity X decreases, under *ceteris paribus* conditions, the consumer is better off. His real income increases—either in the sense of being able to purchase the original quantities prior to the price change and still have some money income left over, or in the sense of being able to purchase more and achieve a higher level of utility. The ordinary demand curve represents the response to a change in the price of commodity X relative to the price of other goods, but it also includes the response to the change in real income accompanying the change in p_x.

Following Hicks and Allen[7] it has been generally accepted that there are actually two components to the consumer's reaction to a price change—a substitution effect due to a change in the relative price structure as if there had been no change in real income or after the change in real income is compensated), and the (real) income effect of the price change due to the change in real income (as if there had been no change in relative prices and no change in money income).[8]

The indifference map provides an excellent means of clarifying the income and substitution effects. In probing further into these two components of a price change, an interesting question arises regarding the measurement and meaning of real income. J. R. Hicks defined a given level of real income to be any combination of goods to which the consumer was indifferent—that lay on a given indifference curve; that is, he defined real income in terms of utility or anticipated psychic satisfaction as represented by the consumer's preferences. Following Hicks's definition of real income we can distinguish graphically the two effects shown in Fig. 3.12. A dashed line is drawn *tangent to the original indifference curve* that contains the point E_1—the equilibrium combination chosen before the price of product X had declined from \$100/unit to \$40/unit. The new dashed line is drawn *parallel to the new price line*, whose slope represents the relative prices (p_x/p_y) when the $p_x = \$40$; that is, after p_x had changed.

Once this interpretation of real income is accepted, the identification

[7] J. R. Hicks and R. G. D. Allen, "A Reconsideration of the Theory of Value," Parts I and II, *Economica*, February 1934, pp. 52–76; May 1934, pp. 196–219.
[8] The same increase in purchasing power or real income which results from a decrease in price may arise from an increase in money income without any change in the relative price structure of consumer goods. The equivalency may be questioned and qualified from the point of view of the psychological effect on the consumer, who may have a money illusion and prefer an increase in money income to a decrease in one or more product prices (even though purchasing power is the same in both cases). The two ways that "real" income can increase are likely to have different consequences in terms of the manner in which a consumer decides to allocate his income.

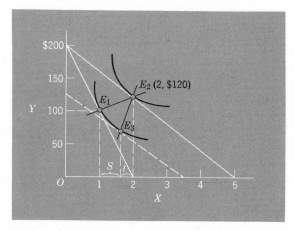

Fig. 3.12

of the two "effects" of a price change is a simple matter. E_3 to E_2 is the income component of the price change (as if the change in relative prices did not take place). The income effect of the price change is conceptually identifiable here, since any point along the old indifference curve (the utility level attained before the price decrease) contains by definition the same level of real income. The new dashed budget line (parallel to the new budget line and tangent to the original indifference curve at E_3) reflects the price change but at the *original* level of real income. The curve passing through the points E_2 and E_3, where the parallel price lines are tangent to the indifference curves, is called the *income-consumption* curve. It represents the income effect of a price change.

The substitution effect is depicted along a given indifference curve from the point of tangency of the first price line to the point of tangency of the new price line—E_1 to E_3. Recall that the substitution effect of the reaction relates only to the change in the relative price structure with real income constant. The reaction is restricted to points along the original indifference curve. The substitution effect of the price change is the rational consumer's response to the price decrease supposing he cannot increase his level of satisfaction (real income)—he cannot move from the original indifference curve. We may suppose there is some *compensating variation* in income, say a tax, which just offsets the increase in real income—shifts the new budget line until it is tangent to the original indifference curve. This is the dashed budget line that contains the same slope (same relative prices) as the new budget line. With convex indifference curves, the substitution effect of a change in p_x must always be inversely related to the change in the rate of purchase of X. The substitution effect is measured along a given indifference curve with real income constant; as p_x decreases, the slope of the budget line (p_x/p_y) becomes smaller (more horizontal) than the slope of the convex indifference curve (MU_x/MU_y): $p_x/p_y < MU_x/MU_y$. To once again maximize satisfaction, the rational consumer will increase his rate of purchase of X until the new budget line is tangent to the indifference curve at some point to the right of the original point of tangency.

The two equilibrium positions before and after the price change—E_1 and E_2—connect two points on what has been called the *price-consumption* curve (or *offer* curve). In Fig. 3.12, the price-consumption curve is positively sloping, indicating that demand is inelastic (since money spent decreases as p_x decreases). The price-consumption curve, from which the demand curve is derived, reflects both the income and substitution effects of a price change.

The income and substitution effects of the change in the price of product X can also be represented in terms of units of product X by dropping vertical lines from the points E_1, E_2, E_3, down to the x-axis. We did this previously with respect to E_1 and E_2—the two points on the price-consumption curve—in deriving the ordinary demand curve with money income and other prices constant.[9]

The Engel curve, depicting the effect of a change in real income on the rate of purchase, can be derived from the indifference curve analysis in a similar way. Consider the two points on the x-axis that correspond to the rates of purchase of product x associated with the two levels of real income at points E_3 (the level before the price change) and E_2 (the level of real income attained after the price change). Drop vertical lines from E_2 and E_3—the two points on the income-consumption curve—down to the x-axis. Hicks did not deal directly with the problem of measuring the two levels of real income; this would require assigning cardinal measures to the indifference curves representing the levels of real income.

Slutsky[10] tried to solve the problem of the measurement of real income by defining real income in a manner independent of the individual's indifference curves or preference system. Recall that a budget line is the locus of combinations attainable with the same money expenditure.

---

[9] The two points on the x-axis, where vertical lines from E_1 and E_3 touch the axis, reflecting the substitution effect of the change in relative price, lie on the real income (or income-compensated) demand curve (always negatively sloping).

[10] Eugene Slutsky, "On the Theory of the Budget of the Consumer," *AEA Readings in Price Theory*, Homewood, Ill., Irwin, 1952, pp. 27–56.

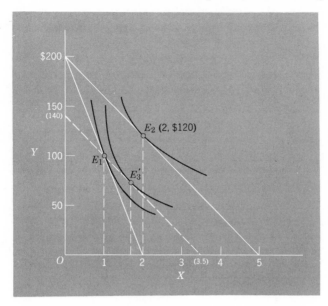

Fig. 3.13

Slutsky argued that a budget line (the dashed line in Fig. 3.13) passing through the original equilibrium combination at E_1 but parallel to the new budget line through E_2 represents approximately the same real income the consumer had achieved prior to the price decrease. Notice the difference between the Slutsky and Hicksian analyses. The dashed budget lines in Figs. 3.12 and 3.13 are both drawn parallel to the new budget line with $p_x = \$40$. The Hicksian budget line representing a compensating variation in income is tangent to the indifference curve passing through the initial equilibrium combination, E_1, while Slutsky's budget line representing a compensating change in income is rotated around and passes through the initial equilibrium position, E_1. Slutsky's dashed "compensating change" budget line would cut the Y-axis at \$140 (\$200 — 60). A tax of \$60 from the \$200 money income would enable the consumer to purchase the original combination, E_1 (one unit of x at the new price of \$40/unit and still save \$100 of Y). Slutsky's real income is measured in terms of purchasing power over the original combination, E_1. The compensating change in income after the price decrease just permits purchase of the original combination of commodities at E_1. (Note Slutsky's dashed budget line should cut the x-axis at 3.5 = \$140/40.)

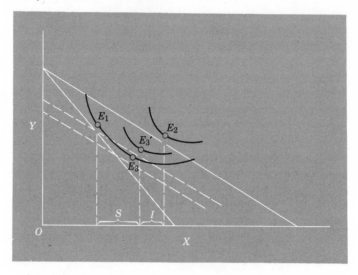

Fig. 3.14

The income and substitution effects of the price change can now be represented. Point E_3' is crucial here. It is the point that the consumer would move to along the new pivoted price line (which has the same real income as other price lines passing through E_1 and the same relative prices as the line passing through E_2).

E_3' is the point of tangency between the pivoted price line and a new indifference curve. This combination E_3' is the combination the rational consumer will purchase if the gain in real income ($60) following the price decrease were taxed away. E_1 to E_3' would represent the substitution effect of the price change.

The substitution effect (according to Hicks) from E_1 to E_3 in Fig. 3.14 tends toward equality with the substitution effect (according to Slutsky) from E_1 to E_3', as the price change converges to zero.

E_3' and E_2 would now be two points on the income-consumption curve. If we drop perpendiculars from E_1, E_2, and E_3' to the x-axis, we can measure the substitution (S) and income (I) effects of a price change in terms of product X. The two points on the X-axis from perpendiculars through E_3' and E_2 represent the income effect—the change in rate of purchase of X as a function of the change in real income.[11]

---

[11] By the simplifying device of assuming the marginal utility of money income Y a constant, Marshall assumed away any income effect of a price change; so that E_2 and E_3 would lie on the vertical line drawn through these points to the x-axis.

The slope of the indifference curve is MU_x/MU_y. If MU_y is a constant, the slope

Classical Indictment of an Excise (Indirect) Tax in Favor of an Income (Direct) Tax

Suppose with an income of $200, the price of X to the consumer had increased (instead of decreasing as in our illustration of the income and substitution effect) from $40 to $100, and that this price increase was the result of an excise tax of $60/unit levied on commodity X. With the higher price due to the excise tax, the consumer will be in equilibrium at E_1, where he will purchase one unit at $100 (with $60 of the $100 going to the state as tax revenue). Now instead of the excise tax, suppose an income tax was levied to yield the same revenue as the excise tax, yet permitting the consumer to purchase E_1, as under the excise tax. In Fig. 3.13, the reduction of the consumer's income is represented by Slutsky's dashed budget line, cutting the y-axis at $140 (= $200 − 60) and parallel to the original budget line, but passing through E_1—the equilibrium position after the excise tax. This income tax yields $60 to the state, as did the excise tax. The consumer can (with an income tax) move along the dashed budget line through E_1 to a new equilibrium position, E_3', which is on a higher indifference curve than was E_1.

The consumer can reach a higher utility level with the income tax than he could have with the excise tax (with both taxes yielding the same revenue to the state).

Income-Consumption Curve, Engel Curve, and Income Elasticity

The income-consumption curve was defined as a curve passing through points of tangency between indifference curves and parallel price lines

---

MU_x/MU_y will be constant (for given values of x) along any vertical line on an indifference map. This assumes neutrality between X and Y, so that MU_x is constant for a given amount of X purchased, independent of quantity of Y. It follows then that with MU_y constant, the indifference curves must be vertically parallel.

Referring back to Fig. 3.14, Marshall's assumption would put E_3 directly (vertically) beneath E_2, since the slopes of the new dashed budget line tangent to the indifference curve at E_2 is drawn with the same slope as the new budget line tangent to the indifference curve at E_2. The indifference curve with a slope equal to the dotted budget line must be tangent to the budget line at a point E_3 vertically beneath E_2. Marshall's substitution effect and price effect are identical. There is no income effect. This was in his view a reasonable approximation for analyzing the first-order partial equilibrum effect of a price change.

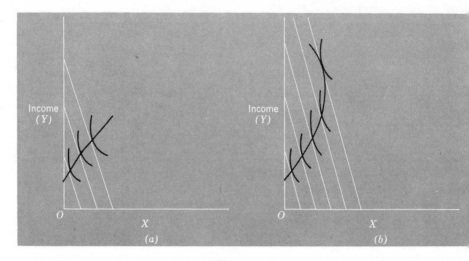

Fig. 3.15

(i.e., assuming the relative price structure fixed and the price lines representing different levels of real income).

Usually, as real income increases, the indifference map showing consumer preferences will be such that the rate of purchase of a particular good will increase (Fig. 3.15a) and the slope of the Engel curve will be positive. This is the normal good case. In Fig. 3.15b, good x is normal at lower income levels, but becomes an inferior good as real income increases. The income-consumption curve bends back toward the y-axis and income elasticity becomes negative.

Comparing the Income and Substitution Effect

The substitution effect of a decrease in price on the rate of purchase must be positive—there is an inverse relation between a change in relative prices (with real income constant) and the change in the rate of purchase. It is possible, however, for the real income effect of a price decrease to be positive or negative. It is rare (particularly for products that use up a small part of the consumer's budget) that the income effect of a price decrease will be as great as the substitution effect (which is always positive).

Rare Conditions Where Demand Curve Has Positive Slope

1. Where a negative income effect of a price decrease does occur and in the unusual case where this negative income effect is greater than the substitution effect.
2. Where preference and price are not independent. Value is judged on the basis of price rather than price serving as a measure of value. This is due mainly to ignorance about the commodity. If this were not the case, it would follow that a person would prefer to pay more rather than less for the same commodity.[12]

Giffen Paradox

The first condition for a positively sloping demand curve, where the income effect of a decline in price dominates and offsets the substitution effect, has rarely occurred. In fact, although theoretically possible, there is no strong evidence that such a situation has ever occurred. The case is often referred to as the Giffen paradox.

Giffen was puzzled by the simultaneous increase in the demand for potatoes and in potato prices. This occurred during the famine in Ireland toward the middle of the nineteenth century. A generally poor crop of most agricultural commodities caused severe famine, since a goodly share of the population depended on agriculture for their livelihood. Potatoes were an important part of the typical family's budget. An increased rate of potato purchase was made possible by increased imports following the repeal of the corn laws (which had placed a high duty on imported grain). A more likely explanation is that it was a local phenomenon. The unusual Giffen case of an increase in potato price accompanied by an *increase* in the rate of purchase is illustrated in Fig. 3.16.

Suppose the price of potatoes increased from p_{x1} to p_{x2}. The rate of purchase was x_1, but when the price of potatoes increased to p_{x2}, the equilibrium rate of purchase increased to x_2. The substitution effect of the *increase* in price must, of course, lead to a *decrease* in the rate of purchase (the substitution component of the price change is x_1x_1'), but the income effect, in the case of this inferior good, leads to an

[12] Snob appeal is sometimes incorrectly given as an explanation of a positively sloping demand curve. A person may prefer a more expensive to a less expensive commodity for this reason, but this is quite different from preferring to buy more of the more expensive good the more expensive it is.

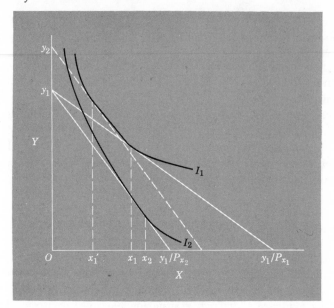

Fig. 3.16

increase in the rate of purchase in response to the decrease in real income (the income component of the price increase is $x_1'x_2$). So for this very special inferior good, which constitutes an important part of the consumer's budget, the income effect swamps the substitution effect. If this very special case applied to enough individuals, then the market demand curve could conceivably be positively sloping.

Consumer Surplus

Where Y is money or all other goods, and with the unit price of all other goods or money (p_y) constant and equal to $1, the equilibrium condition for the rational consumer is

$$\frac{MU_y}{p_y = 1} = \frac{MU_x}{p_x} \quad \text{or} \quad p_x = \frac{1}{MU_y} \cdot MU_x$$

Marshall assumed in his discussion of consumer surplus that each individual's marginal utility of money (MU_y) expended at the margin was not affected by expenditure on commodity X (any single commodity). He assumed MU_y remained unchanged with respect to expenditure on any one of the many commodities in a typical consumer budget. If MU_y is taken as some constant k, $p_x = 1/k \cdot MU_x$ or $kp_x = MU_x$, where the constant marginal utility of money may be taken as dollars—the unit in which price is measured.

When MU_y is constant (so that price in dollars can be taken as a measure of utility) Marshall defined consumer surplus to mean the difference between the maximum amount of dollars that the consumer would be willing to pay for so many units of commodity x rather than go without it, and the amount he actually had to pay (the market price times the number of units purchased).

Let us look at an individual's demand curve (Fig. 3.17), which (under the assumption of constant marginal utility of money) is identical to a curve representing the (diminishing) marginal utility of commodity X. The individual would have been willing to pay $10 for the first unit of X, $9 for the second unit, $8 for the third unit, and $7 for the fourth unit. The market price was $7, and he was able to purchase four units at an outlay of $28. Each unit cost only as much as the last unit purchased, but the value to the consumer of previous units (with diminishing marginal utility) was higher than the market price ($= MU$) of the last unit purchased.

The consumer surplus, in this case, would be $[(\$10 + \$9 + \$8 + \$7) - \$28] = \$6$—the shaded area in Fig. 3.17. The $6 (or 6 utils) is a measure of the surplus satisfaction the consumer receives by being able to buy all four homogeneous units of commodity X at a uniform price ($7) in an impersonal mass market.[13]

---

[13] If the consumer had to deal with an all-powerful single seller (a monopolist) to obtain this commodity, the monopolist might be able to extract the entire consumer surplus in an "all-or-none" type bargain: first-degree price discrimination, where the monopolist stipulates the price that must be paid for each additional unit and the total number of units the consumer must buy if he is to buy any at all.

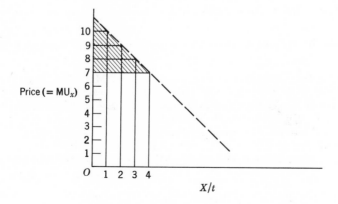

Fig. 3.17

Various interpretations of what may be meant by "consumer surplus" are possible if we relax the assumption that the marginal utility of money is constant (as more is spent and less remains to be spent). However, Marshall believed that the price an individual would be just willing to pay for the last unit of a commodity purchased would be an approximate measure of what the last unit was worth to him. "The price will measure the marginal utility of the commodity to each purchaser individually: we cannot speak of price as measuring marginal utility in general, because the wants and circumstances of different people are different."[14]

Reformulation of the Consumer Surplus Doctrine

In assuming constant marginal utility of money, Marshall ignores the income effect of a price change in his discussion of consumer surplus. Hicks gives greater precision to the concept of consumer surplus.[15] Explicitly considering the income effect of a price change, he distinguishes between equivalent variation EV and compensating variation CV of price increases and decreases.

EV is the money income that must be taken from (a tax) or given to (a subsidy) a consumer so that he may attain the level of real income that would have resulted from a price change that *does not* actually occur.

CV is the money income that just compensates the consumer for a price change that *does* actually occur. It is the tax or subsidy that exactly offsets the price change and thus leaves the consumer at his original level of real income—the level of income prior to the price change.

To clarify the various definitions of consumer surplus (refer to Fig. 3.18), suppose the price of commodity X decreased from p_1 to p_2, enabling the individual to move from one level of real income to another

[14] Alfred Marshall, *Principles of Economics*, 8th ed., Macmillan, New York, 1949, p. 100. Note, on p. 95 of this same edition, Marshall was convinced that the marginal utility of money for a poor man was greater than for a rich man; therefore, although both the poor man and the rich man paid the same price (two pence) for the last ride to work each was only just induced to take, the utility of the last ride to work was greater for the poorer man than for the richer man. $p_x \cdot MU_y = MU_x$ and if p_x is the same for both, but MU_y is greater for the poor man than for the rich man, then MU_x—the extra utility from the last ride—is greater for the poor man.

[15] J. R. Hicks, *A Revision of Demand Theory*, Oxford, 1956.

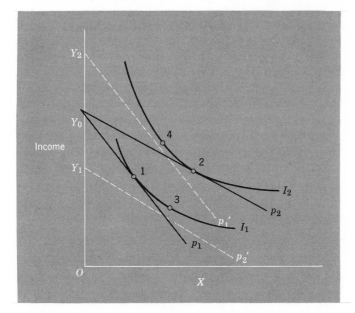

Fig. 3.18

(indifference curve I_1 to I_2). CV would be the amount of the tax that would just counterbalance this price decrease and leave the consumer with the same level of real income (I_1) as he enjoyed before the price decrease took place. It is the maximum amount (Y_0Y_1) that the individual would pay to retain the price decrease. His new position after the tax would be 3, while his original position before the price decrease was 1.

If a price increase from p_2 to p_1 were proposed, the consumer would expect to move from 2 to 1. EV would be that amount of money income (Y_0Y_1) taken from the individual, which leaves him at the same reduced level of real income (I_1) that would have resulted from the price increase. He would go from position 2 on I_2 to position 3 on I_1 after the tax was imposed. Note that the CV accompanying a price decrease is identical to the EV of a proposed price increase. The converse is also true—the CV of a price increase equals the EV of a price decrease.

The EV of a proposed price decrease is the minimum sum of money (Y_0Y_2) the individual would accept in lieu of a price decrease. Either a price decrease from p_1 to p_2 or the sum Y_0Y_2 would enable the consumer to move from a real income of I_1 to a real income of I_2. The subsidy Y_0Y_2 would enable him to go from position 1 to position 4. Unless the

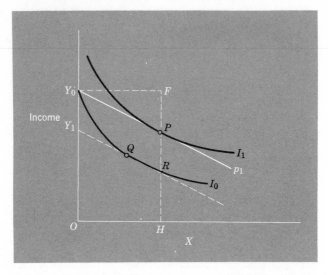

Fig. 3.19. (Based on A. Henderson, "Consumer Surplus and Compensating Variation," *R.E.S.,* Vol. 8, No. 2, p. 117.)

income effect is zero, the EV (or CV) of a price increase is not equal to the EV (or CV) of a price decrease.

Marshall's definition of consumer surplus was restricted to the given amount of the commodity the consumer purchased at the existing price. The free-market price provided the consumer with a bonus—the consumer's surplus or the additional amount he would be willing to pay over and above what he was presently paying rather than do without the present bundle of goods.

In Fig. 3.19 the consumer paid an amount FP for OH, but rather than do without OH of the commodity, he would be willing to pay FR. Note that the indifference curve I_0 passes through R and touches the income axis at Y_0, so the consumer is indifferent between going without commodity X altogether and paying FR for the given quantity OH.

Marshall's consumer surplus is PR. It is the difference between FR—the amount he is willing to pay—and FP—the amount he must pay in a free market for the fixed quantity OH.

Without the market price, p_1, the consumer would have money income Y_0 and an initial real income represented by the indifference curve I_0. It is worth Y_0Y_1 to the individual to be able to buy commodity X at the existing market price, p_1. The individual could pay a tax of Y_0Y_1 and just maintain his initial real income along I_0 at point Q.

This corresponds to Hick's compensating varation without any restriction on the quantity purchased.[16]

Revealed Preference[17]

In the situation represented in Fig. 3.20 there is no apparent way of determining which combination, C_1 or C_2, is preferred. Which is actually preferred depends on the unknown preference system. If I_1 were, in fact, the indifference curve, then C_1 would be preferred to C_2; but if I_2 represented the individual's preferences, then C_2 would be preferred.

In Fig. 3.21 we see the basic principle involved in the method of revealed preference. If the individual purchases combination, C_1, at prices represented by the slope of the budget line (l_{12}) through $C_1(p_{x1}/p_{y1})$, presumably he prefers C_1 to any other combination attainable with the same real income required to purchase C_1. This includes all combinations on this budget line through C_1, and of course all combinations below this budget line that could have been purchased (but were not).

[16] The usefulness of the concept of consumer surplus as a foundation for economic welfare remains in doubt. For more detailed analysis and critical comment, see I. M. D. Little, *A Critique of Welfare Economics,* 2nd ed., Oxford University Press. 1957.

[17] For more advanced treatment, see H. S. Houthakker, "Revealed Preference and the Utility Function," *Economica,* **17**, May 1950, pp. 159–74.

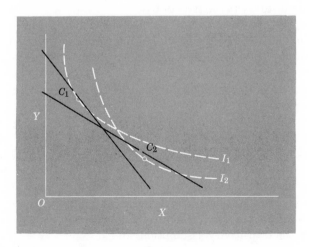

Fig. 3.20

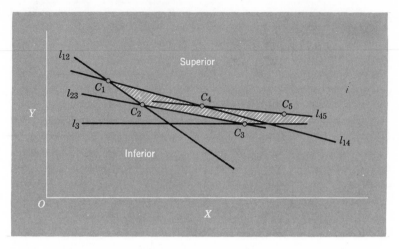

Fig. 3.21

If this individual when confronted with a new set of prices (p_{x2}/p_{y2}) — the slope of the budget line through C_2—shifts his purchases to C_2, we can be quite certain that C_2 is inferior to C_1, since C_2 lies on the budget line (l_{12}) and therefore could have been purchased at the previous prices and income but was not (C_1 was). C_1 is preferred to C_2, and C_2 is prefered to all other combinations on or below the new budget line (l_{23}) through C_2. If transitivity applies and the individual has consistent (well-ordered) preferences, then C_1 is preferred to all those combinations inferior to C_2 (as well as to C_2).

The nonpreferred region can be extended further by considering a combination C_3, chosen after prices and income have changed sufficiently (to budget line l_3) to cause the individual again to shift his preferences to combination C_3 from C_2. (Previously he chose C_2 to C_3 when both combinations were attainable with the prices and the income represented by the budget line l_{23}.)

To carve out a region of combinations preferred to C_1 (and eventually to identify the indifference curve passing through C_1), let us consider new sets of prices and incomes. With the budget line l_{14} passing through C_1 and C_4, the individual does not choose C_1; instead he chooses C_4, so C_4 is preferred to C_1 and to all points on and below l_{14}—the line of attainable combinations. When prices and income again change so that l_{45} applies, C_5 is preferred to C_4, and to all points on or below l$_{45}$, and (by the transitivity assumption) to C_1.

The line segments connecting C_1-C_2-C_3 are an upper boundary of all combinations revealed inferior to C_1, whereas the line segments connecting C_1-C_4-C_5 are a lower boundary of all combinations revealed superior to C_1. The shaded region of indifference (or zone of ignorance) in Fig. 3.21 would converge to a narrower, more continuous indifference curve if we had considered revealed preferences related to smaller price and income changes.

The method of revealed preference is an important attempt to supply an empirical foundation for utility analysis. It attempts to put highly subjective personal preferences on an objective basis. In principle, the individual's preference system is ascertainable by the method of revealed preference. The application of this method, however, would require that the individual's tastes be stable and consistent throughout, and that his purchases be observable as he is confronted with many sets of prices and incomes. It is assumed that at some set of prices and incomes, the individual can be induced to buy any combination of goods.

4

Production

In the abstract, production is any process or activity that adds to utility. The choice of what goods to produce does not follow in any direct mechanical way the preferences of consumers. There is a constant and dynamic interaction between the wants of consumers and the costs and activities of producers. The decision to produce and the implementation of this decision are vital to any economic system; the determinants of the production decision provide a basis for distinguishing between economic systems.

The decision to produce usually involves some risk and uncertainty regarding consumer acceptance, particularly in the case of a new product. The risk and uncertainty are minimized if the product is produced to conform to consumer preferences, but it is lack of perfect knowledge of consumer preferences which gives rise to risk and uncertainty. It is difficult to know beforehand what products will find consumer acceptance. The solutions to production decisions affect the solutions to the other interrelated economic problems confronting societies. How much of a given product is to be produced may determine the choice of production method, which in turn affects the distribution of income and consequently influences the choice of goods to be produced. The production process itself may modify and condition consumer preferences and market demand. The costs of producing a product depend in general on the way resources are combined in the production process, the productivity of the resources in various combinations, and the prices of the resources involved. Before considering the costs of production, let us first examine the production function, which is independent of market phenomena.

Production Function

A production function is an economic summary or description of technological possibilities; it is the framework the economist uses to record

46

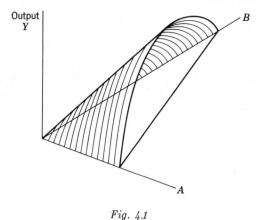

Fig. 4.1

what he needs to know about the physical aspects of the production process.

Although technology (methods of combining resources) may change rapidly, at any particular time it can be taken as given; the producer surveys production possibilities within the limits of available technical knowledge. The production function can be presented as a schedule or as an algebraic function with output dependent on possible input combinations. The information contained in a simple two-factor production function is portrayed graphically in Fig. 4.1 by a production surface in three dimensions on two input axes and an output axis.

The points on the production surface represent the maximum output for each combination of inputs.[1] The attainment of these maximum outputs is possible with existing technical knowledge, although it may require considerable ingenuity and sophisticated techniques.

The use of a surface, covering all input combinations, implies infinite possibilities for substitution between, say, labor A and capital B. Figure 4.1 shows a cross section of the conical surface—a likely shape for a production surface. As the number of units of homogeneous inputs are increased, the surface extends outward. The production surface need not extend quite to each of the axes; some minimum amount of one input may be required before any output is possible. No matter how many man-hours of labor are available, little if any coal or iron ore would be extracted from the ground without some tools, however crude.

We see in Figs. 4.2a and 4.2b an illustration of two important cases.

[1] The terms *inputs, resources,* and *factors of production* are synonymous and used interchangeably.

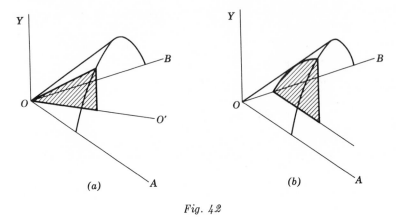

Fig. 4.2

In Fig. 4.2*a* all inputs expand at the same percentage rate and remain in the same proportion along a linear ray from the origin. In Fig. 4.2*b*, input *B* is held fixed at some level and output increases as an increasing number of units of the variable factor *A* is applied to the fixed factor *B*—there is a nonproportionate variation in inputs with *A/B* constantly changing.

Variable Proportions

There are situations where it is not possible or feasible to expand all inputs in the same proportion—according to scale. A special case occurs when one or several of the inputs remain fixed, while one or several (the combination may be taken as a unit) are varied with respect to the fixed factor(s), which may be land, plant, equipment, and managerial capacity. Which factors are fixed and which are variable really depend on the problem being analyzed. The Marshallian time periods, which bear no direct or necessary relationship to clock time, are useful concepts in the economic analysis of production problems. In the one case (long-run) the problem permits expanding all inputs according to scale so that no one input is necessarily more variable than another. Most often this situation, where all factors are variable, applies to the problem of planning the optimal size of the enterprise. In the other case (short-run) some inputs are fixed and some (or one) are variable. The major focus in the short-run is on the effect of changing factor proportions. The long-run situation involves considerable planning and capital investment, which often cannot be quickly reversed or modified. The short-run situation arises more commonly in day-to-day operation; it usually requires some investment in working capital (inventory, manpower, materials, etc.) to be used with preexisting fixed inputs.

The Law of Diminishing Returns

In production problems, where one or several factors are taken as fixed (because of limitations imposed by time or available money capital, etc.) while one or several factors are varied, attention is often focused on the productivity of a particular input. Certain generalizations emerge in this situation. They are most easily understood if we look at the simple two-factor case. If one factor is held constant at some given level and the number of units employed of the other is increased, observe the trace on the production surface that results from the intersection of the production surface with a plane set at right angles to one input axis (holding that factor fixed at a certain level) and parallel to the other axis (increasing the use of the other factor), as in Fig. 4.3.

Let us look at this same production situation from a different viewpoint so that we can focus on the likely shape of the trace in two dimensions (see Fig. 4.4).

First, we notice that although five units of the fixed factor A are employed initially, no output is achieved until at least one unit of the variable factor B is used in complement with A—this is depicted in Fig. 4.4 by the fact that this cross-sectional trace of the production

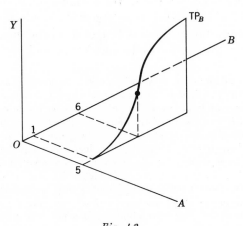

Fig. 4.3

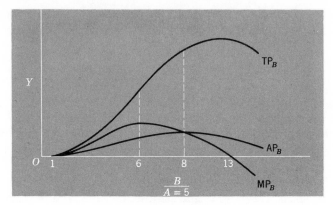

Fig. 4.4

surface does not pass through the origin but touches the input axis at
$B = 1$.

Second, until six units of input B are employed there are increasing
returns: the total product increases at an increasing rate prior to the
inflection point on the total product curve, and up to that point the
marginal product of input B rises. Marginal product may be interpreted
as change in output as a unit of the variable input is added, $\Delta Y/\Delta B$
for discrete changes in input units. (In mathematical language where
the term marginal is strictly defined, the marginal product of the variable
input B is the partial derivative of the production function with respect
to input B.) At the inflection point of the total product curve, marginal
product is a maximum. This rising phase of the marginal product of
B represents increasing returns to the variable input. This phenomenon
is not present in all operations. It is largely the result of the indivisibility
and the underutilization of the fixed input or of the imperfect adaptability of form of the fixed factor to the variable factor.[2]

[2] The problem of adaptability arises whenever there is a change in factor proportions. Where inputs are assumed homogeneous there is a presumption that in the
short run no change of form takes place in the fixed factor as units of the variable
factor are added. Over time the form of the fixed factor may be changed; for example: a machine may be modified so that two men, instead of one, can direct
its operation. Where output is expected to fluctuate, adaptability may be incor-
porated into the basic design; usually this will require additional money outlay for
the fixed factor, but the gain is a generally higher degree of efficiency with varying
factor proportions. Perfect adaptability implies that maximum output could be
achieved with varying factor proportions without incurring any costs of modifying
the form of either factor. Zero adaptability implies no substitution between factors:
fixed factor proportions if there is to be nonzero output.

The empirical generalization sometimes called the Law of Diminishing Returns refers to the eventually declining marginal product of the variable factor—in this example it occurs after the sixth unit of the variable factor is added. Whereas the size of the total product continues to rise after the sixth unit, the *additions to* total product become smaller and smaller. This is one of the few generalizations in economics dignified by being alluded to as a law, since in theory and in practice it is inviolable. As an increasing number of units of the variable input B are added to the fixed input A,[3] eventually a point is reached where the marginal product of the variable input ceases to become larger and begins to become smaller. In itself this principle or law describing a physical relationship is of great significance wherever resources are organized into a producing unit. For example, the application of fertilizer to a given plot of land will eventually result in smaller additions to output. Another example is the problem confronting developing economies. If people are regarded as variable resources—human factors of production—increasing numbers of people working a relatively fixed acreage of arable land may eventually lead to diminishing marginal product. If advances in technology and capital formation cannot keep pace with a rapidly expanding population, the force of diminishing returns can dominate upward shifts in the marginal product function.

General Relationships Among Total, Marginal, and Average Functions

The following comments may help to clarify the relationship among the total, marginal, and average functions. These relationships hold true in general although they are presented here in terms of product functions. Where total product is at a maximum, marginal product is zero.[4] Where average product is at a maximum, marginal product equals average product. This relationship may be extended and understood intuitively. By definition, B's Average Product = Total Product/Number of Units of Input B; this is the average productivity of input B when a certain

---

[3] Notice the proportion B/A may change even in the more general situation where A is not fixed but simply not changing in the same proportion as B. The general case is referred to as the Law of Variable Proportions. The special case, where one or more inputs do not vary at all describes the situation to which the Law of Diminishing Returns applies.

[4] Marginal product is the slope ($= \Delta y/\Delta x$) of the total product function; therefore, whenever the slope of the total product function is zero—maxima, minima, or horizontal plateaus—marginal product is zero. For continuous functions, where the slope of the tangent to a function is roughly a measure of the first derivative, this can be stated in terms of derivatives.

number of units of B are employed (*ceteris paribus*). Average product rises if marginal product is greater than average product (when as a result of adding another unit of input B the addition to total product is greater than the average product), and average product falls when marginal product of an additional unit of input is less than average product. It follows that when average product is a maximum, the marginal product function cuts the average product function at its maximum point from above.

Note there is nothing inconsistent in the fact (as seen in Fig. 4.5) that marginal product may be rising, at a maximum, and falling, over the range where average product is rising. It is only when marginal product falls below the level of average product that average product too begins to fall. It is important to understand that when average is constant, marginal and average coincide. Average product is greatest in Fig. 4.5 when eight units of input B have been added. The average can be depicted diagrammatically as the tangent of the angle formed by the input (horizontal) axis and a ray from the origin to a point on the total product function.[5] It follows that if the total product function were linear and if it passed through the origin (the one in Fig. 4.5 does not meet these conditions), average product of input B would be constant as additional units of B are added.

[5] Recall that the total product function here is a cross section of the production surface, since input A is fixed (at $A = 5$ units).

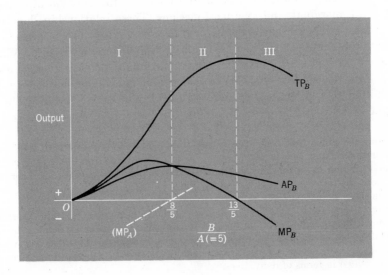

Fig. 4.5

Table 4.1

Stage	A	B	TP$_B$	MP$_B$	AB$_B$
I	5	0	0	—	0
	5	1	100	100	100
	5	2	250	150	125
	5	3	420	170	140
	5	4	620	200	155
	5	5	850	230	170
	5	6	1,110	260	185
	5	7	1,365	255	195
	5	8	1,600	235	200
II	5	9	1,800	200	200
	5	10	1,950	150	195
	5	11	2,057	107	187
	5	12	2,136	79	178
	5	13	2,184	48	168
III	5	14	2,184	0	156
	5	15	2,100	−84	140

In discrete terms, average, marginal, and total product are identical when only one unit of the variable input is used. The total product is the sum of the marginal products up to the given input level. These relationships are illustrated in Table 4.1.

Three Stages in a Short-Run Production Problem

The boundary between stage I and stage II corresponds to the point where the average product of *B* is a maximum (which is also the point—if hypothetically we move from right to left along the input axis—where the marginal product of *A*, holding *B* constant, would have become negative).

The boundary between stage II and stage III is similarly marked by the maximum point on the total product of *B* curve, beyond which point the marginal product of *B* becomes negative. This is also the point where the average product of the fixed factor *A* would be a maximum.[6]

[6] Note that the total product curve of the variable factor is directly related to average product curve of the fixed factor. This follows since the total product of *B* is the result of adding units of the variable factor *B* to a fixed number of units of *A*. By dividing the TP$_B$ at any point by some constant number of units of the fixed factor *A* we would get the average product of the fixed factor AP$_A$.

Under conditions of constant returns to scale, $\text{AP}_A = \text{MP}_A$ when $\text{MP}_B = 0$, and the relationship is symmetrical: $\text{AP}_B = \text{MP}_B$ when $\text{MP}_A = 0$. These relationships hold at the boundaries (see Fig. 4.5). Note, too, that when AP_B is rising, MP_A must be negative (in stage I); and again there is symmetry: when AP_A is rising, MP_B must be negative (in stage III).[7]

In the short run, a rational producer would not choose to remain in stage III; if he were there by some error in calculation, he could increase his total product by reducing his use of the variable factor B; that is, in stage III he would be overutilizing his fixed resources, and some of his variable inputs would be economically redundant. Another way of putting this would be to state that even if the variable resource B were free (an abundant noneconomic resource), the producer would not produce beyond that rate at which total product were maximum; he would choose to produce at the boundary between stages II and III. In this particular short-run production situation, the producer is temporarily stymied if demand increases to the point where it would be profitable to produce more than this short-run maximum. If he anticipates this situation, he may even decide to carry redundant variable resources, which he plans to use in the future with expanded fixed resources. The problem then assumes a long-run nature and the producer must consider varying some "fixed" input, say plant capacity, in order to increase the rate of output.

The only reason for operating in stage I (in Fig. 4.5) would be insufficient demand to permit taking advantage of increased average produc-

---

[7] The proofs of these relationships employ Euler's theorem, which applies under conditions where inputs and outputs increase in the same proportion—constant returns to scale (constant returns to scale is illustrated in Fig. 4.6a and defined in the following section). Euler's theorem states that the total product x will be exhausted if each input unit employed receives its marginal product:

$$x = \frac{\partial x}{\partial a} a + \frac{\partial x}{\partial b} b$$

where a and b are positive numbers of units of the two inputs, A and B; and the partial derivatives, $\partial x/\partial a$ and $\partial x/\partial b$, are the marginal products of A and B. From the theorem, it is apparent that if $\partial x/\partial a = 0$, then $x/b = \partial x/\partial b$.

Dividing Euler's theorem through by a, we obtain the following simple transformation:

$$\frac{x}{a} = \frac{\partial x}{\partial a} + \frac{\partial x}{\partial b} \frac{b}{a}$$

Recall that when $x/a(= \text{AP}_A)$ is rising, $\partial x/\partial a > x/a$; therefore $\partial x/\partial b$ must be negative.

tivity (and incidentally lower cost). If the fixed factor were divisible into smaller units, the producer could increase production by using fewer units of the fixed factor.

Suppose the variable and fixed factors were reversed. Instead of adding units of B to A, we hold B constant and vary the proportions by making A the variable factor (reversing the operation and moving to the left along the horizontal input axis in Fig. 4.5). We can maintain the same ratio B/A along the X-axis that existed when B was added to A. If we move to the left into stage I, the marginal product of A would become negative, reflecting the fact that if less of A were used, total product would increase.

In this illustration of three stages of return in a short-run production situation, no cost information was included. Without information regarding the relative costs of resources, a producer can do very little in the way of choosing the optimum resource combination (assuming he has some choice and some substitution is possible); however, even without knowledge of costs (providing they are not negative) stages I and III represent underutilization and overutilization (respectively) of the fixed factor (or factors) involved.

It would pay to operate in stage II (where diminishing returns to factors prevail): this is somewhere between the maximum average product of the variable factor and the maximum total product of the variable factor. Outside stage II, the marginal product of one or the other factor becomes negative. In stage I the fixed factor A is underutilized and redundant, whereas in stage III the fixed factor A is overutilized and the variable factor B is redundant. Where the marginal product of an input is negative, the producer could increase his product by using less of that input.

To clarify the symmetry of the relationship between the fixed and variable factors, we derive in Table 4.2 the implicit total, average, and marginal products of the fixed factor A from the corresponding total, average, and marginal products of the variable factor B. The values for TP_B, AP_B, and MP_B in Table 4.2 are taken from the first few rows of Table 4.1.

To derive TP_A, AP_A, and MP_A, B is scaled down and held fixed at 1 in column 7, while A is similarly scaled down to maintain the identical proportions in column 9 that appear in column 3 of this table. Assuming constant returns to scale (defined in the following section), if inputs are reduced by some constant, output will be reduced by this same constant.

For example, in the second row of Table 4.2, by taking half of the values of inputs B and A, output TP_B is also halved, and we obtain $B =$

56   Production

Table 4.2

(1) B	(2) A	(3) B/A	(4) TP_B	(5) AP_B	(6) MP_B	(7) B	(8) A	(9) B/A	(10) TP_A	(11) AP_A	(12) MP_A $(= \Delta TP_A/\Delta A)$
1	5	$\frac{1}{5}$	100	100		1	5	$\frac{1}{5}$	100	20	
					150						-10
2	5	$\frac{2}{5}$	250	125		1	$\frac{5}{2}$	$\frac{2}{5}$	125	50	
					170						-18
3	5	$\frac{3}{5}$	420	140		1	$\frac{5}{3}$	$\frac{3}{5}$	140	84	
					200						-36
4	5	$\frac{4}{5}$	620	155		1	$\frac{5}{4}$	$\frac{4}{5}$	155	124	
					230						-60
5	5	$\frac{5}{5}$	850	170		1	$\frac{5}{5}$	$\frac{5}{5}$	170	170	

1, $A = \frac{5}{2}$, and $TP_A = 125$ in columns 7, 8, and 10. And in the third row, by taking $\frac{1}{3}$ the values of B, A, and TP_B, we obtain $B = 1$, $A = \frac{5}{3}$, and $TP_A = 140$.

The proportions B/A in columns 3 and 9 are identical: $\frac{2}{5} = (\frac{1}{5})/2$ and $\frac{3}{5} = (\frac{1}{5})/3$. We simply divided the inputs in columns 1 and 2 by a constant in order to scale down input B in column 7 to 1. The proportion B/A in columns 3 and 9 remain the same. The values in columns 5 and 10 are the same, since AP_B in column 5 and TP_A in column 10 are both derived by dividing TP_B by the value of B in column 1. (If we had decided to hold B fixed at some value other than 1, the values of AP_B and TP_A would not have been identical.)

The values of B/A in Table 4.2 lie in stage I. As more units of input B are applied to $A = 5$, AP_B in column 5 increases. On the right-hand side of Table 4.2, input B remains constant at $B = 1$. Reading up from the bottom row, and increasing the number of units of A applied to B, AP_A (column 11) decreases in stage I, while in column 12 MP_A is negative. B/A is too small (or A/B too large—the variable factor B is overutilized). Table 4.2 corresponds to the data in the first six rows of Table 4.1, and to that part of stage I in Fig. 4.5 where MP_B is still rising. Table 4.2 emphasizes that it is the proportion B/A, not the absolute number of input units, that is crucial in the short-run theory of production.

If producers operate rationally, we can expect them to operate in the stage II—the region where the law of diminishing returns applies or where the marginal products of all inputs are positive and declining. (Note that marginal product begins to decline in stage I.) Just how rapidly marginal product declines depends on the adaptability of the particular operation—the inputs and outputs involved. Where certain factors must be used in fixed proportions (the case of limitational factors) no substitution between the factors is possible. The marginal product of either factor is zero and the production surface is reduced to a linear trace. An example is two parts hydrogen and one part oxygen to form water. The marginal product of the third unit of hydrogen is zero when only one unit of oxygen is available and water is the output being measured.

It is difficult to find cases where *all* inputs must be used in fixed proportions, if we consider the total process. Most patent drug products such as aspirin require fixed proportions of certain basic ingredients, but these may be combined with varying quantities of other factors to bring the completed product to market. One man operating one tractor may be a part of a farming operation requiring fertilizer, tools, storage facilities, other men, and machines. Certain grades of steel or blends of tobacco are examples of products that require fixed proportions of basic ingredients but permit variable proportions between the basic ingredients in combination with such other factors as machines and labor-skills.

Where fluctuations in demand are expected, the producer may purposely choose less productive forms of the fixed factor in order to achieve greater adaptability of form, so that the impact of diminishing returns is contained; the marginal product of the variable factor would decline more gradually over a broader range as short-run increases in the rate of output are required.

The short-run has been referred to several times as a situation where one or more of the resources are fixed. For one reason or another a production problem arises that calls for a decision involving only the variable resources. The short-run then really refers to a type of problem. An apparently short-run problem situation may be treated as a long-run problem where there exists the possibility of selling "fixed assets" or allowing them to depreciate without making provision for replacement. In the long-run all inputs are variable in quantity or form. It is to this case that we now turn our attention.

Returns to Scale: Constant, Increasing, and Decreasing

We now consider the long-run situation where all inputs are variable and can be increased proportionately (according to scale).[8] This case is represented by a linear ray, 0-0′, going out from the origin. Any

---

[8] Increasing all inputs proportionately is not necessarily the least expensive way to expand output. In the case of zero substitutability we have no choice but to vary all inputs proportionately along a given linear ray.

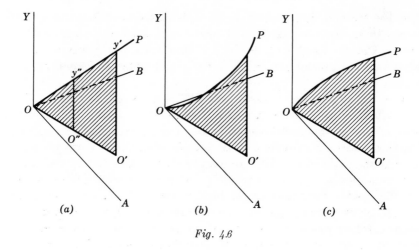

Fig. 4.6

point on such a ray represents a *fixed proportion* of inputs A and B. As we move out from the origin along a linear ray, all inputs increase at the same rate: $\frac{2}{1}$ to $\frac{4}{2}$ represents a 100% rate of increase for A and for B. See Fig. 4.6.

If we examine the outputs on the production surface vertically above this linear ray we see that three general shapes are possible. These three shapes, illustrated in Fig. 4.6, represent constant, increasing, and decreasing returns to scale.[9]

The constant returns to scale case (Fig. 4.6*a*) mean that if all inputs are varied at a certain percentage rate, output will change by the same rate. In mathematical language this is called a linear homogeneous production function.

In Fig. 4.6*a*, output increases by some constant amount per unit change

---

[9] Note there is no inconsistency between the nonlinear trace in a short-run production situation and the long-run constant returns to scale production function. If the short-run total product curve contains an inflection point so that marginal product initially rises (increasing returns), a portion of the cross-sectional trace on the production surface must be concave prior to the inflection point. It is quite possible to have a linear homogeneous production function together with a short-run total product curve containing an inflection point and a maximum point. See comments in *AER*, Sept. 1964, No. 5, pp. 739–753, by H. H. Liebhafsky, Warren Nutter, Ryuzo Sato, et al. Professor Sato provides an example of such a production function:

$$Y = F(K,L) = \frac{K^2L^2}{b_0L^3} + b_1K, \qquad b_0 > 0, \qquad b_1 > 0$$

where Y = total product, K = capital, and L = labor.

in input A (and B). A doubling of each input implies that the input combination $0'$ is twice $0''$ along the straight line ray. Under constant returns to scale, a doubling of the input combination results in a doubling of output—y' is double output y''. The output/input ratio $y''/0''$ is a measure of physical efficiency. Figure 4.6a is an example of constant returns to scale, where no gain or loss in physical efficiency occurs as we increase the scale of operation.

Figures 4.6b and 4.6c represent cases of increasing and decreasing returns to scale, respectively, where physical efficiency increases or decreases as the scale of operation is expanded.

The decreasing returns to scale case (Fig. 4.6c) cannot be accounted for on the grounds that the quality of the input units deteriorates, since the input units are assumed homogeneous. One might reasonably question why increasing or decreasing returns should occur (Figs. 4.6b and 4.6c) if the process or operation is expanded according to scale, except as a result of relaxing the assumption of homogeneous units. Relaxing this assumption would explain, for example, lower productivity (say yield per acre on farm output) as less fertile acres are added and combined in the same ratio with other inputs of uniform quality; or higher productivity as an operation expands according to scale might be explained by an experience or learning factor that improves the quality and efficiency of certain inputs with time.

Specialization of process and division of labor account for some cases of increasing returns to scale. The Laws of Probability have been used to explain why inventories need not increase as rapidly as sales to maintain an optimal sales/inventory ratio. This interesting example of the advantage of large-scale operations is related to the greater stability and predictability of large numbers.

There are cases of increasing returns to scale that result from certain physical relationships. Larger diameter pipe lines may permit increased rates of oil flow per unit of pumping energy because of the smaller energy loss due to friction. The materials necessary to enlarge the storage capacity of a warehouse are related to the square of the surface dimensions, whereas the actual increase in storage capacity is related to the cube of the surface dimensions.

We should be careful in making premature judgments of increasing returns to scale. Increased physical efficiency of operations in developing economies, sometimes used as an illustration of increasing returns to scale, is often the result of the improved quality of input units, the availability of new complementary inputs (whether internal or external to the firm's operation), or unavoidable excess capacities in certain inputs at low operating rates.

The physical characteristic of particular processes requires certain

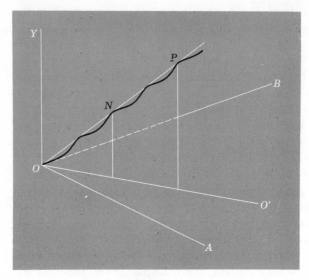

Fig. 4.7

optimal sized components; for example, the relative sizes of tractor motor to tractor weight to land size. Discrepancies between actual and optimal input sizes do occur since certain inputs are simply not available in certain sizes. This problem is the *indivisibility* of input units, as contrasted to *adaptability*, which refers to malleability of form of the inputs rather than to size of the input unit.

Indivisibility might explain why only discrete points exist along input ray 0-0′ and along the output ray *OP* in the Constant Returns to Scale case; the adaptability problem might explain a "wiggly" output ray (these two suggestions are illustrated in Fig. 4.7). Lack of perfect divisibility or adaptability really does not explain the existence of the general cases of increasing and decreasing returns to scale, if the operation is able to expand proportionately and by large enough increments to overcome the problems of divisibility and adaptability (say from *N* to *P* in Fig. 4.7).

The managerial function is often singled out for special treatment as an input, which at some decision-making level (whether it be adapting to the unexpected, coordination, or control) cannot be expanded proportionately. Even if identical units of trained and talented management personnel were available, it is argued that beyond some size, managerial capacity becomes less efficient. This size would vary for different operations and over time with changes in technology; for example, automation, control systems, or advances in management science. Decentralization and competing semiautonomous units—as the case of General Motors—sometimes seem to belie this argument. The area remains a fertile field for research and discussion.

The classical argument for diseconomies of large-scale production units, necessary for the stability of purely competitive markets, rests in part on the limitations of entrepreneurial capacity; perhaps as operations expand and become increasingly complex, a part of the managerial function cannot be expanded, so that its capacity to control efficiently is limited.

5

Production and Cost

While demand derives from consumer preference and budgetary constraints, supply drives from production possibilities, resource costs, and the objectives of business firms.

In this chapter our focus is on the costs of supplying goods and services—a function of physical production possibilities (production functions relating physical output to inputs) and resource prices (factor supply functions relating factor prices to rate of use). We shall examine cost of production in general terms prior to considering objectives of business firms and optimum price-output combinations in the context of various market structures.

The factors influencing the decision to produce will differ according to the type of problem. Recall that long-run production problems require a time period long enough (no definite time span is implied) so that all factors of production can be varied. The long-run problem involves a projection of costs and revenues over time to ascertain whether it is profitable to undertake capital investment. In the short-run certain inputs are fixed and production decisions can properly disregard fixed costs paid to the owners of fixed inputs. Consider a situation where market demand has weakened *after* an irreversible investment in plant and equipment. Choosing a particular rate of production or schedule of operation is then independent of the fixed costs previously incurred. Usually the short-run refers to the day-to-day operation of the firm, whereas the long-run involves the planning function of the firm.

The quantity a producer would be willing to supply in a given period of time can be depicted by a hypothetical functional relationship: the supply function. The phrase "willing to supply" correctly implies that the supply function is a behavioral function. The quantity supplied will depend on the manner and extent to which the producer reacts to one or another variable which he considers pertinent to his decision.

Supply Curve

A simple supply curve focuses on the price-quantity relationship—the rate at which a producer is willing to supply a product as a function of the price he expects to receive: $q = f(p)$. Using price as the primary independent variable has a long historical precedent.

The supply curve applies principally to perfectly competitive markets where price responds freely to market forces, and where individual producers independently react to the price established in the market (without themselves being able to affect that price). By contrast, in market situations dominated by a few large producers who are active price setters, the supply curve as an independent functional relationship may cease to be meaningful. Price remains a variable of considerable significance, but it is no longer an independent variable to which the producer responds.

Cost—Several Viewpoints

The concept of cost is among the most interesting of economic concepts. Historically cost was viewed by the Classical School as a "real" cost of production in terms of the effort, pain, or sacrifice (disutility) of producers; later the Austrian School viewed cost as essentially demand determined—derived from consumer preferences. The Classical viewpoint was that the "real" costs involved in producing do not change simply because consumer tastes or preferences change. On the other extreme, the Austrians reasoned that the cost or value of the resources used (if supply is given) is derived from market demand, independent of the "real" cost experienced by the producer. If no one wants the product, the Austrians reasoned, it is not worth much, however arduously the producer or seller labors to produce the product. The Austrians viewed cost as an *opportunity cost*. They considered that if labor, material, land, capital, and entrepreneurial effort could be used more productively in some alternative employ, then the cost of the resources must reflect the value of their contribution in some best foregone opportunity.

The opportunity cost of a resource in a particular use is equal to what the resource could earn elsewhere or the maximum value of its contribution in some best alternative use. The opportunity cost of a resource in its present use is the value of its contribution foregone by not using it in its best alternative use.[1]

If a resource is paid less than its opportunity cost, the implication is that the resource could earn more and be more productive elsewhere. Net product would increase if a reallocation or transfer were to take place.[2] Usually a firm has no choice but to pay an amount equal to the opportunity cost of the particular resource. If it does not, there will be an incentive for resources to withdraw and relocate. Resources will transfer until opportunity cost is no longer greater than current earnings. Certain "implicit" opportunity costs to owned-resources may not appear as a cash outlay or business expenditure, but must be imputed. Examples are the salary for managerial services of the owner-manager, or the return to the owner's equity capital which is tied up in the business; both the owner and his money might earn more elsewhere—the implicit opportunity cost must be imputed. Suppose the owner could sell the business for $100,000 and reinvest the sum at 10% per year in some equally risky best alternative venture. The imputed opportunity cost of capital would be $10,000 per year.

There may be certain psychic benefits from remaining in present employment (or self-employment), and there may be market imperfections that prevent or inhibit transfer even if present money earnings are less than opportunity costs. Nevertheless, the cost of employing a resource is its opportunity cost, whether it requires a cash outlay (explicit cost) or not (implicit cost). If the cash payment is less than the opportunity cost, then the part of the opportunity cost not paid is an implicit cost. When we consider cost in this text, we mean opportunity cost.

A General Approach to Production Possibilities and Cost of Production

There are often several ways of combining resources to achieve a given output, but perhaps only one way results in lowest cost. In deriving cost functions, the production function is taken as a constraint; the cost functions describe the minimum cost of producing various rates

---

[1] The broader social cost interpretation of opportunity cost is intended. We shall postpone discussion of the distinction between social (total) costs and private costs borne by private producers. See A. C. Pigou, *The Economics of Welfare*, 4th edition, London, Macmillan, 1932, Part II, Ch. 9.

[2] Rent is the earnings surplus that results when a resource makes a contribution in its present use over and above its opportunity cost.

of output. The cost functions summarize and convey information derived from production and factor supply functions. If factor supply functions are infinitely elastic with respect to output (as in purely competitive factor markets), resource prices can be taken as constant. In the analysis that follows in this chapter, we shall assume resource prices remain constant so that we can simplify the relationship between production and cost. A change in the parameters of the production function or a change in factor supply conditions will affect the cost function.

What is the least cost combination of inputs required to produce a given output? This manner of putting the question assumes the output rate is given, as in practice it may be, particularly if the production process takes considerable time and planning; in such cases price information and sales forecasts must be transformed into output requirements well in advance of shipment for the final market and perhaps for inventory. Alternatively, but perhaps less realistically, the question could be formulated as follows: For a given outlay (cost), what is the maximum physical output attainable? We focus our attention on the formal aspects of the first case—minimizing the cost of a given physical output. Later we shall consider the determination of the level of output.

Isoquants

An isoquant is a convenient device for compressing the three-dimensional picture of a production function, two input axes and output surface, into two dimensions. Each isoquant (or isoproduct curve) represents the various input combinations that can be used to produce a given output. Each point on the various isoquants is a maximum output that can be achieved with that input combination. Isoquants are contour lines on the production surface similar to the lines showing equal altitudes on a topographic map. The further the isoquant from the origin, the larger is the output represented. The input axes, A and B in Fig. 5.1, are the same as those used previously to depict production surfaces; however, instead of an output axis, each isoquant (I_1, I_2, and I_3) in Fig. 5.1) represents a certain output level. Isoquants do not intersect; if they did we would have different outputs with the same input combinations, or violating the definition, we would have the same and different outputs on each of the intersecting isoquants.

By representing the isoquants as continuous curves, we imply that the inputs are perfectly divisible; that is, they come in any size units

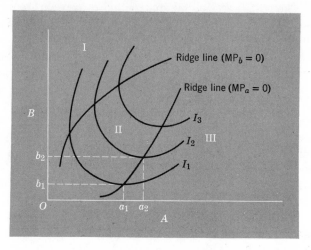

Fig. 5.1

or fractions of a unit. This makes more sense in terms of tons of coal or hours of work than it does in terms of numbers of locomotives. Even in the latter case, however, the indivisibility problem can be overcome if we can change the measure and form of the input unit from numbers of locomotives to units of diesel power. At any time there may, of course, be limitations on the available sizes of a given input.

The equation of an isoquant can be represented by $\Delta A\,(\mathrm{MP}_A)\ +\ \Delta B\,(\mathrm{MP}_B)\ =\ 0$. This follows from the definition of an isoquant. As we move from one point to another along an isoquant, the loss in output from using less of B must be just offset by the addition to output from using more of A—no change in output can result from the substitution of A for B along a given isoquant: $-\Delta B\,(\mathrm{MP}_B)\ =\ \Delta A\,(\mathrm{MP}_A)$; therefore the slope $\Delta B/\Delta A\ =\ -\mathrm{MP}_A/\mathrm{MB}_B$. The slope of an isoquant is called the rate of technical substitution. We can also identify the (marginal) input coefficient MI, which is simply the change in input required to produce an additional unit of output. The input coefficient of input B is the reciprocal of the marginal product of B. [$\mathrm{MI}_B = 1/\mathrm{MP}_B$ $= 1/\Delta Y/\Delta B = \Delta B/\Delta Y$.] The rate of technical substitution RTS, which is the slope of an isoquant, can be represented in terms of the input coefficients:

$$\mathrm{RTS} = -\,\frac{\mathrm{MP}_A}{\mathrm{MP}_B} = -\,\frac{1/\mathrm{MI}_A}{1/\mathrm{MI}_B} = -\,\frac{\mathrm{MI}_B}{\mathrm{MI}_A}$$

The degree of input substitutability is represented by the curvature of the isoquants (or isoproduct curves).[3]

If factors are substitutes, the slope or rate of technical substitution RTS is negative. Convexity—decreasing RTS as we move downward and to the right along an isoquant—indicates that the inputs are not perfect substitutes. Convexity follows as the input proportions change, if the law of diminishing returns (decreasing marginal product) applies.[4]

In the case of perfect substitutes, the slope (rate of technical substitution) would be a constant. A given amount of one input could always be exchanged for some given amount of the other along a given isoquant (isoproduct) curve. The zero substitutability case is one where a given output requires fixed amounts of each input; no additional amount of A can be substituted for B, or vice versa. With a given amount of one input, units of the other become completely redundant beyond a certain level.

In Fig. 5.2 we illustrate the extreme cases of perfect substitutability

[3] Note the similarity between the analysis that follows and the representation of consumer choice using indifference curves. In fact isoquants are sometimes referred to as producer indifference curves. There is one difference, which results from the way the problem is formulated: in the theory of consumer choice we focused on the equilibrium conditions that exist if utility is to be maximized subject to income or budget restrictions; here, cost is to be minimized subject to the constraint offered by the production function.

[4] Again, as with indifference curves, diminishing returns does not necessarily imply convexity. We need the additional qualification that the input be sufficiently neutral so that the change in rate of use of one input does not affect the marginal product of the other, at least not enough to offset the decreasing $\mathrm{MP}_A/\mathrm{MP}_B$ ratio as more of input A is substituted for input B.

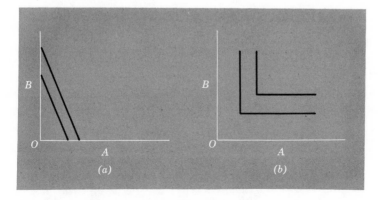

Fig. 5.2

(Fig. 5.2*a*) and zero substitutability (Fig. 5.2*b*). With ingenuity, substitutability is often possible, even though in the early stages of planning, fixed input proportions may be specified for a particular process. Flexibility in the use of resources may be planned, or it may emerge in implementation of the production process, sometimes after considerable experience with the operation.

In Fig. 5.1 the short-run total product function with *A* the variable input and *B* the fixed input can be derived by holding *B* constant at, say, $B = b_1$, and moving out along the dotted line parallel to the *A*-axis.

The lower ridge line in Fig. 5.1 cuts the isoquants at points where the isoquants begin to turn in and assume a positive slope. It is at these points that the slopes (RTS) of the isoquants become horizontal (or vertical in the case of the upper ridge line). Along the lower ridge line the marginal product of input *A* is zero.

I_1 represents the maximum output that can be achieved with b_1 of *B* (if b_1 is combined with a_1 of *A*). At (a_2, b_2), $\text{RTS}_{AB} = \text{MP}_A/\text{MP}_B = 0$.

If *B* is fixed at b_2 and we add units of *A*, output increases up to a_2 units of *A*. When a_2 units of *A* are used, total product, I_2, is the maximum attainable with b_2 units of *B*. Beyond a_2, total product decreases and marginal product of *A* becomes negative. At a_2 where total product of *A* (TP_A) is maximum (with *B* fixed at b_2), the average product of *B* ($= \text{TP}_A/b_2$ units of *B*) is maximum. The same reasoning applies to other points on the isoquants where the marginal product becomes zero. The two ridge lines pass through these points and mark the boundaries of Regions I, II, and III (similar to the stages of production shown for the special case of $A = 5$ in Fig. 4.5). In Stages or Regions I and III (outside of the two ridge lines) one of the inputs is redundant in the sense that output would actually increase if less of the input were used until production were again located in Region II.

In production theory there is no essential difference between the approach utilizing product curves and the approach utilizing the more general expository device, isoquants. But with isoquants we can present, in two dimensions, information on resource costs as well as technical information summarized by the production function, to analyze what the optimum (least cost) combination of resources should be to produce a given output. A measure of technological efficiency, based completely on the knowledge of physical production possibilities, may be of some interest to someone, but it is of little concern to the economist. The economist is concerned with *economic efficiency*, the determination of which requires knowledge of input prices as well as physical possibilities.

Resource price information is represented by price (or isocost) lines.

Every point on a given price line represents the same cost outlay (C), while every point on a given isoquant represents the same output rate. The equation of the price line is

$$C = P_a \cdot a + P_b \cdot b \quad \text{or} \quad b = \frac{C}{p_b} - \frac{P_a}{P_b} a$$

Since the axes represent units of inputs, the slope of the price line equals the relative input costs, $-P_a/P_b$.[5] The parallel linear price lines in Fig. 5.3 represent constant relative input prices, independent of the intensity or proportion of factor use.

Least Cost Factor Combination

By "maximum economic efficiency" we mean the least cost combination of resources to produce a given output. Both knowledge of production possibilities and input prices are required to identify economically efficient resource combinations. In general, the least cost of producing a given output (a point on a given isoquant) lies at the point where the isoquant touches the price line representing the smallest possible outlay (the price line nearest to the origin). At any point other than the point of tangency, the isoquant intersects higher budget lines; thus away from the point of tangency, greater cost will be incurred in producing a given output. The point that fulfills the cost-minimizing objective is the point where the isoquant (which is likely to be convex to the origin) is tangent to the linear price line. At this point of tangency, the slope of the price line equals the slope of the isoquant, $P_a/P_b = \text{MP}_a/\text{MP}_b$. This most important result—the total cost of a given output will be minimized if the resources are so employed that the ratio of the marginal products of the factors are proportional to the ratio of their prices—can easily be generalized to include more than two factors. Alternatively, this may be written $\text{MP}_a/P_a = \text{MP}_b/P_b$. The meaning of this equation can be better understood if we look at a situation where the equality does not hold, $\text{MP}_a/P_a > \text{MP}_b/P_b$. The rational (cost-minimizing) producer would react [as did the rational (utility-maximizing) consumer] by substituting input A for input B. The inequality means that additional output (marginal product) per dollar (or any money measure) of A

[5] Suppose a total outlay (C) of \$4000, a unit price of $B = \$80$ and a unit price of $A = \$100$; then \$4000/\$80 $= 50$ units (q_b) and \$4000/\$100 $= 40$ units (q_a). A little algebra will convince you that $P_a/P_b = q_b/q_a$, which is the slope of the price line.

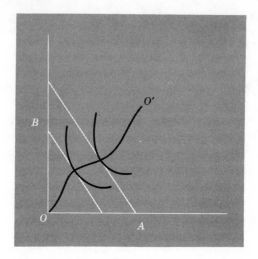

Fig. 5.3

is greater than the additional output per dollar of *B*. If the producer has made a mistake and uses too much of *B* (and/or too little of *A*), he can reduce his costs by reallocating his dollar outlay (assuming the law of diminishing returns holds so that the marginal product of *B* will increase and the marginal product of *A* will decrease as he spends fewer dollars on *B* and more dollars on *A*) until eventually the contributions per dollar of each resource will be in balance, $MP_a/P_a = MP_b/P_b$.

Equilibrium

A change in relative input prices may induce a producer to vary his use of inputs, depending on the degree of substitutability of the inputs and the strength of the expansion effect (recall the income and substitution effects considered earlier). We have assumed that the relative prices of the inputs remain constant, so that the price lines will be parallel (equal slopes, $-P_a/P_b$). The expansion path 0-0' in Fig. 5.3 connects the points of tangency between the price lines and isoquants where the slopes are equal:

$$\frac{P_a}{P_b} = \frac{MP_a}{MP_b} \quad \text{or} \quad \frac{MP_a}{P_a} = \frac{MP_b}{P_b}$$

The expansion path of a linear homogeneous production function is a straight line ray from the origin.[6] Recall that with such a function, if each input is increased by a constant k, output increases by this same constant k (to the first power). The locus of least cost input combinations of various outputs are represented along the expansion path. With constant returns to scale and constant input prices, the least cost of various outputs requires constant input proportions, as indicated by the linear expansion path.

Cost of Production

The minimum costs of various rates of outputs are represented along the expansion path in Fig. 5.3. The average cost function relating average costs per unit to rates of output y, and the marginal cost function relating changes in total cost TC to unit changes in output are easily derived from the total costs of various outputs: $AC = TC/y$ and $MC = \Delta TC/\Delta y$.

The ratios, marginal product to input price, are equal for all inputs when the cost of producing a given output is minimized along the expansion path. The reciprocal of any of the ratios (MP_a/P_a, MP_b/P_b, . . .) equals the long-run marginal cost (MC) of producing one additional unit of output:

$$MC = \frac{P_a}{MP_a} = \frac{P_a}{\Delta y/\Delta a} = \frac{P_a \cdot \Delta a}{\Delta y} = \frac{\Delta TC}{\Delta y}$$

(We could have used $MC = P_B/MP_B$ or $MC = P_c/MP_c$, instead of $MC = P_A/MP_A$, since for small changes in the vicinity of the expansion path, $P_A/MP_A = P_B/MP_B = P_c/MP_c = \ldots$.) For the case of a single variable, consider the meaning of P_a/MP_a—the additional cost of hiring resource A at constant price P_a divided by the marginal product MP_a. If $P_a = \$10$ and $MP_a = 2$ is the contribution to output of a unit of A, then the marginal cost per unit of output would be $\$5$; to produce an

---

[6] With a linear homogeneous production function, marginal products do not change with scale but only as factor proportions change. If all inputs and output increase proportionately by some constant k (as along a linear ray from the origin), factor proportions remain constant and *changes* in the inputs and output increase in the same proportion: $ky_2 - ky_1 = k(y_2 - y_1) = k\Delta y$. Since $MP_a = \Delta y/\Delta a = (k\Delta y/k\Delta a)$ and $MP_b = \Delta y/\Delta b = k\Delta y/k\Delta b$ MP_a/MP_b remains constant for proportionate input changes. So, if the slopes of the isoquants remain constant along a linear ray from the origin and if the price lines are parallel (P_a/P_b constant), the expansion path $MP_a/MP_b = P_a/P_b$ will be linear. With constant returns to scale and constant input prices, input proportions remain constant along the linear expansion path.

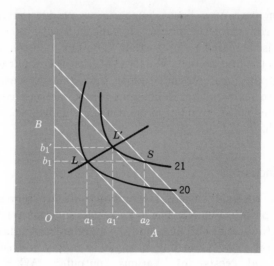

Fig. 5.4

additional unit of output would require one-half unit of resource A; therefore MC $= \frac{1}{2}$ ($10) $=$ $5.00.

The long-run total cost function relating the minimum total cost to various output levels is derived from the points of tangency between the price lines and isoquants. The expansion path represents the minimum total cost for the long-run situation since all factors are variable. There are, of course, various ways to increase output and as many ways for cost to vary. We assumed that resource prices were fixed and independent of output, and that total cost represented the minimum total cost of producing various outputs, subject to the constraint of available technical knowledge. In Fig. 5.4 the short-run adjustment is illustrated and compared to the long-run adjustment.

The least cost of expanding the rate of output from 20 to 21 units would be along the expansion path where inputs A and B are both varied and according to the condition $\mathrm{MP}_A/\mathrm{MP}_B = P_A/P_B$; the least cost combination of inputs is maintained as we move from L to L'. If, however, in the short run, input B is fixed at b_1, then to increase output by one unit, input A must be used more intensively from a_1 to a_2. The short-run marginal cost of increasing output by one unit, moving from L to S, is greater than the long-run marginal cost of going from L to L' along the expansion path. At S, $\mathrm{MP}_A/\mathrm{MP}_B < P_A/P_B$. By reallocating expenditure from A to B and moving back onto the expansion path at L', the marginal cost of producing the extra unit would be less, since L' is on the same isoquant but on a lower isocost curve than S.

Along the expansion path where both inputs are variable, and where ΔA and ΔB are the least cost input changes required to increase output, $\text{MC} = \Delta\text{TC}/\Delta y = (P_a\Delta A + P_b\Delta B)/\Delta y$. Along the expansion path, ΔTC to produce Δy will be minimized, since all factors are varied in optimal proportions:

$$\text{MC} = \frac{P_A\Delta A}{\Delta y} + \frac{P_B\Delta B}{\Delta y} = \frac{P_A}{\Delta y/\Delta A} + \frac{P_B}{\Delta y/\Delta B} = \frac{P_A}{\text{MP}_A} + \frac{P_B}{\text{MP}_B}$$

$$\text{or} \quad \frac{1}{\text{MC}} = \frac{\text{MP}_A}{P_A} + \frac{\text{MP}_B}{P_B}$$

In the short run, adjustment is to some extent incomplete since the change in the rate of output does not take place along the expansion path; to complete the adjustment and minimize the total cost of producing a given output, we must move along a given isoquant onto the expansion path.

The analysis in the preceding section can be summarized and restated more formally:

Given: Factor prices and output level.

Objective: Minimize total cost of production, subject to constraint of the production function.

Optimizing Condition: To the extent possible, choose the factor combination such that the ratio of factor prices is equal to the ratio of the corresponding marginal products.

Total, Marginal, and Average Cost

Most statistical studies have concentrated on total cost functions; however (as we have seen), average and marginal costs are easily derived from the total cost function. Average cost, defined as TC/Output, is the tangent of the angle θ formed by the output-axis and a line from the origin to a point on the total cost curve (NO''/OO'' in Fig. 5.5 is the minimum value for the tangent of θ—minimum average cost). The marginal cost of a particular output, defined as $\Delta\text{TC}/\Delta$ Output is given by the slope of a straight line drawn tangent to the total cost function. In Fig. 5.5 the output O' corresponding to the inflection point M of the total cost function is the output at which marginal cost is a minimum, since the slope of the total cost function decreases up to the inflection point M and increases thereafter. At output O'' where average cost (equal to the tangent of θ) is a minimum, marginal cost

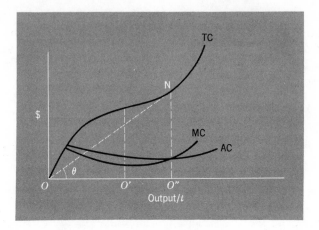

Fig. 5.5

equals average cost. At the point N, the slope of a line drawn tangent to the total cost curve is identical to the tangent of θ.

Note that for a linear total cost curve beginning at the origin (implying there are no fixed costs or overhead), marginal cost and average cost are equal and constant (as is the case in the long run with a linear homogeneous production function with constant input prices).

The typical short-run total and marginal and average cost functions are considered to have the general shapes sketched in Fig. 5.6.

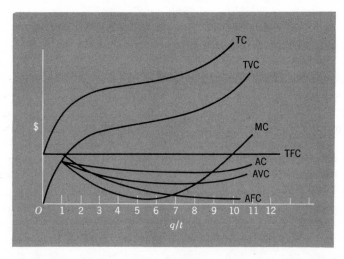

Fig. 5.6

These relationships among the various costs are illustrated in Table 5.1. Note that TC and TVC are vertically parallel. The difference at any output is equal to TFC. AFC is a rectangular hyperbole: $AFC \cdot q = TFC$, which is a constant. AVC and AV converge due to declining AFC. AC reaches its minimum point at a higher output than does AVC, since AFC is still declining, offsetting for a while the increase in AVC $(AC = AFC + AVC)$. The initial decline of the average cost function is due principally to relatively high fixed costs at zero output. The initial decline of the marginal cost function is attributable to under-utilization of the fixed factor (recall the discussion in the theory of production). The subsequent increase in marginal cost is related to the law of diminishing returns—the declining marginal product of the variable factors.

Table 5.1

(1)	(2)	(3)	(4)	(5)	(6)	(7)	(8)	(9)	(10)	(11)	(12)
					$(a = 5, P_A = \$50)$		$(P_B = \$100)$				
A	B	TP_B	MP_B	AP_B	TFC	AFC	TVC	AVC	TC	AC	MC
5	0	0	—	0	250	—	0	—	250	—	—
5	1	100	100	100	250	2.50	100	1.00	350	3.50	1.00
5	2	250	150	125	250	1.00	200	0.80	450	1.80	0.67
5	3	420	170	140	250	0.60	300	0.71	550	1.28	0.59
5	4	620	200	155	250	0.40	400	0.65	650	1.04	0.50
5	5	850	230	170	250	0.29	500	0.59	750	0.88	0.43
5	6	1,110	260	185	250	0.23	600	0.54	850	0.77	0.38
5	7	1,365	255	195	250	0.18	700	0.51	950	0.70	0.39
5	8	1,600	235	200	250	0.16	800	0.50	1,050	0.66	0.43
5	9	1,800	200	200	250	0.14	900	0.50	1,150	0.64	0.50
5	10	1,950	150	195	250	0.13	1,000	0.51	1,250	0.64	0.67
5	11	2,057	107	187	250	0.12	1,100	0.53	1,350	0.66	0.93
5	12	2,136	79	178	250	0.11	1,200	0.56	1,450	0.68	1.27
5	13	2,184	48	168	250	0.11	1,300	0.60	1,550	0.72	2.08
5	14	2,184	0	156	250	0.11	1,400	0.64	1,650	0.75	∞
5	15	2,100	−84	140	250	0.12	1,500	0.71	1,750	0.83	—

$$TFC = a \cdot P_A$$

$$AFC = \frac{TFC}{TP_B} = \frac{(6)}{(3)}$$

$$TVC = b \cdot P_B = (2) \cdot P_B$$

$$AVC = \frac{TVC}{TP_B} = \frac{(8)}{(3)} \quad \left(AVC = \frac{P_B}{AP_B} = \frac{P_B}{(5)}\right)$$

$$TC = TFC + TVC = (6) + (8)$$

$$AC = \frac{TC}{TP_B} = \frac{(10)}{(3)}$$

$$MC = \frac{\Delta TC}{\Delta TP_B} = \frac{\Delta TVC}{\Delta TP_B} = \frac{\Delta(10)}{\Delta(3)}$$

This typical cost function is consistent with the situation where the slope of the total cost function is approximately constant over a broad

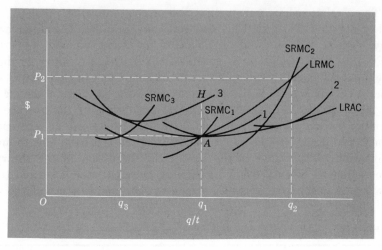

Fig. 5.7

range of operation; in Fig. 5.6 the marginal cost of increasing the rate of output between outputs 2 and 6 appears to be roughly constant.

Long-Run Average Cost (LRAC)

The long-run average cost function (LRAC) is useful for planning purposes, as in selecting the optimum scale of plant or firm, one capable of producing at lowest possible unit costs (Firm 1 in Fig. 5.7). Implicit in any such long-run planning is a capital investment decision.

A firm planning a long-run investment decision must consider both the size of the market that will support the investment and the optimum size of the capital investment on plant and equipment that will maximize the rate of return on the investment. There is an avoidable risk involved in choosing to build a larger than optimum-sized firm (e.g., Firm 2 in Fig. 5.7).

Suppose Firm 1 is an optimum-sized (most efficient) firm, and Firm 2 is a higher-cost profit-maximizing-sized firm (if price = P_2). Purely competitive theory (as discussed later) tells us that in long-run equilibrium, firms of size 1 will survive. Positive economic profit at price P_2 will induce entry of new firms into the market until the market is divided among more and more competitors. Supply will increase and price will decline to P_1. At the long-run equilibrium price P_1, only optimum-sized firms of size 1 will prevail, and no longer will new firms want entry in hopes of obtaining higher than competitive returns.

Where entry barriers exist, an investment in a firm of size 2 may be attempted, but the risk is greater than investment in an optimum-sized firm. Investors would have to be convinced that the market would not decline, or that smaller, more efficient firms would not enter and bring about a price below that anticipated by a firm of size 2.

The Planning Curve

Instead of the short-run average cost curves representing different firms, more commonly they represent possible sizes (of plants or any producing unit) a firm may choose to build, buy, or lease. Once the decision is made, the firm is temporarily saddled with SRAC related to plant sizes 1, 2, or 3. (Refer back to Fig. 5.7).

If 3 is chosen because it is estimated that the optimum average output will be q_3, a long-term commitment is involved. During this time, if, say, demand increases and the firm would like to increase production to q_1, the firm will be able to produce at a rate q_1 with a plant the size of 3 at a cost H—an average cost quite high compared to average cost using the lowest cost "optimal scale" plant 1.

The firm's LRAC curve is often referred to as a planning or envelope curve. If there are an infinite number of sizes to choose from, the planning curve will be a smooth envelope of the possible plant sizes the firm can consider—this is the LRAC curve in Fig. 5.7.

Note that only plant 1 would be able to produce a given output at lowest unit cost and still be used at its optimal capacity (minimum cost), since only 1's short-run average cost curve is tangent to the long-run average cost curve at its minimum cost point.

If LRAC is bowl-shaped at points other than A—the lowest cost point—its slope will be positive or negative so it will not touch any of the short-run cost curves, with the exception of 1, at their lowest cost points where their slope is zero.[7] At the tangency points where

---

[7] In a supplementary note to his classic article "Cost Curves and Supply Curves," reprinted in Readings in Price Theory, *AEA*, 1952, p. 227, Jacob Viner amusingly writes, "If I had known what an 'envelope' was I would not have given my excellent draftsman the technically impossible and economically inappropriate assignment of drawing an (LR) AC curve which would pass through the lowest cost points of all the (SR) AC curves and yet not rise above any AC curve at any point." This is the famous Vinerian error.

costs of producing a given output are at a minimum, the firm's SR and LR marginal cost of producing that output will be equal, since SR and LR average and total costs are equal at the tangency point and have the same slope in the immediate neighborhood of that point.

Let us consider the calculation of the per period (1 year) total cost from which LRAC is calculated. Suppose the total investment cost can be spread over the length of life of the investment so that an annual depreciation charge represents capital investment. To this charge the going rate of interest—a competitive rate, say 4% per annum (this means $4 on every $100 each year)—is added after converting the rate into dollars by multiplying the rate by the number of 100 dollars involved in the investment. A $5000 capital investment would require an annual interest charge of $4 \times 50 = $200. Even if the money capital is owned, an equivalent implicit opportunity cost must be imputed for planning and control purposes. A similar rate of interest should be charged on working capital.

To find the expected rate of earnings, we can multiply expected average cost and revenue by the expected yearly output rate, and compute total revenue and total cost (which includes depreciation and interest charges) to find expected net earnings (after tax) for the year. The implicit time horizon is assumed infinite; the investment, whatever its size, is completely amortized at the end of its life and the initial capital investment plus the opportunity cost of capital is assumed recovered.

If we assume a constant and continuing stream of revenue and cost, the rate of earnings then reduces to the ratio of net earnings (TR − TC) divided by the size of the initial investment. Information regarding the size or length of life of the investment is often omitted in explanations of the traditional LRAC curves. The implicit assumptions are that product price and unit costs will continue indefinitely, and the depreciation included in the long-run total cost function will be sufficient to recover the capital outlays. The investment criterion, based on yearly cost and revenue, also implicitly assumes the continuation of the average rate of output.

Some of the operational problems in long-run planning involving capital investment are often overlooked when the problem is framed in terms of the static long-run average cost curve.[8]

---

[8] In a more operationally oriented method to determine whether an investment of limited duration is worthwhile, the investor must consider the discounted stream of expected future earnings (annual revenues less annual expenses excluding depreciation) against the discounted capital expenditures, to see if the expected rate of return $\geqq$ competitive rate of return plus an appropriate risk premium, reflecting the uncertainty of the investment.

Research in Aggregate Production Functions

Measuring and estimating the parameters of the production function in physical terms is often feasible for a particular firm but not at higher levels of aggregation, where indexes (of physical quantities or deflated values) have to be employed. Where more than one industry or technological process is involved, value-added estimates are used to approximate physical data.

No attempt is made here to elucidate in detail the problems of measurement that econometricians face when confronted with the task of fitting production functions for the firm, an industry, all manufacturing, a region, a national economy, etc.[9]

The Cobb-Douglas Production Function

One of the notable attempts to estimate statistically a generalized production function for manufacturing industries is the Cobb-Douglas production function.[10] This pioneering study has served as a basis for many research studies of the nature of production functions.

Cobb and Douglas found that the nonlinear exponential function fit quite well their sample of inputs and outputs drawn from a variety of industries. This function takes the form

$$x = zl^a c^b u \qquad (5.1)$$

where x is output, l is labor input, c is capital input, u is a disturbance term, and z, a, b are parameters. The production elasticities, a and b, representing the output response with respect to labor and capital, respectively, are assumed constant in this form of the production function. The logarithmic transformation of this exponential function has the convenient property (for estimation purposes) of linearity in the parameters.[11]

---

[9] A good introduction to these problems is provided by Lawrence R. Klein, *An Introduction to Econometrics*, Prentice-Hall, Englewood Cliffs, N.J., 1962, pp. 83–139.
[10] C. W. Cobb and Paul H. Douglas, "A Theory of Production," *A.E.R.*, *Supplement*, Vol. XVIII, 1938, pp. 139–65. From sample data of U.S. Manufacturing running from 1900 through 1922, they fit the following function: $x = 1.10 \ l^{.75} c^{.25}$, with x an index of total production per year, l an index of labor input, and c an index of capital input.
[11] If $x = 1.10 \ l^{.75} c^{.25}$, the linear logarithmic form is $\log x = \log 1.01 + .75 \log l + .25 \log c$. The partial derivatives of the logarithmic form yield the elasticities. (See footnote 12): $\partial (\log x) / \partial \log l) = .75$ is the constant elasticity of production with

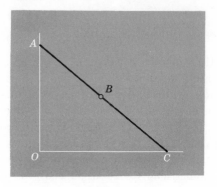

Fig. 5.8

If each of the exponents (constant elasticities) is less than one, the function reflects diminishing returns (declining marginal product). Depending on the combined values of a and b, the production function may exhibit increasing returns to scale $(a + b > 1)$, constant returns to scale $(a + b = 1)$, or decreasing returns to scale $(a + b < 1)$. For example, if $a = \frac{3}{4}$ and $b = \frac{1}{4}$ and each input in Eq. 5.1 is increased proportionately by k, it can be shown that output x increases by k:

$$x = zl^{3/4}c^{1/4}u$$
$$= z(kl)^{3/4}(kc)^{1/4}u$$
$$= zl^{3/4}c^{1/4}u(k)$$
$$= x(k)$$

This then is the constant return to scale case $(a + b = 1)$—a homogeneous function of the first degree. If $x = f(l,c)$, $kx = f(kl,kc)$. Output increases in the same proportion as the inputs.

We distinguished earlier between elasticity and slope, using the demand curve as an example. Figure 5.8 is a two-variable linear function whose slope is, of course, a constant $(= -1$ in this case), and B is a point midway between A and C (so that $BC/AB = 1$). We find that in the region between A and B the line is elastic, between B and C it is inelastic, and only at B does the degree of elasticity (unit elastic) equal the slope.

In general, given the function $y = f(x)$, elasticity e is defined as the

respect to the labor input, and $\partial (\log x)/\partial (\log c) = .25$ is the constant elasticity of production with respect to the capital input. These elasticities are the exponents of the original function. If the labor input were increased by 1%, output would increase by .75%; if capital were increased by 1%, output would increase by .25%. If both labor and capital were increased by 1%, a 1% increase in output would result.

slope times the inverse ratio of the level of the two variables, or simply as the ratio of percentage (or relative) changes in the variables.[12] The marginal productivity theory of wages for purely competitive conditions gives the result that real wages tend to equal the marginal product. From this result and the definition of elasticity, it can be shown that under purely competitive conditions a factor's share of income will equal the exponent (elasticity), if a Cobb-Douglas type production function or any other production function with constant elasticity is empirically correct.[13] Since $dy/dl = w$, $e = dy/dl \cdot l/y = w \cdot l/y$, which is a proportionate share of wages in total output.

Over an extended time period the relative wage share of national income has been relatively stable at about two-thirds, which Cobb and Douglas found to be very roughly (though with considerable dispersion) the average value of elasticity with respect to the labor input, a, when exponential production functions were fit to cross-section and time series data for manufacturing industries covering various countries and time periods.

The original research was suggestive rather than conclusive. Some evidence of diseconomies of scale was found. The Cobb-Douglas production function is sometimes incorrectly offered as *the* explanation of the relative constancy of the wage share; in several cases other functions fit the data as well as the exponential type. There is no necessary reason why factors must be combined in this particular way with the properties noted. Of considerable interest in the original study are the broad com-

---

[12] By definition $e = (dy/y)/(dx/x) = \%$ change in $y/\%$ change in x [$= d(\log y)/d(\log x)$]. The slope, or limiting value of the slope for infinitesmal increments, is the derivative dy/dx. If this were a production function, dy/dx would be the marginal product, Rewriting the definition of elasticity in the form: $e(y/x) = dy/dx$, where elasticity e is assumed constant (as in the Cobb-Douglas production function), we can see that marginal product (dy/dx) is proportional to average product (y/x).

In terms of a Cobb-Douglas type exponential production function with one independent variable, $y = zl^a$, elasticity e equals the exponent a:

$$e = \frac{dy}{dl} \cdot \frac{l}{y} = azl^{a-1}\left(\frac{l}{zl^a}\right) = a$$

(The proof can be extended to many variables by using partial derivatives).

[13] For greater detail and criticism of this research effort, see L. R. Klein, *op. cit.*, pp. 90–111, and of course the original source cited above. Of particular theoretical interest, Klein indicates on p. 99 that given the Cobb-Douglas production function and the marginal productivity theory of wages, the labor share under noncompetitive conditions would be a function of the elasticity of demand for output, the elasticity of supply of labor, in addition to the elasticity of production a—the exponent of the labor variable in the production function.

parisons between countries and time periods, and solutions to some of the technical problems in the fitting of production functions to data available for manufacturing industries.

Constant Elasticity of Substitution (CES) Production Function

In a study by Arrow, Chenery, Minhas, and Solow, a constant elasticity of substitution (CES) production function, more general than the Cobb-Douglas production function, was suggested.[14]

Earlier we demonstrated that the rate of technical substitution (RTS)—the slope of an isoquant relating a given output to two inputs—equalled the ratio of the marginal products of the two inputs. The RTS is a measure of the substitutability of one input for another, maintaining the same output. Possibilities for input substitution vary among the many different types of production functions. At a given cost-minimizing point on an isoquant, a certain, say, capital/labor ratio applies. If relative input prices change, costs can be lowered by moving to a new point on the same isoquant, where the slope of the new price line again equals the slope of the isoquant—the RTS. A new capital/labor ratio applies at the new cost-minimizing point.

The elasticity of substitution σ[15] measures the relative change in the input ratio in response to a relative change in the RTS (or in response to a relative change in the input price ratio, which is equal to the RTS along the cost-minimizing expansion path).

The CES production function contains an unspecified constant elasticity of substitution, σ. If $\sigma = 1$, the CES production function reduces to the Cobb-Douglas function as a special case. When σ approaches zero, the CES function reduces to the fixed proportion (constant input coefficient) production function.

The complex equation of the CES function can be written

$$x = z[bc^{-\rho} + (1 - b)l^{-\rho}]^{-1/\rho}$$

where $\sigma = 1/(1 + \rho)$, x is output, c and l are variables representing the levels of the capital and labor input, respectively, and z, b, and ρ are constants. $\sigma[= 1/(1 + \rho)]$ is the elasticity of substitution.[16]

Empirical estimates of σ vary, and particularly at the industry level

---

[14] Kenneth Arrow, Hollis B. Chenery, Bagicha Minhas, and Robert M. Solow, "Capital-Labor Substitution and Economic Efficiency," *The Review of Economics and Statistics*, Aug. 1961, XLIX, No. 3, pp. 225–250.

[15] The elasticity of substitution is considered in greater detail in Chapter 13 in its relationship to income distribution.

[16] While σ (or ρ) takes on some constant value in a CES-type function, in an even more general type production function σ may be a variable.

there is considerable dispute over which production function best applies. Presumably no one function is better for every industry. At the aggregate level, estimates of σ for the American economy derived from CES-type functions have tended to vary between 0.5 and 0.7.[17]

The likelihood of change in technology being present in any historical time period (as contrasted to the Marshallian "long run" where technology is assumed unchanged in the time required for complete and optimal adjustment of all inputs including capital) has offered a challenge to economists involved in the estimation of production functions in dynamic growth models. If technical change has taken place during the period to which the time series data apply, the universe from which the sample data are taken will have changed, and the meaning of the fitted function would be unclear. If the data are carefully selected from a limited period during which methods of production were unchanged, the results may be of historical interest but obsolete for many operational purposes.

Progress in technology involves a change in the production function. Such a change in technology may be classified as neutral, labor-saving, or capital-saving.

A neutral advance in technology is illustrated in Fig. 5.9a by a parallel

[17] See Ronald G. Bodkin and Lawrence R. Klein, "Aggregate Production Functions," *The Review of Economics and Statistics,* Feb. 1967, Vol. XLIX, No. 11, pp. 28–43. Among other interesting suggestions, Professors Bodkin and Klein found evidence of increasing returns to scale in the American economy. The bibliography at the end of the article will be useful for those interested in recent empirical work on production functions.

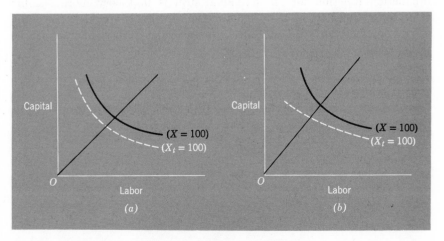

Fig. 5.9. (a) Neutral technological change. (b) Labor-saving technological change. Solid line-before technological advance; dashed line—after technological advance.

shift in the isoquant ($X = 100$) toward the origin. Along any production ray from the origin, representing a constant capital/labor ratio, the slope of the isoquant remains constant for neutral changes in technology. The solid-line and dashed-line isoquants represent the same output levels before and after the change in technology. With a neutral technological advance, the same output can be generated with a certain proportionate decrease in all inputs.

A labor-saving (capital-using) technological advance is represented in Fig. 5.9b by the dashed isoquant, which is more horizontal than the solid-line isoquant (before the labor-saving technological change). After the labor-saving technological advance, the rate of technical substitution—$RTS_{CL} = MP_L/MP_C$—decreases. The labor-saving change in technology is one where fewer units of capital need be substituted for a unit of labor, as along the new dashed isoquant.

Attempts have been made[18] to measure the effect of the change in technology by introducing a time variable—a proxy variable which hopefully stands for changes in technology, or by examining the residuals in the fitted function. The Cobb-Douglas type production function and equilibrium conditions suggested by theory are used to isolate an aggregate measure of technological change.

A more direct way to estimate a production function for a particular firm or for a typical firm in an industry is to survey engineering knowledge of production possibilities rather than historical data that may reflect nonoptimal operating procedures.[19]

The production function is basic to supply, analogous to the manner in which the utility function underlies demand. The estimation of the production function for an individual firm is in theory more feasible than the estimation of a utility function for an individual, since the production function rests on objective knowledge rather than subjective preferences.

---

[18] See R. M. Solow, "Technical Change and the Aggregate Production Function," *RES*, Vol. XXXIX, 1957, pp. 312–320.
[19] See Vernon L. Smith, *Investment and Production*, Harvard University Press, Cambridge, Mass., 1961.

6
Linear Programming

Linear or mathematical programming has many uses over a broad area from welfare economics and economic development to plant location, transport routing and many other management problems. One of the contributors to its development has stated that "The most useful applications of mathematical programming are probably to problems . . . concerned with finding optimal production plans using specified quantities of some or all of the resources involved."[1]

The generalized production problem considered in Chapter 5 supposes a single output and unlimited opportunities for substitution between inputs A and B along a given isoquant. The least cost combination of resources at any level of output was found at the point of tangency between the isoquant, which was a continuous curve convex to the origin, and a linear isocost line representing constant relative factor prices. There were no limits on the availability of either factor.

Linear programming is applicable to a rather special case of this problem, illustrated in Fig. 6.1, where (1) limitational factors are used in fixed proportions along a process ray, (2) constant returns to scale apply for each process, and (3) relative factor prices are constant. These assumptions imply constant unit costs at any output or scale of operation.

The production rays, 1 and 2, represent alternative processes, each requiring a fixed proportion of the two inputs. Process 1 requires relatively more of B than A. If B were labor and A were capital, process 1 would be the more labor intensive process—many men digging a hole with shovels—as contrasted to process 2, the more capital intensive process—a man operating a bulldozer. The same output could be achieved using either process. Point J may represent an output of 400 cubic feet of dirt removed using men with shovels (process 1), and point K the

[1] Robert Dorfman, "Mathematical or Linear Programming: A Non-Mathematical Exposition," *AER*, Vol. XLIII, Dec. 1953, No. 5, p. 810.

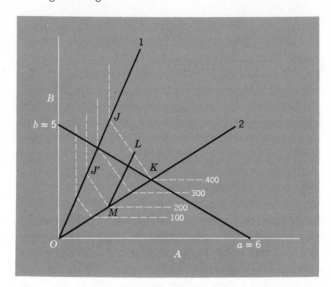

Fig. 6.1

same output using a man with a bulldozer (process 2). The only thing the two processes have in common is that they employ the same categories of resources, A and B. The dashed line segments connecting equal output points like J and K can be considered isoquants, since the same output can be produced using some combination of the two processes. (If the unit price of the output varied, the isoquants could be converted to isovalue lines.) A point L on the dashed line segment between points J and K on rays 1 and 2 represents some combination of the two processes, which, taken together, uses exactly the same amounts of each factor as is indicated at point L. Point L represents the same output as either point J on production ray 1 (process 1) or point K on production ray 2 (process 2). The particular combination of the two processes indicated by point L may be found by drawing a line from L to M parallel to process 1. $LM(=J'J)$ represents the output produced by process 1, and OM the output produced by process 2.

As many processes as desired can be considered in this graphic representation, with each process involving limitational factors or fixed factor proportions and each production process a case of constant returns to scale (indicated by the equal spacing of the isoquants as we move out from the origin).

A single linear isocost or price line is sketched in Fig. 6.1 connecting $a = 6$ on the A-axis and $b = 5$ on the B-axis. The slope of this price line is $b/a = -p_a/p_b$. Input A (capital) is less expensive than input B (labor), and at these relative prices $[p_a/p_b = -5/6$ or $p_a = -5/6p_b]$ we would use the capital intensive process 2 exclusively to remove 400 cubic feet of dirt (OK). Exclusive use of process 2—a man and a bulldozer—would be the lowest cost method of removing this much dirt. This is a corner solution, not a tangency solution as in our general analysis. If the slope of the price line were steeper than the isoquant segment JK, then point J would be the corner solution requiring exclusive use of process 1 to remove 400 cubic feet of dirt. If the price line had the same slope as the isoquant segment JK, the least cost solution would allow use of *either* process or *any combination* of the two processes.

So far, the analysis of the least cost combination of resources required to produce a given output does not differ in any essential way from the general analysis, except that with linear isoquant segments and linear price line the tangency solution does not apply. With no limitation on the rate of factor use and with a single price line, no matter how many processes are available, only one of the processes need be used whatever relative prices obtain.[2]

Linear programming is most appropriate where there are constraints or side conditions that are not easily handled by the standard maximizing or minimizing methods. Suppose, for example, that only a limited quantity, OS, of one of the factors, A, is available (see Fig. 6.2). We can illustrate this by drawing a factor-limitation line parallel to the B-axis. Such a line marks a boundary of the feasible region beyond which no production can take place. The feasible region for the factor-limitation line ST would be all points on or to the left of ST in Fig. 6.2.

The factor-limitation line ST happens to pass through the corner that was an optimal solution (refer back to Fig. 6.1) prior to the inclusion of the factor limitation; therefore this constraint does not affect the solution that now lies on the upper boundary of the feasible region.

The least cost solution for producing a given output will be affected if, with the inclusion of the factor-limitation line as a constraint, the "solution" (or what would have been the solution) now lies in the nonfeasible region. There are cases where the introduction of a constraint places the target output in the nonfeasible region. If the target output were 400 and the factor-limitation line had been to the left of the vertical isoquant segment through J in Fig. 6.2, an output of 400 would not be possible since it would lie outside the feasible region.

If the factor-limitation line UV applies and if we wish to produce an output lying at some point on this same isoquant (400), we can no longer use *only* process 2. With the factor-limitation line UV, the

[2] This is explained and elaborated upon later in this chapter.

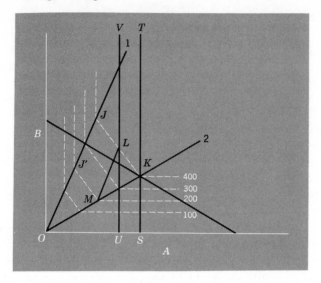

Fig. 6.2

least cost combination of resources represented by point K (the corner solution in Fig. 6.1) is no longer feasible. There is an insufficient quantity of resource A to rely solely on process 2. Instead, with the two constraints—a factor limitation and a fixed output—the optimal (lowest cost) feasible solution would now require some combination of the two processes. As indicated previously, point L represents LM ($= J'J$) of process 1 and OM of process 2. This combination of the two processes requires exactly the same rate of use of factors A and B as is represented by point L, lying on factor-limitation line UV, just at the upper boundary of the feasible region. A basic theorem of linear programming states that the optimal solution will require no more processes than there are constraints. A solution where the number of activities or processes equals the number of side-conditions or constraints is called a basic solution. Since there are two constraints in the preceding example, the optimal solution will be a basic solution and involve just two processes (even if more processes were available).[3]

Suppose maximum output were the objective and there were two factor limitations. In addition to UV, suppose a horizontal line passing through L represented a limitation on factor A. The solution would remain the

---

[3] If the price line were steeper than the isoquant segment JK in Fig, 6.2, point J would be optimal. If it were less steep and cut JK at some point to the right of point L, an output of 400 would no longer be feasible.

same. It would involve the combination of the two processes implied by L. There are still two side conditions—both factor limitations; however, the objective function would now be to maximize output subject to the two resource limitations, whereas previously we tried to minimize cost subject to one factor limitation and a given output requirement.

Common Structure of Linear Programming Problems[4]

All linear programming problems contain an objective function to be maximized or minimized subject to certain constraints or side conditions, usually in the form of inequalities. If the solution is to be accurate, both the objective functions and the constraints must be linear in form. This implies that variables are in additive relation in each equation, and no variable is raised to a power higher than one. All prices and production coefficients are constant.

Previously we considered the graphic illustration of the problem of minimizing the costs of producing a single product where more than one method of production was possible. Now let us turn to a profit-maximizing problem involving two products and two inputs. We want to allocate limited supplies of the inputs among the products selected in such a way as to maximize profit P.

Let the structural variables X_1, X_2 represent the levels of output of the two products; and let $C_1 = 100$, and $C_2 = 50$ be the given capacities of the two inputs in fixed supply—labor time (man-hours) and machine time (machine-hours). The problem is to maximize the objective function:

$$P = 1X_1 + 3X_2$$

subject to the constraints

$$0.2X_1 + 1.5X_2 \leq 100 (\equiv C_1 = \text{available labor time})$$
$$0.4X_1 + 0.6X_2 \leq 50 (\equiv C_2 = \text{available machine time})$$

We must add the non-negativity condition, $X_1 \geq 0$ and $X_2 \geq 0$, since the structural variables—the output levels of the products—cannot take on negative values.

The constants in the objective function are unit profits. There is a profit (in thousands of dollars) of 1 per unit for every unit of X_1 pro-

---

[4] If there is a time constraint, the remainder of this chapter may be omitted without interrupting the main argument. There is some advantage in postponing the discussion of the dual programming problem and its economic interpretation so that it follows Chapter 11 on Income Distribution.

duced, and 3 per unit of X_2. Total profit P will equal $1X_1 + 3X_2$. The constants in the constraints are fixed production (input) coefficients. Every unit of X_1 produced requires 0.2 hours of labor time, and every unit of X_2 produced requires 1.5 hours of labor time. The first constraint tells us that the products cannot be produced in unlimited quantities. $0.2X_1 + 1.5X_2$ is the total amount of labor time used up in producing our outputs, and this total labor time must not exceed the capacity limitation of $C_1 = 100$ man-hours. The constants of the second constraint are hours of machine time per unit of output: 0.4 hours of machine time are required per unit of X_1, and 0.6 hours of machine time are required per unit of X_2. The total amount of machine time used must not exceed our capacity, $C_2 = 50$ machine hours.

The simplest of production functions is involved. Each unit of X_1 produced requires 0.2 man-hours and 0.4 machine-hours. Each unit of X_2 requires 1.5 man-hours and 0.6 machine-hours. Assuming constant returns to scale, these input coefficients hold at any level of output.

Linear Programming Solution

We shall not be particularly concerned with the solution of a linear programming problem, but we shall try to understand the relationship of linear programming to economic analysis. To this end, we shall look at the main outlines of the simplex method, which is the most commonly used method of solving linear programming problems.

To solve the linear programming problem, we make the constraints which are stated as inequalities, into equations by introducing a slack variable into each inequality. The slack variables are unused labor time L or unused machine time M. For example, if $X_1 = 80$ and $X_2 = 30$, the labor time used up in producing outputs X_1 and X_2 would be $0.2X_1 + 1.5X_2 = 0.2(80) + 1.5(30) = 61$. According to our first constraint, $0.2X_1 + 1.5X_2 \leq 100$, so 39 hours of labor time would not be utilized. By introducing a slack variable M_1 for unused labor time, the constraint can be stated as an equality: $0.2X_1 + 1.5X_2 + M_1 = 100$. In the example, with $X_1 = 80$ and $X_2 = 30$, M_1 would equal 39: $0.2(80) + 1.5(30) + 39 = 100$. At these same levels of output, the slack variable M_2, representing unused machine time, would be equal to zero, since $0.4(80) + 0.6(30) = 50$, which according to the second constraint is the total amount of machine time available. The non-negativity condition is extended to include these slack variables. The unused time cannot be negative.

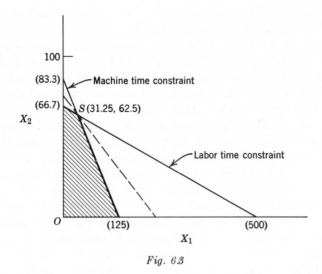

Fig. 6.3

The programming problem can now be expressed as follows:

Objective Function: $\qquad P = 1X_1 + 3X_2$

Constraints: $\qquad\qquad 0.2X_1 + 1.5X_2 + M_1 = 100$

$\qquad\qquad\qquad\qquad 0.4X_1 + 0.6X_2 + M_2 = 50$

Non-Negativity Conditions: $\quad X_1 \geq 0, \quad X_2 \geq 0, \quad M_1 \geq 0, \quad M_2 \geq 0$

X_1 and X_2 are the two structural or ordinary variables, while M_1 and M_2 are the two slack variables in our two-constraint problem.

Figure 6.3 provides an illustration of the problem. The coordinate axes represent levels of outputs (activities), X_1 and X_2. The straight lines diagonally connecting the two axes are the constraint equations, each indicating an upper boundary of output combinations possible with given input capacities. The heavy line segments of the labor time constraint and the machine time constraint form the upper bound of the feasible region—the shaded area in Fig. 6.3 which includes an infinite number of feasible solutions. Recall that a feasible solution is one that does not violate the constraints or the non-negativity condition. In our problem these are the output levels which can be reached with the available resources. It was mentioned earlier that a basic solution to a linear programming problem is one where the number of variables included in the solution (nonzero-valued variables) equals the number of constraints. In the problem illustrated in Fig. 6.3, each of the corners of the feasible region is a basic feasible solution, containing just two nonzero-valued variables from among the four (ordinary and slack) variables and not violating the side conditions.

At the corner marked S, both products are produced, so both ordinary variables are positive. It is here that both constraint lines intersect to form a corner of the boundary. This tells us that at this point on the boundary of the feasible region both inputs are used to capacity, and therefore both slack variables equal zero.

At the origin, where $X_1 = 0$ and $X_2 = 0$, we have another basic feasible solution. At this corner, our inputs are completely unused. The slack variables are here equal to their total capacities: $M_1 = C_1$ and $M_2 = C_2$. The origin is a basic solution since the ordinary variables are equal to zero, whereas the slack variables take on nonzero values equal to their respective capacities and there are as many slack variables as there are constraints. It is often convenient to choose the origin as the initial basic feasible solution, although it is unlikely to be an optimal solution in a profit-maximizing problem; with the ordinary variables X_1 and X_2 zero-valued, the value of the objective function is zero.

We know from the basic theorem of linear programming that a basic solution will always provide an optimal solution to a linear programming problem, and that there will always be a finite number of basic feasible (corner) solutions. An optimal solution will always include one of the corners on the boundary of the feasible region. A corner solution will provide an optimal solution even in the unusual case where the linear contour of the objective function is parallel to one of the line segments of the boundary. In this case, an optimal solution will lie along this line segment as well as at the corner.

In our simple problem with only four corners, each of them a basic feasible solution, the optimal solution can easily be found graphically at the corner that touches the highest of the linear isoprofit lines representing the contours of the objective function. A very direct algebraic solution would be to substitute each of the basic corner solutions into the objective function. The optimal basic feasible solution would be the one that yields the highest profit. In a more complicated problem such a method would not be recommended. Even with, say, three capacity constraints and five activities, where an optimal solution can be found containing only three variables—no more than three activities and possibly less if one or more of the slack variables in the final solution are positive—testing every basic (corner) solution in the objective function would be a cumbersome and inefficient way of finding an optimal solution.

In Fig. 6.3 the corner along the X_1-axis with $X_2 = 0$ occurs where the machine time constraint touches the X_1-axis at $X_1 = 125 (= 50/0.4)$, indicating that if all of the available machine time were allocated to X_1, a maximum of 125 units of X_1 could be produced. The available labor time would permit $X_1 = 500(= 100/0.2)$, where the labor time constraint line touches the X_1-axis, but this lies outside the feasible region. With $X_2 = 0$, the bottleneck is machine time.

The corner on the X_2-axis with $X_1 = 0$ is $X_2 = 66\frac{2}{3}(= 100/1.5)$, where the labor time constraint line touches the X_2-axis. Machine time would permit a little more than 83.3 units of X_2 if all the machine time were allocated to X_1, so labor time is the bottleneck in producing X_2 with $X_1 = 0$. Notice that each of these corner solutions along the axes is a basic solution containing one ordinary variable and one slack variable. At $X_1 = 125$ (and $X_2 = 0$), the slack variable M_2 associated with unused machine time would be zero, but the slack variable M_1 associated with unused labor time at this corner solution would be equal to 25:

$$[0.2(125) + 1.5(0) + M_1 = 100 \therefore M_1 = 25]$$

At the corner S where the constraint lines intersect, both slack variables are zero-valued. The values of X_1 and X_2 may be found here by solving the two constraint equations simultaneously:

$$0.2X_1 + 1.5X_2 + 0 = 100$$
$$0.4X_1 + 0.6X_2 + 0 = 50$$

Multiplying the first equation by 2:

$$0.4X_1 + 3.0X_2 = 200$$
$$\underline{0.4X_1 + 0.6X_2 = 50}$$
$$2.4X_2 = 50$$
$$X_2 = 62.5$$

Substituting this value into either constraint equation we find $X_1 = 31.25$:

$$[0.4X_1 + 0.6(62.5) = 50, \therefore X_1 = 31.25]$$

Simplex Solution

Instead of finding all of the basic feasible solutions—activity combinations at every corner—and then substituting each solution into the objective function to see which is optimal, the simplex method provides a more efficient method of solving a linear programming problem. Begin by choosing an initial basic feasible solution. Often the origin is most convenient, although any corner solution will do. Then see if any improvement is possible by moving to one of the adjacent corners. Move to the one (if any) that offers the most improvement, and repeat the procedure by comparing the new corner with the next adjacent corner. Because of the linear surface of the objective function and the general convexity of the feasible region, by testing only adjacent corners we are assured of moving successively toward an optimum solution. If no adjacent corner of the feasible region offers any improvement, we are at an optimal point.[5]

[5] A simplex solution to our illustrative problem is presented in this lengthy footnote. For greater detail, see William J. Baumol, *Economic Theory and Operations Analysis,* 2nd ed., Prentice-Hall, Englewood Cliffs, N.J., 1965, pp. 70–166.

More formalized methods should be followed if many problems are to be solved; electronic computers provide the fastest solution to programming problems.

It is convenient to place nonzero-valued variables on the left-hand side of the constraint equations and to write our equations in matrix form. We begin by taking the origin as our inital basic feasible solution, and we write our equation with the slack variables M_1 and M_2 on the left-hand side of the equation:

Maximize: $P = 0 + 1X_1 + 3X_2$
Subject to: $M_1 = 100 - 0.2X_1 - 1.5X_2$
$M_2 = 50 - 0.4X_1 - 0.6X_2$

In matrix form these equations may be written:

		X_1	X_2
P	0	1	3
M_1	100	-0.2	-1.5
M_2	50	-0.4	-0.6

In our initial basic solution $M_1 = 100$, $M_2 = 50$, $X_1 = 0$ and $X_2 = 0$. The zero in the upper left corner of the matrix (the first term in the objective function) represents the value of the objective function. The other terms in the first row of the matrix are the profits per unit of X_1 and X_2. The constants in the second and third rows of the matrix are the capacities and production coefficients of the two constraint equations.

The problem of deciding which (if any) of the adjacent corners of the feasible region offers the most improvement is equivalent to deciding which of the zero-valued variables X_1 and X_2, now in position at the head of the matrix columns, is to be added, and which of our nonzero-variables M_1 and M_2, now positioned to the left of rows two and three of the matrix is to be replaced in the next trial basic solution.

Two rules guide us in these selections:

Rule 1. Select as the new variable to be included the one that promises the greatest gain. In our profit-maximizing problem, X_2 offers a unit profit of 3, while X_1 offers a unit profit of only 1. We therefore choose X_2, which has the largest positive coefficient in the objective function. Note that if neither X_1 nor X_2—the zero-valued variables in the initial basic trial solution—offered positive unit profit, then the initial basic solution would be optimal. Having chosen X_2 to replace M_1 or M_2, we must formulate a rule to decide whether to replace M_1 or M_2. The decision is immediately obvious if we look at the corner on the X_2-axis in Fig. 6.3. The corner of the feasible region occurs where the labor time constraint touches the X_2-axis, so $M_1 = 0$ at this corner of the feasible region adjacent to the origin. We will include X_2 as a nonzero-valued variable and replace M_1, which becomes a zero-valued variable in the next trial solution. We replace M_1 in the new solution because, as we add X_2, labor time is used up first. It is the bottleneck—the most limiting constraint. The second rule provides an arithmetic measure for deciding which variable to replace.

Rule 2. Consider the negative coefficients in the X_2-column of the matrix—the column of the variable to be added in our next trial solution. Divide the input coefficients of this column into their respective input capacities in the first column to see whether labor time or machine time is the most limiting factor. The input capacities were the values of the slack variables in the initial basic solution. Ignoring sign, replace the slack variable associated with the most limiting constraint; e.g., $100/1.5 = 66.7$ and $50/0.6 = 83.3$. The smaller quotient, 66.7, is associated with L, indicating that 66.7 units of X_2 will use up all the units of labor time available; it would take 83.3 units of X_2 to use up all the units of machine time available. In the M_1-row 66.7 is the quotient with the smaller numerical value, therefore since labor time is the most limiting factor as X_2 is added, we replace M_1 (which becomes a zero-valued variable in the next trial solution).

Having chosen X_2 the variable to be introduced, and M_1 the variable to be replaced in the next basic solution, we must rewrite our equations with X_2 and M_1 exchanging places in our matrix. To accomplish this, we designate the input coefficient (-1.5) in the X_2-column and M_1-row as the pivot element. It is the amount of labor time used per unit of X_2. To rewrite the constraint equation of the M_1-row, which contains the pivot element, divide each of the elements of this row by -1.5 (the pivot element) and transpose to bring the new nonzero-valued variable, X_2, to the left-hand side of the equation, replacing M_1 without violating the constraint:

$$M_1 = 100 - 0.2X_1 - 1.5X_2$$

Dividing by pivot element, 1.5:

$$\frac{M_1}{-1.5} = \frac{100}{-1.5} - \frac{0.2X_1}{-1.5} - \frac{1.5X_2}{-1.5}$$

Transposing and multiplying by -1:

$$X_2 = \frac{100}{1.5} - \frac{0.2}{1.5}X_1 - \frac{1}{1.5}M_1$$

This becomes the second row of the new matrix. Substitute this new value of X_2 in the other equations, collect terms and rewrite the solution matrix. This procedure accomplishes the exchange in positions of the new nonzero-valued variable, X_2, with the new zero-valued variable, M_1:

$$P = 0 + X_1 + 3X_2$$
$$P = 0 + X_1 + 3\left(\frac{100}{1.5} - \frac{0.2}{1.5}X_1 - \frac{1}{1.5}M_1\right)$$
$$P = 200 + 0.6X_1 - 2M_1$$

This becomes the first row of the new matrix. Substituting the expression for X_2 in the other constraint equation, we get:

$$M = 50 - 0.4X_1 - 0.6X_2$$

$$M = 50 - 0.4X_1 - 0.6 \left(\frac{100}{1.5} - \frac{0.2}{1.5}X_1 - \frac{1}{1.5}M_1 \right)$$

$$M = 10 - 0.32X_1 + 0.4M_1$$

Our new basic feasible solution can now be written with the two zero-valued variables X_1 and M_1, in the top row—the revised objective function—and the two new nonzero-valued variables, X_2 and M_2, on the left-hand side of the revised constraint equations:

$$P = 200 + 0.6X_1 - 2M_1$$

$$X_2 = \frac{100}{1.5} - \frac{0.2}{1.5}X_1 - \frac{1}{1.5}M_1$$

$$M_2 = 10 - 0.32X_1 + 0.4M_1$$

		X_1	M_1
P	200	0.6	-2
X_2	$\frac{100}{1.5}$	$\frac{-0.2}{1.5}$	$\frac{-1}{1.5}$
M_2	10	-0.32	0.4

This second basic solution represents an improvement of 200, but we readily see that further improvement is possible. Applying Rule 1, we next introduce X_1, since the coefficient of X_1 in the objective function is positive. If introduced, X_1 would make a positive marginal contribution to profit. Applying Rule 2, we find X_1 should replace the slack variable M_2 in the next basic solution, since the quotient $10/.32$ is smaller than

$$\frac{66.7 \left(= \frac{100}{1.5} \right)}{0.133 \left(= \frac{0.2}{1.5} \right)}.$$

M_2 is the most limiting variable and reduces most rapidly to zero as X_1 is added.

We move then to the next basic feasible solution at the corner where the two ordinary variables X_1 and X_2 are nonzero-valued, and the two slack variables M_1 and M_2 are zero-valued—the corner where the two linear constraint lines intersect. This turns out to be the optimal solution, as we see below, since the coefficients of the revised objective function in the top row of the revised matrix are both negative, indicating no improvement can be gained from moving to an adjacent corner. We replace M_2 by X_1 in the final basic solution.

The pivot element is $-.32$ in the X_1-column and M_2-row. We divide this into the other elements of the M_2-row, and transpose, solving for X_1:

$$M_2 = 10 - 0.32X_1 + 0.4M_1$$

$$X_1 = 31.25 - \frac{1}{0.32} M_2 + \frac{0.4}{.32} M_1$$

This becomes the third row of the final matrix. Next we substitute this expression for X_1 in the other two equations:

$$P = 200 + 0.6X_1 - 2M_1$$

$$P = 200 + 0.6\left(\frac{10}{0.32} - \frac{1}{0.32} M_2 + \frac{0.4}{0.32} M_1\right) - 2M_1$$

$$P = 218.75 - \frac{0.6}{0.32} M_2 - 1.25M_1$$

This becomes the first row of the final matrix.

$$X_2 = \frac{100}{1.5} - \frac{0.2}{1.5} X_1 - \frac{1}{1.5} M_1$$

$$X_2 = \frac{100}{1.5} - \frac{0.2}{1.5}\left(\frac{10}{0.32} - \frac{1}{0.32} M_2 + \frac{0.4}{0.32} M_1\right) - \frac{1}{1.5} M_1$$

$$X_2 = 62.5 + \frac{1}{2.4} M_2 - \frac{5}{6} M_1$$

This is the second row of the final matrix. The final matrix representing the optimal basic feasible solution is:

		M_2	M_1
P	218.75	$-\dfrac{0.6}{0.32}$	-1.25
X_2	62.5	$\dfrac{1}{2.4}$	$-\dfrac{5}{6}$
X_1	31.25	$-\dfrac{1}{0.32}$	$\dfrac{0.4}{0.32}$

The optimal profit-maximizing solution, $X_1 = 31.25$ and $X_2 = 62.5$, yields a profit of 218.75. This is the basic (corner) solution at S in Fig. 6.3 that we obtained earlier by solving the two constraint equations simultaneously.

Where the linear programming problem is a minimizing problem with certain minimum constraints, the origin may not be a feasible solution and so cannot be chosen as an initial basic (corner) solution. The problem is surmounted by introducing an additional artificial slack variable in each constraint equation, and setting these "artificial" slack variables equal to zero in the initial basic solution of what is called a feasibility program. The artificial slack variables are also included in the objective function, but together with coefficients arbitrarily chosen large enough to ensure that they will not remain in the optimal solution to the minimizing problem.

Dual Linear Programming Problems

Every linear programming maximizing problem has an associated minimizing problem, and vice versa. Either may be referred to as the *primal* problem. Each primal problem has a closely related *dual* problem. The solution of the one provides a solution to the other. At times it is easier to solve the primal problem by first solving the related dual problem. Let us look at the structure of the profit-maximizing "two output-two input" problem together with its minimizing dual problem.

Primal Problem	Dual Problem
Maximize: $P = \pi_1 X_1 + \pi_2 X_2$	Minimize: $V = C_1 Y_1 + C_2 Y_2$

Subject to: $a_{11}X_1 + a_{12}X_2 \leq C_1$ $\qquad$ Subject to: $a_{11}Y_1 + a_{21}Y_2 \geq \pi_1$
$\qquad\qquad\ a_{21}X_1 + a_{22}X_2 \leq C_2$ $\qquad\qquad\qquad\ \ a_{12}Y_1 + a_{22}Y_2 \geq \pi_2$

$\qquad\qquad (X_1 \geq 0, X_2 \geq 0)$ $\qquad\qquad\qquad (Y_1 \geq 0, Y_2 \geq 0)$

Notice the complete inversion. The inequalities in the constraints of the dual are the reverse of those in the primal. The column coefficients of the constraints in the primal become the row coefficients of the constraints of the dual. There is a juxtaposition of a_{12} and a_{21} in our example of the primal problem and dual problem. Notice, too, that the capacities C_1 and C_2 in our primal constraints become the coefficients in the objective function of the dual. The inverse is also true. The coefficients of the objection function in the primal problem become the limiting values on the right-hand side of the constraint equations of the dual problem. Adding the slack variables M_1 and M_2 in the constraints of the primal problem and subtracting the slack variable L_1 and L_2 in the constraints of the dual problem, we can express both sets of constraints as equalities.

Primal Problem
Maximize: $P = \pi_1 X_1 + \pi_2 X_2$

$\qquad$ Subject to: $a_{11}X_1 + a_{12}X_2 + M_1 = C_1$
$\qquad\qquad\qquad\ \ a_{21}X_1 + a_{22}X_2 + M_2 = C_2$

$\qquad\qquad (X_1 \geq 0, X_2 \geq 0, M_1 \geq 0, M_2 \geq 0)$

Dual Problem
Minimize: $V = C_1 Y_1 + C_2 Y_2$

Subject to: $a_{11}Y_1 + a_{21}Y_2 - L_1 = \pi_1$
$$a_{12}Y_1 + a_{22}Y_2 - L_2 = \pi_2$$

$$(Y_1 \geq 0, \ Y_2 \geq 0, \ L_1 \geq 0, \ L_2 \geq 0)$$

To solve the primal and the dual, the variables to be included in the initial basic solution to the primal and dual are brought to the left-hand side of the constraint equations written as follows:

Primal Problem

Maximize: $P = 0 + \pi_1X_1 + \pi_2X_2$

Subject to: $M_1 = C_1 - a_{11}X_1 - a_{12}X_2$
$$M_2 = C_2 - a_{21}X_1 - a_{22}X_2$$

Dual Problem

Minimize: $V = 0 + C_1Y_1 + C_2Y_2$

Subject to: $L_1 = -\pi_1 + a_{11}Y_1 + a_{21}Y_2$
$$L_2 = -\pi_2 + a_{12}Y_1 + a_{22}Y_2$$

In matrix form, these equations become:

		X_1	X_2
P	0	π_1	π_2
M_1	C_1	$-a_{11}$	$-a_{12}$
M_2	C_2	$-a_{21}$	$-a_{22}$

		Y_1	Y_2
V	0	C_1	C_2
L_1	$-\pi_1$	a_{11}	a_{21}
L_2	$-\pi_2$	a_{12}	a_{22}

The dual matrix can be formed from the primal matrix simply by interchanging columns and rows and changing the signs of all of the elements in the primal matrix, except for C_1 and C_2 in the first column of the primal matrix. These elements retain their same sign in the first row of the dual matrix. In the trial basic solution to the dual, $L_1 = -\pi_1$ and $L_2 = -\pi_2$. These variables, L_1 and L_2, are the nonzero-valued variables of the initial basic solution to the dual problem. The Y_1 and Y_2 at the top of the dual matrix are zero-valued variables in the initial basic solution to the dual.

Some economy is achieved by writing a single combined matrix for the primal and the dual problems. The dual variables are written in ( ) at the right and at the bottom of the combined matrix.

		X_1	X_2	
P	0	π_1	π_2	
M_1	C_1	$-a_{11}$	$-a_{12}$	(Y_1)
M_2	C_2	$-a_{21}$	$-a_{22}$	(Y_2)

$$(V) \qquad -(L_1) \qquad -(L_2)$$

In the objective function of the dual, C_1 and C_2 are the coefficients of the variables Y_1 and Y_2, which are the zero-valued variables of the dual basic solution, since Y_1 and Y_2 formerly appeared at the top of the dual matrix where were placed the variables excluded from the basic solution.

V, L_1 and L_2, which equal 0, $-\pi_1$, and $-\pi_2$, respectively, in the initial basic solution to the dual problem are moved from the left of the dual matrix to the bottom of the combined matrix, where they equal the elements (with their signs changed) in the top row of the combined matrix. The dual variables at the bottom of the combined matrix are the nonzero-valued variables with a negative sign in front of the (L_1) and (L_2) to indicate that these variables equal the negative of those values in the first row of the combined matrix.

It is important to note that the same variables are paired and positioned opposite each other throughout the process of seeking an optimal basic feasible solution. In the initial basic solution the structural variables of the primal program (X_1 and X_2 at top of combined matrix) are positioned in opposition to the slack variables of the dual program (L_1 and L_2 at the bottom of the combined matrix). Also, the slack variables of the primal program (M_1 and M_2 at the left of the combined matrix) are positioned in opposition to the structural variables of the dual program (Y_1 and Y_2 at the right of the combined matrix).

Economic Interpretation of the Dual Problem

In the primal problem, we wish to select profit-maximizing output levels for our two products. Each of the two products uses the limited supplies of the two inputs according to the requisites indicated by the fixed input coefficients. The production function is presumed to be linear homogeneous—constant returns to scale. The coefficients of the objective function tell us the unit profit contributed by each product.

The coefficients a_{11} and a_{12} in the first constraint equation of the primal problem tell us the amounts of input 1 required per unit of product 1 and 2, respectively. In the second primal constraint equation a_{21} and a_{22} tell us the amounts of input 2 required per unit of products 1 and 2. The first constraint equation of the primal problem tells us that the amount of input 1 required must not exceed C_1. The second constraint equation of the primal problem tells us that the amount of input 2 required must not exceed C_2.

If we look at the coefficients a_{11} and a_{21} in the first column of the constraint equations of the primal problem, we see the various input requirements per unit of product 1. a_{12} and a_{22} in the second column are the input requirements per unit of product 2. It is these column coefficients of the primal problem that become the row coefficients of the constraint equations of the dual problem.

The ordinary structural variables Y_1 and Y_2 of our dual minimizing problem are "shadow prices" assigned to each resource. They are an artificial accounting valuation per unit of input such that the profit to be maximized in the primal problem is imputed among the inputs included in the optimal solution. The shadow prices of the dual problem reflect the marginal contribution of each input included in the optimal solution.

The connection between the valuation of a scarce resource (shadow price) and its contribution to profit may be seen in terms of the change in profit that would result from withdrawing a unit of the scarce resource from use.

In the dual problem, the cost-minimizing objective function $V = C_1Y_1 + C_2Y_2$ represents the total value of inputs at the firm's disposal—input capacities times their respective shadow prices, Y_1 and Y_2. The coefficients C_1 and C_2 are the input capacities of the primal problem.

The first constraint inequality in the dual problem—$a_{11}Y_1 + a_{21}Y_2 \geq \pi_1$—tells us that the amount of input 1 required to produce a unit of product 1 (a_{11}) multiplied by the shadow price per unit of input 1 (Y_1) plus the amount of input 2 required to produce a unit of product 1 (a_{21}) multiplied by the shadow price per unit of input 2 (Y_2) must be at least as large as the unit profit of product 1 (π_1). This means the profit from a unit of product 1 must be completely imputed or overimputed to the inputs employed in its production. If the value of the resources used in producing a unit of product 1 exceeds the unit profit of product 1, a loss would occur. The amount of the loss is the slack variable L_1 in the first constraint equation of the dual problem.

The second constraint equation—$a_{12}Y_1 + a_{22}Y_2 - L_2 = \pi_2$—tells us the value of the resources used to produce a unit of product 2 less any loss that might be incurred in producing a unit of product 2 must equal the profit per unit of product 2.

Two theorems are of considerable importance in understanding the dual problem and its relation to the primal problem. The first duality theorem tells us that the shadow prices per input unit will be such that there will never be any profit left over—all will be distributed to scarce resources; in the optimal feasible solution to the primal problem, the maximum profit P will exactly equal the minimum valuation V placed on available resources in the optimal solution to the dual. In fact, in any feasible solution to the primal problem, profit can never exceed the input valuation of the dual problem. If all resources, optimally allocated in the optimal feasible solution to the profit-maximizing primal problem, are valued according to their marginal contribution, total profit is exhausted. The total value V of the resources allocated to yield maximum profit would be a minimum and would exactly equal the maximum profit P.

A second duality theorem tells us that where the value of the resources (their imputed cost) required to produce a unit of the product is greater than the unit profit from the product (so that a loss occurs), that product will not be included in the optimal solution. The optimal solution will include only those products whose loss is zero. Wherever L_1 or L_2—the slack variables—are positive, indicating a loss would occur, the related activity is not included in the optimal solution. Included (nonzero-valued) in the optimal solution to the primal problem are those activities (products) whose related slack variables in the final solution to the dual are zero-valued. The optimal solution will include only those products that can be produced without a loss. The loss is a signal that a further reallocation of resources would be profitable. The slack variables L_1 and L_2 may be viewed as the opportunity costs of pursuing a given activity.

The second duality theorem also states that only fully utilized (scarce) resources will receive positive shadow prices. Where the slack variable M_1 or M_2 in the primal problem is nonzero-valued, the respective shadow-price Y_1 or Y_2 will be zero-valued. This is symmetrical to the first part of the theorem, which stated that where L_1 or L_2 (losses in dual constraint equations) is nonzero-valued, then the associated output X_1 or X_2 must be zero-valued.

The optimal feasible basic solution to our primal problem is $X_1 = 31.25$ and $X_2 = 62.5$. The same paired opposition of variables holds in the final combined matrix—the optimal basic feasible solution—as appeared in the combined matrix of the initial basic feasible solution.

		M_2	M_1	
P	218.75	$-\dfrac{0.6}{0.32}$	-1.25	
X_2	62.5	$\dfrac{1}{2.4}$	$-\dfrac{5}{6}$	(L_2)
X_1	31.25	$-\dfrac{1}{0.32}$	$\dfrac{0.4}{0.32}$	(L_1)

$$(V) \qquad -(Y_2) \quad -(Y_1)$$

In the solution to the dual program, the zero-valued (excluded) variables are the slack variables L_2 and L_1 at the right of the combined matrix ($L_2:X_2$ and $L_1:X_1$ remain in paired opposition as in the initial basic solution). $Y_2 = 0.6/0.32$ and $Y_1 = 1.25$ represent the optimal dual solution. Recall the change in sign required for these elements in the first row of the combined matrix—the elements that yield the solution to the dual. The dual objective function—$V = C_1Y_1 + C_2Y_2$—is now solved: $V = 218.75 = 100(1.25) + 50(0.6/0.32)$. [The solution to the primal objective function—$P = 1X_1 + 3X_2$—is $P = 218.75 = 1(31.25) + 3(62.5)$.] Using the convenient device of a single combined matrix, the optimal solution to the profit-maximizing level of outputs (and allocation of inputs) in the primal problem yields directly an optimal solution to the imputed valuation of resources in the cost-minimizing dual problem. The solution to the resource allocation problem implies a solution to the resource valuation problem. In the optimal solution, no transfer of scarce resources from one product to another would add to profit, and resources are so allocated that the opportunity cost of producing a unit of any product included in the optimal solution is zero.

Where resources are used in fixed proportions, it is impossible to measure the marginal product of one input holding the other constant. However, the shadow prices assigned to scarce resources in fixed supply—the values imputed to scarce resources in the optimal solution to the dual problem—are closely related to their marginal contributions. If the restrictive assumptions of the linear programming model apply, the shadow prices of the dual solution represent the contribution of a unit of resource in fixed supply at the margin. To equate the total contribution of a resource to an enterprise with its marginal contribution multiplied by the number of units employed requires a strict adherence to the assumption that all units of the resource are homogeneous and optimally employed—that each unit of a given resource is as productively employed as any other unit of that resource. The imputed valuations of the dual problem may be useful in deciding whether it is profitable to expand or contract current activities, and whether to increase or decrease the available stock of resources currently employed.[6]

[6] The shadow prices imputed in the solution to the dual problem may serve a useful role in decentralizing control, particularly in situations where leaving all decisions regarding resource requirements and output selection to central control places too great a burden on centralized decision-making machinery.

7

The Purely Competitive Market

Previously we discussed the problem of the firm's objectives in general without specifying the particular character of the market within which the firm operates. We supposed that the average or "representative" firm has a profit-maximizing objective, and that it was able to implement this objective—that it exhibited rational behavior. The market defines certain aspects of the firm's external environment within which the firm tries to fulfill its objectives. The particular market structure may influence the firm to modify its objectives. As we shall see, there are instances where the market may force certain responses by the firm. The usefulness of the simple profit-maximizing rule—produce each product to the point where marginal cost equals marginal revenue—may be questioned for a large, multiproduct firm operating in a noncompetitive market. Programming, information theory, organization theory, and other methods of analysis may help firms to solve their complex problems and implement their objectives. Often these alternative approaches are consistent with marginal analysis. Considerable market information, technical knowledge, and managerial skill may be required to arrive at optimal (profit-maximizing) solutions.

We shall examine social implications of resource allocation and firm behavior under various market conditions. We begin with a definition of a market, and then proceed to consider a single-product firm operating in a perfectly competitive market.

A Market

What is a market? Where buyer and seller negotiate to buy or sell, we have a market. If they agree on terms of price and quantity, a sale—a specific transaction—takes place. Usually a market involves many transactions on a continuing basis. The same product may be offered for sale in various places by the same producer. The result may be several distinct markets, each with a separate market demand and supply function. Often there are technical problems in trying to determine where one market ends and another begins. A useful criterion for identifying the proper boundary for a market involving a standardized or homogeneous product is price uniformity (net of transportation or delivery charges).[1] Where the product is not standardized or where several grades or variations of the product are offered on the market by different sellers, it is more difficult to use price as a basis for identifying separate markets or for evaluating the efficiency of a market.

A perfectly efficient market is one where adjustment to change in market conditions is instantaneous. This requires perfect knowledge of market conditions by buyers and sellers, and perfect resource mobility. Buyers and sellers must have complete price information at all times, so that the buyer can buy at the cheapest prevailing asking price, and the seller can sell to the highest bidder at the best offered price. Resources must be able to respond immediately to all possibilities of gain. In a perfect market a single price will prevail throughout at any given time.

A Purely Competitive Market

In the model of price and output determination under purely competitive market conditions, price is "determined" by the impersonal market forces of supply and demand, not by the individual actions of buyers or sellers. Each buyer and seller sees the market price as a parameter—the price is given.[2] The individual firm in such a market may be said to be a "price taker." The forces behind market demand and supply are supposed to be separate and distinct. Firms and consumers react independently to changes in market price; they do not set price or make price decisions. Price is permitted to move freely in response to changes in market forces—supply or demand. In a purely competitive market, as distinct from a perfectly competitive one, some price dispersion is likely at any given time since adjustment is not instantaneous. Perfect knowledge

---

[1] "Thus the more nearly perfect a market is, the stronger is the tendency for the same price to be paid for the same thing at the same time in all parts of the market." Alfred Marshall, *Principles of Economics*, p. 325.

[2] The costs of searching out, contracting, and enforcing market exchange are implicitly included in the costs of supplying goods. Effective allocation via the price system requires that these exchange costs be a relatively small part of the price of the goods being exchanged.

and perfect mobility are lacking. Under pure competition, buyers, at least, are assumed to possess knowledge of product prices and availability.

For a market to be purely competitive, the following necessary conditions must, in general, prevail:

1. There must be *many firms* acting independently, with each small enough relative to the size of the market so that a single firm's decision to either cease producing entirely or to produce to capacity will not have a perceptible enough effect on market supply to cause a change in market price.

2. Entry (and exit) into (from) the market must be *free* (unimpeded, but not necessarily frictionless or instantaneous, as in a perfectly competitive market).

3. Individual consumers and producers are assumed to act independently (no collusion among buyers or sellers).

4. The products offered for sale are assumed divisible into small units with each unit homogeneous (identical to any other).

5. General knowledge of market prices must exist among buyers and sellers.

6. Market prices must be free to vary in response to changes in market forces.

For a market to be perfectly competitive, two additional conditions must be added to the six necessary conditions of a purely competitive market:

7. Perfect knowledge of prices and profits.
8. Perfect factor mobility.

If these necessary conditions prevail the firm can expect to lose its entire market if it sets its price above the market price, and can expect no gain by lowering price since it can sell all it wishes to produce at the market price. Remember the competitive firm has no price discretion; market price will not be affected by the independent action of a single firm. With general knowledge of market prices and homogeneous products, no firm is able to influence market price; the demand curve facing the purely competitive firm is then infinitely elastic (as, for example, is d_0 in Fig. 7.1*a*).[3]

---

[3] The firm as buyer of resources in a purely competitive market is not able (by its own action) to influence resource price; resource supply curves facing the firm are horizontal or infinitely elastic. Resource prices will be constant to each firm acting independently.

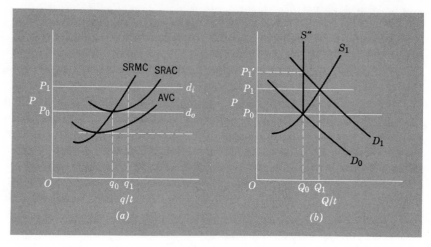

Fig. 7.1. (a) Firm. (b) Market.

Few markets in the United States fit exactly the conditions of perfect or even pure competition, and it is unlikely that a completely purely competitive economy has ever existed; however, early eighteenth-century agrarian societies approximated this situation, and economists from the eighteenth century to the present have been impressed with certain properties of a purely competitive economy. Such a market offers a solution to some of the difficult economic problems common to every society.

Price Determination in the Market Period

Suppose market demand has increased from D_0 to D_1 (see Fig. 7.1b). If the available stock is fixed, the immediate response to the increase in market demand is an increase in market price to P_1'—this is the "market" period or very short-run response along S'' in Fig. 7.1b, before any change in supply or any change in firms' output rates is possible. In this simplest of market period cases, supply S'' at any point in time is perfectly inelastic (see Fig. 7.1b). As with certain perishable commodities, the existing stock is fixed and sellers have no effective control over it.

The equilibrium price occurs where the demand curve intersects with the vertical supply curve S''; price is said to be *demand determined*. Of course, the equilibrium (market-clearing) price depends on the size of the available supply, but once this fixed stock is determined, price will vary with market demand. This vertical supply case is approximated by the daily supply of fresh fish or by a parcel of land in a crowded urban area.

Reservation Demand: Storable Commodities

In the market period stocks of goods are defined as fixed. But even with total supply fixed at any point in time, the market supply may not be perfectly inelastic. At various prices sellers may decide to reserve or withhold part of the available stock from the market. This is particularly feasible where goods are storable, where the likelihood of damage or deterioration is slight, and where storage cost are minimal. The decision to reserve part of the total supply at certain prices is usually related to the expectation of an improvement in price at some later time.

In Fig. 7.2, OT is the total available stock. At prices above P_r sellers are willing to sell their total stock, but at prices below P_w they withhold their total stock from the market. The dashed line beginning at O and running through S is a supply curve representing the amounts of the total stock that sellers are willing to offer for sale at various prices.[4] D_B is

---

[4] That sellers can substantially affect the quantity supplied to the market, by deciding to store (or destroy) parts of the available supply, suggests that the sellers are not operating independently, as under perfectly competitive conditions.

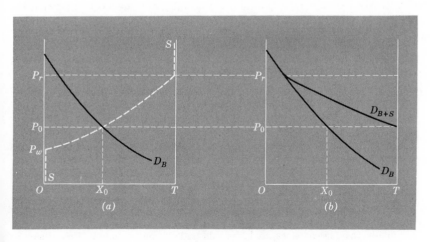

Fig. 7.2

the ordinary buyers' demand curve. It intersects the supply curve at (X_o, P_o)—the equilibrium price and quantity. At P_o, the quantity (X_o) that buyers demand is equal to the quantity that sellers are willing to supply.

The same results can be obtained (without resorting to the dashed supply function in Fig. 7.2a) by introducing the concept of seller's demand or reservation demand. The total stock OT less the amount sellers are willing to supply yields the reservation demand—the amounts the sellers want to hold on to at various prices. In Fig. 7.2b these amounts are added to buyers' demand to derive total demand (D_{B+S}). At any price, the difference between D_{B+S} and D_B is of course equal to the difference between the total stock OT and the supply curve SS.

Notice that the same equilibrium price (P_o) is obtained by considering either the intersection of supply (SS) and buyers' demand (P_B), or the intersection of total demand (D_{B+S}) and total stock (OT).[5]

Over a period during which total stock is relatively fixed, suppliers may vary the amount they are willing to place on the market for sale. In reserving part of the total stock, suppliers must make some guesses regarding future supply, future demand, and future price. The shape of the supply curve reflects suppliers' future expectations; the shape of the supply curve also reflects the various carrying costs: storage costs, risks of damage (these may be avoidable by incurring an insurance cost), the opportunity cost of money capital invested in inventory,[6] and the uncertainty related to future demand, future supply, and price. In general, supply becomes less elastic over the period as opportunities for disposing of the stock (prior to the time when the stock will be replenished) become fewer, and the various carrying costs increase the more extended the carrying time. The later market period supply curves tend to lie above the earlier supply curves.

Futures Markets: Rationing Over Time

The existing (spot or cash) market and reservation demand in the market period are often influenced by the existence of a secondary or futures market.

---

[5] Buyers and sellers need not be separate and distinct parties. A trader may buy and sell at various prices: he may augment his stock at one price and sell off part of his stock at another price.

[6] Presumably the present stock could be sold and the money invested elsewhere, so the cost of carrying the stock must include the interest foregone.

Where a futures market exists, traders can hedge by taking "long" and "short" positions on a commodity. When you own a commodity and hold on to it betting that its price will increase, you have taken a long position. You may decide to hedge (against the possibility of a price decline) by selling a futures contract. When you sell a futures contract you promise to deliver at some future date at an agreed price. Here you take a short position—you sell short (prior to possessing the commodity). A speculator may sell short, gambling that future prices will fall; if he guesses correctly he can take his profit by buying when the price falls (covering his earlier promise to sell at some predetermined price). The buyer of a futures contract benefits if price rises. He has bought a promise from someone to deliver at agreed price, so if the cash price goes up, he stands to gain.

For storable standardized goods, a futures market facilitates the rationing function of a commodity over time. If the demand is expected to increase relative to supply, and so a price rise is expected, speculators may buy long at present price, gambling on a price increase more than sufficient to cover interest costs, storage, insurance, and other carrying charges. If it is expected that price will fall, they will sell short for future delivery at present prices.

Futures markets play an important role in rationing over time and reducing risk, particularly when there is seasonal variation in supply or demand.

If speculators correctly guess the course of future market supply and demand, they will tend to have a stabilizing influence on price over time by taking goods off the market when supply is plentiful, spreading the available supply over time. The activities of speculators in futures markets also make it possible for producers to protect themselves against the uncertainties of price changes by hedging; if producers want to insure delivery of some material in the future at some determined price, they can hedge against the uncertainty of a possible price change by buying a futures contract: a promise that the commodity will be delivered in, say, May at the currently listed price for May futures.

The Short-Run Response to a Change in Price

In the short run some inputs can be varied so firms will adjust output rate up to point q_1 in Fig. 7.1a, where marginal revenue (equal to price along the firm's new horizontal demand curve d_1) from extra output no longer exceeds the marginal cost of extra output. The short-run market supply S_1 is the horizontal summation of firms' supply curves—their short-run marginal cost curves such as SRMC in Fig. 7.1*a*.[7] At any given market price, each firm will attempt to vary its output rate to the point where marginal cost equals marginal revenue. This applies only to marginal costs above average variable costs (AVC). After the short-run response by firms, P_1 would be the short-run market equilibrium price, and Q_1 the short-run equilibrium quantity supplied by the market. At (Q_1, P_1) the short-run market supply curve (ΣSRMC) intersects with the new market demand curve D_1.

Even if price were to drop below short-run average cost (providing $P >$ AVC), the firm in the short run, if it expected the price decline to be temporary, would continue to operate, minimizing its loss by producing that output rate where MC = MR. As long as price exceeds average variable cost, some contribution to overhead would result from production even though the firm would be operating temporarily at a loss. At a price greater than average variable cost but below average cost, a firm, by producing to the point where MC = MR, would minimize its short-run loss, even if it were not covering its full (average) costs. Alternatively, if the firm expected the price to remain below average cost, it might well choose the long-run response of going out of business, or liquidating its assets.

Long-Run Response to a Change in Price

In the long run, we suppose a period long enough (no set clock time is implied) to vary the capacity of the firm. (Recall all inputs are variable in the long run.) An existing firm's long-run response to a change in market price (which is expected to persist) will depend on its present size and efficiency and the shape of its long-run average cost curve (LRAC).

In Fig. 7.3*a*, a firm of size *A* has not yet grown to optimum size where the LRAC is a minimum. A size *A* firm could exist at a price P_1, but in a competitive industry such a price would permit profitable investment (by existing firms or new firms). Capital would be attracted to this industry, and the industry would expand. Market supply would shift to the right until an equilibrium was once again attained at a market price that just yielded zero economic profit to a most efficient optimum-sized firms (firm *B* in Fig. 7.3*a*).

---

[7] This assumes no external economies or diseconomies, so that the firm's resource costs and production function are unaffected by industry or general economic changes beyond the firm's control. This simplified concept of a firm's supply curve will be modified in our discussion of external economies and diseconomies.

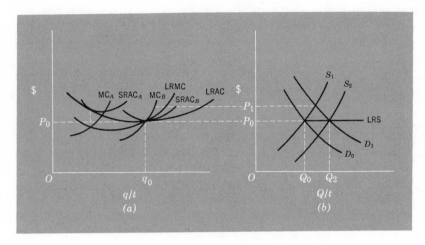

Fig. 7.3. (*a*) Firm. (*b*) Market.

Capital expansion brings about a shift outward in market supply (S_1 to S_2 in Fig. 7.1*b*) until price declines to a point where the economic profit of an optimum-sized firm will approach zero—there will then be no incentive for existing firms to expand or contract capital facilities, nor will new firms be tempted to enter (assuming they cannot improve on the operating performance of the low-cost firms in the industry). The fact that the new long-run equilibrium price (P_0) equals the initial equilibrium price, although the industry output rate has increased to Q_2 (in Fig. 7.3*b*), implies no external effects on the firm's costs as the industry expands. The horizontal long-run market supply curve (LRS) in Fig. 7.3*b* (through the equilibrium points at the intersections of the short-run market supply and demand curves) defines a constant-cost industry, where the long-run equilibrium price tends toward some constant level as the industry expands (or contracts). If price falls to P_0, firm A (in order to avoid running negative profits) would be forced to make a long-run response: either it would have to expand its capital facilities to attain a more efficient size or it would have to leave the industry.

At the long-run equilibrium price P_0, firm B (and all other optimal, most efficient-sized firms) would be in equilibrium. P_0 equals its short- and long-run average and marginal costs. It has no incentive to expand or contract its capital facilities or vary the intensity of use of its existing capital facilities. If market price were to increase from the equilibrium price P_0 to a price P_1, an optimal-sized firm (B) with a bowl-shaped

LRAC curve would be taking an unnecessary risk (under competitive market conditions with no barriers to entry) if it were to expand its capacity and gear its rate of output (according to the simple profit-maximizing rule) to the point where LRMC equalled price. Operating under purely competitive conditions, it may well expect the price increase from P_0 to P_1 to be temporary (in the absence of external diseconomies to be discussed later), since positive economic profit will result in industry expansion and a shift in market supply from S_1 to S_2 in Fig. 7.3b. Instead, firm B may attempt to use its existing facilities more intensively and react to the price increase along its short-run supply curve (MC_B in Fig. 7.3a). (Note the firm's short-run marginal costs will increase more sharply than its long-run marginal costs due to the force of the law of diminishing returns.)

The Shape of the Long-Run Average Cost Function

The shape of the LRAC curve is directly related to input prices and to the physical production function relationship we examined earlier. If we assume constant input prices, constant returns to scale implies a perfectly horizontal LRAC curve; increasing returns to scale implies a downward sloping LRAC curve, that is, internal economies of scale; decreasing return to scale (probably due to eventual stresses on the managerial function) implies an upward sloping LRAC curve, that is, internal diseconomies of scale. A firm's LRAC (planning) curve may exhibit all three shapes over various possible sizes.

The point at which diseconomies set in, how rapidly the LRAC curve turns up, or over how wide a range LRAC remains horizontal will, of course, vary with the industry and the technology involved. There may be pecuniary as well as technological influences governing the shape of the LRAC curve. There are, for example, economies in large-scale purchasing (quantity discounts), financing, and advertising.

The shapes of the LRAC and LRMC are of considerable importance in predicting the long-run response to an increase in market price. If the price increase persists, we should expect some capital inflow into the industry and an expansion of the industry's capacity. The expansion could take place either by expansion of existing firms or by new firms entering. Industry expansion by existing firms will occur if the LRAC is horizontal over a considerable range (and equal to LRMC over this range). If the LRAC curve of firms in an industry were decidedly U-shaped, we would expect existing firms to remain about the same size (as long as there is no change in technology); expansion in response to positive economic profit would then take place by new optimum-sized firms entering the industry. Where a firm's LRMC curve is rising, the only point on its LRMC curve that is relevant to industry supply is that point where it touches the firm's LRAC curve at its minimum. If firm's LRAC curves are bowl-shaped or U-shaped, thus discouraging expansion by existing firms, long-run industry supply can be viewed as the summation of outputs at the minimum points on firms' LRAC curves. Assuming firms' costs are identical at their equilibrium outputs and firms' costs remain constant with changes in industry output (no external effects), long-run industry supply will be horizontal—infinitely elastic.

Faced with a common long-run equilibrium price, all purely competitive firms may be viewed as having the same minimum long-run average costs in equilibrium if resources are identical for each firm. If resources differ, firms of various size may be optimum-sized; that is, the size at which LRAC is a minimum may not be unique. Certain firms may possess advantages such as better location or superior management; they may be low-cost firms due to the greater productivity of certain specialized resources. These specialized resources may earn a rent above their opportunity cost. A perfect market will tend to bid up the actual cost to the firm of a superior resource until its price reflects its superior productivity. A firm's average cost curve reflects opportunity costs of its resources. The greater productivity of a resource to the firm will tend to be offset by the higher resource price. If the rent earned by a superior specialized resource accrues to the firm (a low-cost firm), it will show up as positive profit even in long-run equilibrium (but it is really a rent to some specialized resource). If all rents are included as costs of specialized resources to the firm, all firms in long-run equilibrium may be viewed as having identical average costs.

External Effects on the Firm's Cost: External Economies and Diseconomies

Industry expansion (or even general economic growth outside this particular industry) may have an external effect on the firm's costs.

As new firms enter, the short-run market supply function tends to shift to the right. With factor prices constant, market supply is the horizontal aggregation of firms' short-run marginal cost (MC) functions. If industry expansion is extensive and rapid, however, the firms' short-run supply functions are likely to be more inelastic than they appeared to a single firm acting independently, and market supply will be less elastic than would have been the case if there had been no increase in factor prices. Previously we assumed that resource prices to the firm were constant, as were the marginal products of the various resources (or their inverse: the marginal input coefficients). Now, due to industry or general economic changes outside the control of any single firm, input prices or the firm's production functions may change. These are external pecuniary or technological economies (or diseconomies), which will cause the firm's costs to decrease (or increase).

The response of existing optimal-sized firms (such as Firm B in Fig. 7.3a) to a price rise is likely to be a short-run response involving variable resources, since there is a long-run expectation that such a price rise, which permits the firm to earn positive economic profit, is temporary. The initial market period price rise (prior to the short-run response) from P_0 to P_1' in Fig. 7.1b is a signal to existing firms to increase their rate of output by using existing capital facilities more intensively. A short-run (temporary) equilibrium price will then be set at P_1, where short-run market supply S_1 intersects with demand D_1 in Fig. 7.1b. However, short-run equilibrium in a purely competitive market is a temporary or incomplete adjustment. As investment in the industry leads to new plant capacity, price tends to approach the long-run equilibrium price (equal to minimum average cost of an optimal-sized firm). New capital is attracted to the industry by a favorable market price, which permits positive economic profits.

How long will the market price remain above minimum average cost before sufficient resources are attracted to the industry so that market supply will increase (shift to the right) and price will once again reach a new long-run equilibrium position?[8] The answer depends in part on the actual ease of entry: How perfect is the market and how mobile are resources? There may exist various frictions and hurdles that must be overcome before industry expansion takes place. Bottlenecks and shortages of resources of similar quality to those presently used may impede entry and cause certain resource prices to rise if sufficient quantities are to be drawn to the expanding industry. Increased resource prices due to industry expansion is an example of external diseconomies; industry expansion causes the firm's costs to increase (see Fig. 7.4a). In the diseconomy case, the new long-run equilibrium price (P_2 in Fig.

---

[8] The analysis proceeds here according to comparative statics. Demand has shifted and we trace this change in parameter to a new partial equilibrium, assuming income, taste, and other prices are fixed, while we examine the direction and mechanism of change. In fact, other things are constantly changing in a dynamic economy, and it is quite unlikely that a position of long-run equilibrium is ever attained.

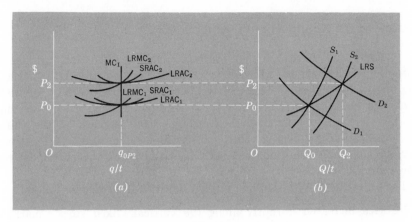

Fig. 7.4

7.4b) remains above the original long-run equilibrium price P_0. In increasing cost industries, the long-run market supply curve is positively sloping. The market short-run supply curves, S_1 and S_2, where there are external economies or diseconomies, are the summation of firms' MC_I curves, which take account of shifts in firm's costs, due to changes in resource prices or technological possibilities beyond the control of the firm. MC_I is perfectly inelastic in Fig. 7.4a, implying an equal proportionate change in all input prices or physical efficiencies. If fixed factors increased in price relative to the price of variable factors, MC_I would have a negative slope and a smaller firm would be optimum sized. (Note S_2 in Fig. 7.4b would still be positively sloping.)

In long-run equilibrium there is no incentive for new firms to enter nor for present firms to expand or leave the industry. Each firm is operating at that rate of output where LRMC = LRAC = price. (If we include "rent" earned by superior resources as a cost to the competitive firm, then *all* firms in long-run equilibrium are operating at that rate of output where price = LRAC = LRMC.) Each firm in a competitive market earns zero economic profit in long-run equilibrium.[9]

[9] Where specialized resources are present, a low-cost firm may earn economic "rent" in addition to a competitive rate of profit, which is included as an opportunity cost in the firm's average cost curve. In our analysis, LRAC was inclusive of rent—allowing for change in the cost (or value) of specialized resources to the firm. Note that the revaluation (rental costs) does not affect the firm's LRMC (change in total costs as output increases).

Resumé of the Adjustment to Equilibrium

It is important to realize that even though our discussion has dealt with the mechanism by which a new equilibrium position is achieved, the analysis has been in terms of comparative statics: we first allowed a change in some particular market parameter, causing a shift in the market demand function; we then examined the response to the shift in demand in an artificially controlled environment, assuming the *ceteris paribus* condition held and that nothing would block the movement to a new equilibrium position.

The adjustment to the shift in market demand proceeded as follows:

1. Price increased abruptly along the vertical "fixed stock" market period supply curve (S'') in Fig. 7.1b.

2. Existing firms without making additional capital investment expanded output along the upward sloping short-run MC curve until the short-run (temporary) equilibrium was reached where $P = \text{MC}$; price declined after its initial abrupt rise due to the expanding output of existing firms.

3. Capital expansion by new (and existing) firms in response to positive economic profit ($P > \text{AC}$) caused a shift in market supply. The shifting market supply curve intersects the market demand curve at higher output rate, bringing about a further price decline (approaching the new long-run equilibrium price).

If the adjustment to the initial shift in demand were allowed to go to completion, a new short-run market supply would intersect the market demand curve at some price, which might be higher than, equal to, or lower than the initial long-run equilibrium price.

We began our analysis with the industry in equilibrium. There then occurred a change in market demand—an increase in demand signalled by an initial market period price increase. In the short run, output expanded by existing firms varying the rate of use of variable resources until the original short-run market supply curve intersected with market demand. In the long run, new resources were attracted to the industry, and price moved to a new long-run equilibrium position.

In reality, adjustment in the market is rarely completed before some new disturbance arises causing a shift in market demand or supply. The partial equilibrium analysis indicates the expected direction of the response by individual firms, and by the aggregate response of all firms supplying a particular market. If the market constitutes a substantial part of total economic output, the results of partial equilibrium analysis may be spurious since demand in the market cannot, without serious error, be assumed independent of supply and income generated in producing for the market.

We must be careful to recognize the limitations of the partial equilibrium analysis, particularly its reliance on the *ceteris paribus* condition. Partial equilibrium and comparative static analysis remain a useful analytic method well adapted to examining the first-order effects of changes in the economic environment on particular markets.

Normative Implications of Pure Competition

Under pure competition, the profit-maximizing firm always produces at that rate of output where its MC equals the market price. (Remember that a purely competitive firm cannot influence price.) All firms in a purely competitive market face a common market price $(\bar{P})$. They attempt to equate MC = MR$(= \bar{P})$. The result is that whatever the industry output, it is always allocated among the firms in the industry in such a manner that their MC's are equal.

The equality of each firm's marginal cost and market price leads to two very important results. The first is that, with the existing producing units, industry output is produced at minimum total cost (maximum efficiency). The second is that industry output is optimal in a purely competitive industry with MC = $\bar{P}$. (The additional benefit from the last unit produced—as measured by price—equals the additional opportunity cost.) If output had fallen short of the competitive output so that MC < P, there would be a net gain to society if resources were transferred to the industry. Also, if MC's were not equal among the firms, output could be produced more efficiently by reallocating resources. In purely competitive equilibrium, firms' MC's are equal.

In equilibrium, when each consumer has maximized utility, the ratio MU_i/P_i is equal for any of the ith products the consumer purchases with his given income. This common ratio is the marginal utility of each consumer's income (MU_Y)—the marginal utility from the last dollar spent on each commodity:

$$\frac{\mathrm{MU}_i}{P_i} = \mathrm{MU}_Y \quad \text{and} \quad \frac{\mathrm{MU}_i}{\mathrm{MU}_Y} = P_i$$

Under pure competition, the utility-maximizing consumers will purchase to the margin where their MU from the last dollar spent on each product (divided by MU_Y) equals the price of the product; thus price can be taken as an "approximate" measure of the MU that consumers derive from a product.[10] A purely competitive profit-maximizing producer will produce to the point where MC equals market price. In equilibrium, then, the output of a purely competitive industry will be carried to a point where P = MC, where price is a measure of utility of the marginal unit, and marginal cost is a measure of the value of the resources used to produce the marginal unit.

A third advantage of a purely competitive market is that price to the consumer will be no higher than necessary in long-run equilibrium. The purely competitive firm in equilibrium will be an optimum size; and long-run equilibrium price (with free entry and exit) will tend to equal the minimum average cost (= LRMC = SRMC) of an optimum-sized firm—operating a lowest-cost plant at its economic capacity (minimum AC). An optimum number of such firms will be able to sell enough at this price to cover their opportunity costs including a normal or competitive rate of return on capital. In equilibrium, there will be no tendency for the industry to expand or contract its capital facilities. There will be no tendency for firms to enter or leave the industry, since firms will be earning zero economic profit.

Problems

The tendency for autonomous adjustment to zero-economic profit in response to changes in the market environment does not imply that income will be distributed among individuals in any "best" way. A change in income distribution due to, say, a tax is likely to lead to a different allocation of resources among different commodities with a different optimum output in each industry. Consumer sovereignty takes the existing income distribution as given.

If external diseconomies in consumption exist, the purely competitive result may not be optimum. The pleasure anticipated when one person in a big city buys a car is likely to be quite different from the pleasure experienced when eight million of his neighbors also buy cars. The congestion may be such that he may not find room to drive the car a place to park it (in fact he may not find the car if it was parked in violation of city ordinance). The smog and noise from eight million auto exhausts and horns are additional diseconomies in consumption.

Another basis for questioning the optimality of the competitive solution is that net private cost, to which producers adjust their output,

[10] There is a difficulty in that MU_Y may vary among individuals, so that a dollar may be worth more to one person than to another.

may be less than net social cost, due to external diseconomies in production. This discrepancy between the industry's benefit and the community's benefit is recognized by the community when it attempts to impose standards of automotive safety or reduce water pollution.

It has been argued[11] that private costs and social costs will be equalized in perfectly competitive markets (and the optimum output produced where price is equal to marginal social cost), as long as someone sees to it that producers must recognize any discrepancy between marginal private and social costs (by taxing, penalizing, or bribing) so that the firms will adjust their output to social cost. If firms attend only to that part of (total) social cost that is private, there will very likely be overproduction (in terms of net social benefit).

It has also been suggested that where there are external economies—as a decreasing cost industry expands (e.g., better transport facilities, better trained work force, or lower prices from supplying industries with their own economies of scale)—industry output under perfect competition will be smaller than optimum. The MC (for industry expansion) would lie below price. The firm's AC and MC curves would shift downward as the industry expands, but the individual firms making zero economic profit ($MC = AC = P$) and acting independently will not be able to affect the potential benefits from an expanding industry.

A different type of problem, which at least in part accounts for the instability of a purely competitive equilibrium and for the existence of noncompetitive market structure in certain industries, is that the market may not be large enough to support a sufficient number of firms if the existence of internal economies (declining LRAC) gives one or a few large firms a competitive advantage over many relatively small firms. (Remember that in a purely competitive market the firms are presumed to act independently and are "price-takers.") All of the preceding discussion of the normative implications of pure competition assumed that internal economies of scale and the size of the market permitted the existence of a purely competitive industry. The number of firms in a purely competitive market will be large and determinate if the LRAC curve is bowl-shaped for each firm and the market will permit a sufficiently large number of optimum-sized firms, each operating at the bottom of the (LRAC) bowl.

The purely competitive market solution is sometimes criticized in terms of dynamics, that is, operating over time. In an unstable economy with deep cyclical swings in the economy, there would be frequent and

[11] Ronald Coase, "The Problem of Social Cost," *Journal of Law and Economics*, **3,** 1961.

wasteful resource transfers into and out of an industry. It has also been argued that without the guarantee of some positive economic profit over time, advances in technology and economic innovations would not be generated at a sufficient pace by purely competitive firms. (They would have neither the financial power to continue in the face of adverse economic conditions nor the incentive to plan for and implement improvements in products or technology.)

Market Equilibrium

Under purely competitive conditions in a perfect market, price would adjust to the market clearing static equilibrium position at a point where quantity supplied Q_s equals quantity demanded Q_d as in Fig. 7.1, where P_0 is the equilibrium price. Equilibrium exists since excess demand equals zero at this price: $Q_d - Q_s = 0$ at P_0. At this equilibrium price neither a surplus nor a shortage exists. At some price P_1 below the equilibrium price, where excess demand is positive $(Q_d > Q_s)$, a shortage exists since suppliers are only willing to supply Q_1 at this price, while some buyers who are not able to purchase all they want at that price would be willing to pay much more than P_1 and would offer more, eventually bidding the price up to the market-clearing equilibrium price, P_0. Of course at the price P_1 some may be fortunate and enjoy a privileged

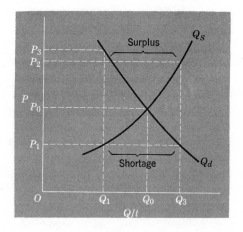

Fig. 7.5

buyer status for one reason or another; for example, someone may have been an old, valued customer or simply first on line. If for some reason the market price were not free to move, there would be a strong possibility that other markets would arise since a rate of output Q_1 could find takers at a price as high as P_3. There would exist a situation with a positive "excess demand price" ($P_3 > P_1$ at Q_1).

Occasionally the market mechanism is circumvented and price is artificially kept below the equilibrium price. This occurred in World War II when certain food products were in short supply. Because of the extreme scarcity—the reduced supply available to the public and the increased demand—it was judged unfair to allow the market to perform its normal allocating function through the automatic price system. An alternate rationing device—blue stamps—was introduced to supplement money and a free market price. However, it was rather difficult to prevent some of the supply from being diverted into illegal "black" markets, further reducing the legal supply.

A surplus exists at prices above the equilibrium price. Here we have negative excess demand ($Q_d < Q_s$) or excess supply. This surplus situation is also likely to be temporary unless the price is rigged or maintained by some authority at a price above the equilibrium price. The tendency in this surplus situation is for unsold stocks to pile up; the capacity to produce or the willingness to supply at a price P_2 (in Fig. 7.1) is greater than the willingness of buyers to purchase at this price above the equilibrium price. Under purely competitive conditions there will be some price reductions as suppliers try to unload their unwanted surplus, and the rate of production will decrease as price falls, until the equilibrium price P_0 is reached.

There are extreme situations where the market pricing mechanism does not work well. The wartime shortage situation has been mentioned. Another is the case of price instability resulting from very inelastic market supply and demand functions so that even slight shifts in market demand or supply trigger exaggerated price changes (see Fig. 7.6a). At the other extreme, very elastic supply and demand functions coupled with variability in demand may cause wasteful transfers of resources, especially in perfect markets where adjustment is immediate (see Fig. 7.6b).

Adjustment in a Regulated "Competitive" Market

If market price is regulated at a support price P_1 (Fig. 7.7) inducing producers to produce at a rate of Q_1, while the market is willing to

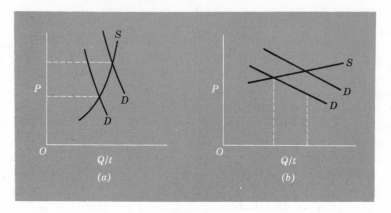

Fig. 7.6

absorb Q_2, a surplus Q_1-Q_2 would result. There would then be competitive forces at work to depress the market price to P_0; however, if the price is inflexible due to producer agreement or governmental decree, a "managed" equilibrium could be maintained by government standing ready to purchase any surplus, as with the agricultural price support of certain storable commodities such as wheat. The demand curve would become horizontal at price P_1 and the effective demand facing the producers would be D-D_g rather than the private market demand D-D. The government would buy and store an amount equal to the shaded

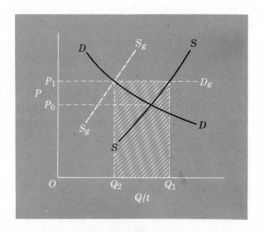

Fig. 7.7

area.[12] Alternatively, producers might be persuaded to restrict supply so that supply shifts back to S_g-S_g. A farm acreage restriction program has been attempted; however, the program has not been a rousing success. Through intense cultivation and care of limited acreage, former levels of farm output were in many cases maintained or surpassed. More direct methods of restricting output, such as marketing quotas, may be necessary to achieve the desired result of restricting supply so that price support need not require substantial government purchase and storage of surplus produce (presuming restricted output is a desirable end).

Comparative static analysis is concerned with equilibrium positions before and after change has occurred. The process of adjustment and the stability of equilibrium positions are of considerable importance. The concept of equilibrum was discussed previously in terms of surplus and shortage (negative and positive excess demand). If a surplus exists, competition among sellers causes price to fall, eliminating the surplus; if a shortage exists, competition among buyers causes price to rise, eliminating the shortage. The question of exactly how the adjustment takes place remains unanswered. How the price system affects equilibrium in any particular market—the path of adjustment—belongs to economic dynamics. In some situations *price* may be the initial equilibrating variable and in other situations *quantity* may be the initial equilibrating variable.

Stability of Equilibrium

We cannot take it for granted that the adjustment will always be toward the equilibrium position. Not all equilibrium positions are stable in the sense that if there is a movement away from equilibrium, forces are set in motion that induce a return to equilibrium. The cases of stable, neutral, and unstable equilibrium can be explained by a physical analogy. Suppose we have a marble sitting in the bottom of a rounded concave soup bowl. If the bowl is bumped, the marble may be dislodged but it will tend to return to its position in the bottom of the bowl; this is stable equilibrium. If we turn the bowl over so that the convex side is up, we may still be able to balance the marble in the middle of the outside of the bowl, but a slight disturbance will cause the marble

---

[12] The mechanics of the farm price support program involved crop storage loans for farmers who wished to bring their crop to certain central locations. The crop was held in storage as collateral. The farmer then had the option of selling the crop held in storage in private markets or receiving a check from the government for an amount equal to the quantity times the support price.

to roll down the side and away from the original position; this is unstable equilibrium. Neutral equilibrium may be likened to a marble sitting on a flat surface; if jostled it may move to a nearby position, but there will not be any tendency for it to return to or move further away from the original position of rest.

Appraisal of whether a particular equilibrium is stable or not must depend on an examination of the process and path of adjustment. The adjustment process is never really instantaneous, although this is often overlooked in comparative static analysis where the time period is chosen so that adjustment is assumed completed within the period. The problem of the stability of equilibrium in a market is essentially a dynamic problem that can be resolved only by considering the adjustment process in a particular market.

Walrasian and Marshallian Interpretations of Stable Equilibrium[13]

Marshall and Walras agreed on what constitutes equilibrium in a market, although they used slightly different nomenclature in their explanations. Marshall defined equilibrium as the intersection of the supply and demand curve. Walras stated that equilibrium exists when excess demand equals zero. Using the standard Walrasian definition of equilibrium in terms of the price at which excess demand equals zero, we discussed the shortage and surplus situations when price was below or above equilibrium price, and excess demand was positive or negative.

In discussing the stability of equilibrium, Marshall viewed the demand price as the maximum price at which a certain quantity could be sold, and supply price as the minimum price at which that certain quantity would be offered for sale. At quantities where demand price exceeds supply price ($P_3 > P_1$ at Q_1 in Fig. 7.5), Marshall judged that the quantity offered for sale would increase. When the supply price exceeds the demand price ($P_2 > P_1$ at Q_3 in Fig. 7.5), the quantity offered for sale would decrease. The quantity offered for sale was, in Marshall's judgment, the equilibrating variable to which market price responded.

In the more generally accepted Walrasian approach to the problem of what constitutes a stable equilibrium, price is the equilibrating independent variable to which Q_d and Q_s respond. When excess demand is positive ($Q_d - Q_s > 0$), price rises. When excess demand is negative

---

[13] Leon Walras, *Elements of Pure Economics,* trans. William Jaffe, Richard D. Irwin, 1954; Alfred Marshall, *Principles of Economics,* 8th ed., Macmillan and Co., London, 1936.

$(Q_d - Q_s < 0)$, price falls. These were shortage and surplus situations illustrated in Fig. 7.5.

In the usual case of a positively sloping supply curve and a negatively sloping demand curve (the situation illustrated in Fig. 7.5), there is no disagreement regarding the stability of the equilibrium at (Q_0, P_0). Whichever adjustment mechanism applies—whether price adjusts when excess demand is not equal to 0 or whether quantity adjusts when the demand price is not equal to the supply price—there will be a tendency to approach the equilibrium position at the intersection of the supply and demand curves.

A difference of opinion over what constitutes a stable equilibrium arises in the exceptional cases where the supply curve is negatively sloping (or forward falling) and cuts the negatively sloping demand curve from either above or below, as in Fig. 7.8.

In these exceptional cases, the Walrasian and Marshallian assumptions regarding the dynamics of the adjustment process lead to opposite estimates of which of the situations in Fig. 7.8 constitutes a stable equilibrium. What will happen if, say, demand shifts to the right in Figs. 7.8*a* and 7.8*b*? Let us look first at the case in Fig. 7.8*a*, where a negatively sloping supply curve intersects a more steeply negatively sloping demand curve. Walras, assuming that a positive excess demand would induce a rise in price, considered the situation in Fig. 7.8*a* unstable. Buyers would bid up the price when demand shifted, and instead of price moving from the original equilibrium position at E_0 to the new equilibrium position at E_1, the price would tend to increase from E_0

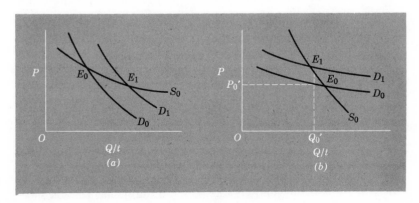

Fig. 7.8. (*a*) Walras: unstable; Marshall: stable. (*b*) Walras: stable; Marshall: unstable.

in a direction away from the intersection at E_1, where the market would be cleared.

Marshall viewed the same situation—where the demand curve was steeper than the negatively sloping supply—as a stable equilibrium, since when demand shifted, the demand price would exceed the supply price and suppliers would increase the amount offered for sale in the direction of the new equilibrium at E_1. Of course, they reached opposite conclusions regarding the stability of equilibrium in the Fig. 7.8b case, where the supply curve cuts demand from above (the supply is steeper than the demand curve).

The disagreement over which of these unusual cases constitutes a stable equilibrium can be demonstrated without a shift in the demand curve, as in our illustration. Suppose in 7.8b, suppliers had underestimated demand D_0, and market supply was somewhere to the left of E_0 at Q_0'. Walras would judge E_0 to be a stable equilibrium since this output Q_0' could be sold at a price no higher than P_0', and so excess demand would be negative (a surplus); price would fall in the direction of the equilibrium at E_0, where excess demand equals zero. Marshall would judge the equilibrium in Fig. 7.8b to be unstable, since at Q_0' the supply price exceeds demand price, inducing suppliers to reduce the quantity offered for sale in a direction away from the equilibrium at E_0. In terms of Marshall's criterion for stable equilibrium, E_0 in this case would be judged unstable, since for quantities smaller than the equilibrum quantity at E_0, the excess demand price would be negative, inducing suppliers to supply less (a move further away from E_0); if a quantity larger than the equilibrium quantity at E_0 were supplied, the "excess demand price" would be positive, inducing suppliers to increase their rate of supply again away from E_0, the unstable equilibrium.

No doubt the discrepancy over the definition of stable equilibrium was in reality an argument over the generality of the assumptions regarding the process of adjustment. Marshall was concerned with the long-run market adjustment under purely competitive conditions in decreasing cost industries (Fig. 7.8a). The downward sloping long-run supply curve represents the market supply, where there are external economies of scale. Underlying Marshall's view that this case was one of stable equilibrium was an elaborate dynamic adjustment process applicable to external economy situations, where market output is likely to increase in response to increased demand. Walras was concerned with an adjustment process where suppliers cannot (or will not) so quickly respond to an increase in demand—perhaps the period of adjustment is too short, as in the market period when stocks are in fixed supply.

Imperfect Adjustment toward Equilibrium

Complete and instantaneous adjustment to market forces requires a perfect market mechanism: perfect knowledge of the availability and the prices of goods and services and perfect mobility of resources in response to market signals. Imperfections in the market tend to lengthen the period of adjustment to equilibrium.

Time lags in the production process between production plans and their fruition can result in a dynamic (time) path of adjustment away from equilibrium; or it can result in a situation where several periods elapse before an equilibrium is achieved; or it can result in a situation where the market price and quantity neither converge toward nor move further away from equilibrium. Imperfect and lagged adjustment to market signals may cause stable oscillations toward an equilibrium position (damped oscillations and the equilibrium position is approached), unstable oscillations (they become larger), or the oscillations may be neutral (of given size about the equilibrium position).

Suppose we consider the market for an agricultural crop, say corn, with an extended growing season, so that the supply is harvested and comes to market the period after it has been planted. The price in the former period will affect the amount planted in that period but it will not further affect the supply harvested and brought to market. This model may be represented using the market supply and demand curves in Fig. 7.9, where quantity supplied Q^S is a function of market price in the previous period, and quantity demanded Q^D is a function of the current period's market price (the period when supply is harvested and brought to market). So while Q^S and Q^D both apply to the current period, they are functions of two different variables:

$$Q_t{}^S = f_1(P_{t-1}) \quad \text{and} \quad Q_t{}^D = f_2(P_t)$$

If price in the current period P_t happens to equal the price in the former period, then $Q^S = Q^D \ (= Q_0)$ at the equilibrium price in the current period (P_0 in Fig. 7.9).

If the market price in the earlier period was P_1, Q_1 would be planted in the earlier period and brought to market in the current period. Unfortunately this quantity (Q_1) cannot be sold at the higher price; Q_1 can be sold only at the lower price P_2 (dictated by the demand curve, which is assumed stable throughout the period under consideration).

The period-by-period analysis can be carried further. Suppliers will react to the price P_2 by planting less. They will plant and bring Q_2

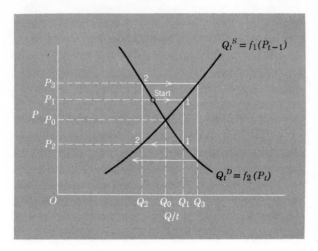

Fig. 7.9

to market in the next period, but Q_2 can be sold at P_3. This higher price will in turn induce an enlarged supply Q_3, and so on. The solid line segments connecting quantities supplied and demanded form a cobweb pattern, from which derives the name *cobweb theorem*. With a time lag on the supply side, the cobweb theorem indicates that the stability of equilibrium depends on the relation between the slopes of the supply and demand curves. In the unstable case, there are oscillations of increasing size away from equilibrium (as in Fig. 7.9). In this case

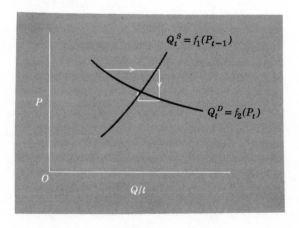

Fig. 7.10

the demand curve sloped more steeply than the supply curve. For market price to approach equilibrium in this model, the absolute value of the slope of the demand curve must be smaller than the slope of the supply curve. The stable oscillation case is illustrated in Fig. 7.10, where the convergence to equilibrium is quite rapid.

We have seen that even in the "normal" case of a positively sloping supply curve and a negatively sloping demand curve (both Marshall and Walras agreed this was a case of stable equilibrium), dynamic considerations such as the production lag in the cobweb case may cause instability and imperfect adjustment to equilibrium.

Effects of an Excise Tax on Market Equilibrium

The short-run burden of an excise tax in a purely competitive market is directly related to the elasticities of supply and demand. Suppose an excise tax (TX in Fig. 7.11) is levied. This tax on each unit sold can be added to the firm's MC (supply) curve to indicate the quantity the firm is willing to supply at various market prices (including the tax). The tax can be represented in the market by a vertical upward shift in market supply (Q_S to Q_{S_t}). We shall assume that market demand is unaffected by the tax—that buyers are indifferent as to how the price they are willing to pay is divided between the seller and the government. From whom the government actually receives the tax is not an important factor in this discussion. We can treat the buyer or the seller as a collecting agent.

If the demand curve were absolutely inelastic (Fig. 7.11a), the whole

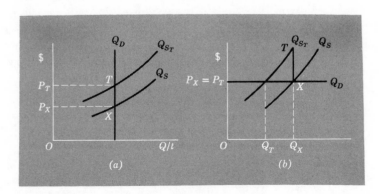

Fig. 7.11

price burden of the tax would be borne by the buyer. The change in market price (ΔP) from P_x to P_t would be equal to the full amount of the tax.

If market demand were infinitely elastic (Fig. 7.11*b*), the whole price burden would be borne by the suppliers. There would be no change in market price. In addition to the price burden—the effect of the tax on the unit price consumers must pay—there may be an effect on the quantity consumers purchase and of course an effect on total revenue ($= \Delta P \times \Delta Q$). In the infinitely elastic demand case (in Fig. 7.11*b*), the effect falls entirely on the quantity purchased—on the reduced rate of sales in the industry (Q_x to Q_t).

Between these two extreme cases, we have the usual case of a negatively sloping demand curve. Here, we find buyers and sellers sharing the price burden of the tax, at least in the short run. The proportion of the price burden borne by consumers is the change in price (ΔP) divided by the tax: $\Delta P/TAX$ in Fig. 7.12. The exact proportion of the tax borne by consumers will depend on the slopes (b) or the elasticities (e) of the demand and supply functions (the subscripts identify the function):

$$\frac{\Delta P}{TAX} = \frac{b_D}{b_D + b_S}\left(= \frac{e_S}{e_S + e_D}\right)^{14}$$

The larger the slope (or elasticity) of the *supply* curve, the larger the share of the tax borne by the consumer; also the smaller (closer to zero) the slope (or elasticity) of the *demand* curve, the larger the share of the tax borne by the consumer.

We have seen that in the short run, if the demand curve is not perfectly inelastic, price will rise by an amount less than the full amount of the tax. Existing firms will adjust their after-tax short-run supply ($SRMC_T$) to the new after-tax price, P_T. Since the new price, P_T, will now lie below the firm's LRMC (and below its LRAC), the firm will not be able to pay all resources an amount equal to what they could earn elsewhere, so resources will leave the industry. In the long run, market supply— ΣSRMC—will shift more to the left and price will rise above P_T, until price again equals LRMC ($=$ LRAC) at a reduced output.

---

[14] *Proof* (refer to Fig. 7.12). The slope of demand curve, $b_D = TA/-\Delta Q$, and $TA = b_D(-\Delta Q)$. The slope of the supply curve, $b_S = AX/-\Delta Q$, and $AZ = B_S$ $(-\Delta Q)$. TAX is the full amount of the tax, and TA is equivalent to the change in price (ΔP) paid by the consumer following the tax and AX is the amount of the tax borne by the producer, $\Delta P/TAX = TA/(TA + AX) = b_D(-\Delta Q)/[b_D(-\Delta Q) + b_S(-\Delta Q)] = b_D/(b_D + b_S)$. [With a little additional effort, it can be shown that $b_D/b_D + b_S) = P_S/(P_S + P_D)$.]

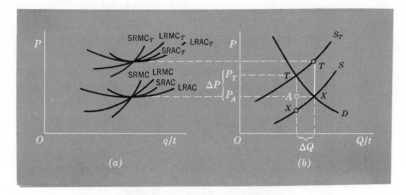

Fig. 7.12. (*a*) Firm. (*b*) Market.

Having adjusted to the tax, all resources will once again be earning their opportunity costs at $P = \text{LRAC}_T = \text{LRMC}_T$. The long-run price burden will be borne largely by consumers. The major long-run incidence of an excise tax on a competitive industry will be a reallocation of resources—a contraction of industry output, and a loss to owners of specialized resources.

The Identification Problem

Equilibrium in a purely competitive market occurs at the intersection of the market supply and the market demand curves at a price that just clears the market. The quantity that sellers are willing to supply at that price equals the quantity buyers are willing to buy at that price. The model of a purely competitive market can be represented by two hypothetical behavioral functions representing market demand and market supply, and a third market-clearing equation representing the equilibrium condition. Q_D, Q_S, and P are endogenous variables, whose equilibrium values are jointly determined by the simultaneous solution of the equations in our model:

$$Q_D = f_1(P) \qquad \text{Demand} \qquad\qquad \text{(I.a)}$$
$$Q_S = f_2(P) \qquad \text{Supply} \qquad\qquad \text{(I.b)}$$
$$Q_D = Q_S \qquad \text{Market Clearing} \qquad \text{(I.c)}$$

This is the model so often displayed graphically (see Fig. 13). The equilibrium values of the three endogenous variables, P, Q_D, Q_S, in the three-equation model (I) can be determined once the form of the

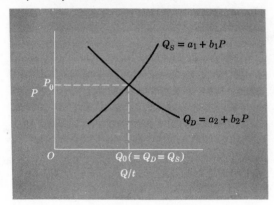

Fig. 7.13

equation is specified and the structional parameters known. At time $t = 0$ in Fig. 7.13 the structural parameters (a_1, b_1, a_2, b_2) in the two linear behavioral functions are assumed known. In equilibrium, $Q_D = Q_S (= Q_o)$ and $P = P_o$ at the intersection of supply and demand.

If the *ceteris paribus* conditions underlying supply and demand are violated, demand or supply may shift over time, and new equilibrium points will be (Q_t, P_t) observed in the market, as in Fig. 7.14 [If the *ceteris paribus* conditions held and there were no shifts in supply or demand (in model I) a single data-point would be observed.]

A curve fitted[15] to the observed market equilibria (assuming market-clearing prices prevail in each period) is more likely to represent some hybrid function than a separate demand or supply curve. There are exceptional cases where one or the other curve can be identified from the observed data. Such a case occurs where one of the curves is known to remain stationary. All of the points generated are then attributed to shifts in the other curve (see Figs. 7.15a and 7.15b).

In Fig. 7.15a, demand may remain constant while, say, changing weather causes shifts on the supply side. In Fig. 7.15b, income changes may cause demand to shift while supply remains constant.

The identification problem is the problem of trying to identify the structural parameters of the separate behavioral equations in the model from observed market data.

---

[15] The student who has had some statistics will no doubt be familiar with mathematical techniques, such as the method of least squares, for fitting mathematical functions to data. Others need only consider here a smooth, freehand curve drawn roughly through the data points.

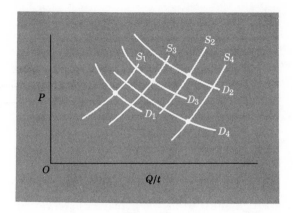

Fig. 7.14

In the simple model (I) above, identification from market data is unlikely. The data presumably represent the intersection of supply and demand, but no shift variables are explicitly considered in the model. We can only guess whether a new observed price-quantity combination is the result of a shift in the variables underlying supply or demand or both.

In econometric studies, where models of the real world are tested, the separate equations are assumed to contain a disturbance term that allows for some error between observed values and values estimated from the model. In model II, the linear demand and supply equations and the market clearing equations are written with a disturbance term—

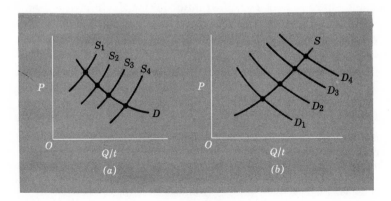

Fig. 7.15

the model is no longer determinate but allows now for some uncertainty. (By including disturbance terms e_1 and e_2, we explicitly recognize that our predictions may be inexact as a result of omission of certain variables, of errors in estimating the form or structure of our model, or the result of those unpredictable elements in human behavior.) Model II follows.

$$Q_S = a_1 + b_1 P + e_1 \qquad \text{(II.a)}$$
$$Q_D = a_2 + b_2 P + e_2 \qquad \text{(II.b)}$$
$$Q_S = Q_D + (e_1 + e_2) \qquad \text{(II.c)}$$

If e_1 were known to be zero over the time period (or even to vary within very narrow limits), while the demand curve varied considerably due to variation in e_2, the data would describe an identifiable supply curve (as in Fig. 7.15b).

The empirical identification of the parameters of the separate equations from observed market data usually requires the inclusion in the model of exogenous variables, whose values are known and independent of the simultaneous solution of the model. Suppose an income variable Y were added to the demand function, as in Model III:

$$Q_S = a_1 + b_1 P + e_1 \qquad \text{(III.a)}$$
$$Q_D = a_2 + b_2 P + c_2 Y + e_2 \qquad \text{(III.b)}$$
$$Q_S = Q_D + (e_1 + e_2) \qquad \text{(III.c)}$$

The shifts in the demand curve in Fig. 7.15b can now be attributed to changing values of the exogenous variable Y. The supply curve equation (III.a) is now "just identified" and we are able to estimate a_1 and b_1—the structural parameters of our supply curve. Equation III.b— the demand curve—is not identified in model III. If all of the behavioral equations (containing at least one endogenous variable) are identified, the model is "just identified," meaning all of the structural parameters can be estimated.[16]

A necessary condition for determining whether an equation can be identified is as follows. Suppose there are v_i variables (endogenous and exogenous) in an equation i. Let n be the number of endogenous variables in the model and let x be the number of exogenous variables in

---

[16] A model is said to be complete if, once the structural parameters are identified and known, we can then solve the equations for the equilibrium values of the endogenous variables. In general, m linear independent equations are required in order to obtain a unique solution for m endogenous variables.

the model; $(n + x)$ is the total number of variables in the model. Find the total number of endogenous variables in the model and subtract one— $(n - 1)$, or one less than the number of endogenous variables in the model. Next find the number of variables in the model that do not appear in our equation $[(n + x) - v_i]$, where v_i is the number of variables (exogenous and endogenous) that appear in our equation. If this number, $(n + x) - v_i$, is at least equal to $(\geq)$ $n - 1$, the equation meets the necessary condition for identification.

Let us apply this rule to Eq. III.a. There are four variables in model III: the endogenous variables Q_S, Q_D, P and the exogenous variable Y, so $n = 3$ and $x = 1$. Of the four variables, two—Q_S and P—appear in Eq. III.a, so $v_1 = 2$. Excluded from this equation are the two variables Q_D and Y, so $(n + x) - v_1 = (3 + 1) - 2 = 2$. There are three endogenous variables, so $n - 1 = 2$.

Is $(n + x) - v_i \geq n - 1$? Yes, since $2 \geq 2$; therefore Eq. III.a meets this necessary condition. Note that Eq. III.b does not meet the necessary condition, $v_2 = 3$, $n = 3$ and $x = 1$, so $[(n + x) - v_2 = 1] < [n - 1 = 2]$. We know 1 is less than 2, so Eq. III.b cannot be identified; that is, its parameters cannot be estimated from the data.[17]

Let us write the system of equations of a new model (IV), where both of the behavioral equations can be identified:

$$Q_S = a_1 + b_1 P + d_1 R \qquad \text{(IV.a)}$$
$$Q_D = a_2 + b_2 P + c_2 Y \qquad \text{(IV.b)}$$
$$Q_S = Q_D \qquad \text{(IV.c)}$$

Data generated by such a model would appear as in Fig. 7.16 (ignoring the error terms). Note Eq. IV.a and Eq. IV.b would each be sketched as a single function (a plane) in three dimensions. A two-variable equation (in terms of Q and P) fitted directly to the observed data points

---

[17] The following is a convenient rule (involving some knowledge of matrix algebra) for determining whether the equations in the model meet the necessary and sufficient conditions for identification: an equation of an m equation model meets these conditions if we can form at least one nonzero $(m - 1)$ ordered determinant from a matrix of the coefficients of those variables which do not appear in the equation being tested, but which do appear in the other $(m - 1)$ behavioral equations (the coefficients of the equation being tested do not appear in our matrix). The proof is given in T. C. Koopmans and W. C. Hood, "The Estimation of Simultaneous Linear Economic Relationships," in Hood and Koopmans (eds.), *Studies in Econometric Method*. Cowles Commission Monograph No. 10, John Wiley and Sons, New York, 1953, pp. 135–42.

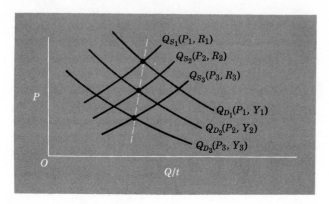

Fig. 7.16

would yield the mongrel function represented by the almost vertical dashed line.

Reduced Form of the Original Structural Equations[18]

The original structural equations usually can be written in reduced form (after a little algebraic manipulation).[19] This means we can express each endogenous variable in the original model as a function of the exogenous variables, whose values are known prior to solving the system of equations. Each reduced-form equation is independent of any other and contains only one endogenous variable.

We can then proceed to estimate (using the least squares technique) the parameters of each reduced-form equation separately, avoiding the bias inherent in applying least squares directly to the original simultaneous system of structural equations.

The original structural equations in model IV may be written in reduced form by substituting Eqs. IV.a and IV.b in IV.c to eliminate Q_D and Q_S; eliminate P using the method of elimination (or direct substitution) to derive the second reduced-form equation. The reduced-form

---

[18] This section describes a convenient solution to the problem of estimating the structural parameters of the original equations suggested by economic theory. It is not essential to the development of the material that follows. It does, however, contain useful information on models.

[19] According to the implicit function theorem, the reduced form of the original structural equations exists if the determinant of the matrix of the parameters of the endogenous variables of the original structural equation is nonzero.

equations are written in IV′ below. [Note that the observed values of Q_S and Q_D are assumed to be the equilibrium values in the reduced-form equation (IV.b′) so $Q_D = Q_S = (Q_{D=S})$.]

$$\text{r-f:} \quad P = \frac{a_1 - a_2}{b_1 - b_2} + \frac{c_2}{b_1 - b_2} Y - \frac{d_1}{b_1 - b_2} R \tag{IV.a′}$$

$$\text{r-f:} \quad Q_{D=S} = \frac{a_1 b_2 - a_2 b_1}{b_1 - b_2} + \frac{b_1 c_2}{b_1 - b_2} Y - \frac{b_2 d_1}{b_1 - b_2} R \tag{IV.b′}$$

When the original model is just identified, we can solve backwards and compute the estimates of the structural parameters in the original behavioral equations from the least squares estimates of the parameters in the reduced-form equations.

If any of the behavioral equations are not identified, the structural parameters cannot be computed from the parameters of the reduced-form equations. A system of equations is said to be overidentified if there are too many relationships or constraints on the variables to identify the structural parameters from the reduced-form parameters (where there are more equations than unknown, there is no unique solution to satisfy all conditions). In an underidentified system, there are too few relationships to identify the structural parameters from the reduced-form parameters (fewer equations than unknowns; thus an infinite number of solutions are possible).

Equations IV.a and IV.b are just identified, and their parameters can be derived from the coefficients of the reduced-form equations IV.a′ and IV.b′.[20]

---

[20] This method in the just identified case leads to unbiased, consistent estimates of the structural parameters, which can be identified from the sample data. The structural parameters of the original model can be derived by substituting the reduced-form equations into the original structural equations, and employing some simple algebra.

8

The Theory of the Firm

The private business firm occupies a central position in a market-oriented economy. Its decisions have important implications for the resource owners, whose incomes depend on the firm's organization of resources, and for consumers, who purchase the firm's output.

The range of problems the business firm must solve covers a broad spectrum. It must make a product selection, arrange to finance the investment necessary to produce and market the product(s); in addition, it must plan, organize, control, and administer on a continuing basis. The theory of the firm considered here serves as a general introduction to the behavior of the firm under various market conditions.

As students of business organization have pointed out, there is in practice no single dimension to the firm's objectives, and no simple criterion for making decisions. Economists have often taken the profit motive to be the primary objective of business firms. The profit-maximizing objective is in fact the backbone of neoclassical economic theory, and the driving force behind a market-oriented economy. Whether a theory based on this single objective is satisfactory for predictive purposes is an empirical question of considerable importance. Independent of the empirical results, the profit motive has a very essential ideological position in neoclassical price theory. Its existence is one of the mainsprings accounting for the efficiency of a market economy.

Once profit is defined and a profit function established, maximizing the profit function yields a solution—what the firm will do (or should do if it wants to maximize profit). The profit-maximizing firm, after its costs and revenue functions are specified, would choose that rate of output that would maximize the difference between total revenue

140

and total cost. The difficulties here lie not in finding the solution once the profit function is known, but in specifying the expected cost and revenue functions. The cost function depends on the method of production, the productivity of the resources, and their cost. The revenue function is based on a prediction of market demand; that is, what the market will absorb at given prices.

If there are several dimensions to the firm's objective function—perhaps including security (minimizing risk), prestige (maximizing power or public image), and domination of market (maximizing sales revenue), as well as profit—there may be no easy solution to the problem of maximizing or even optimizing under certain constraints. The complexity of many corporate enterprises—the separation of management and ownership and the apparent mixture of management objectives—has led to attempts to extend the profit-maximizing theory of the firm in order to improve the predictive power of the theory. A broader utility-maximizing objective, including nonpecuniary variables and discretionary behavior by management, may be particularly appropriate in markets where effective competition is lacking.

Impressed with the multidimensionality of the firm's objectives and unable to prescribe simple optimizing solutions to some of the firm's operating problems, some economists have proposed a theory built on the *satisficing* principle.[1] The criteria for deciding upon a particular action would be that certain minimal requirements are met or exceeded. This does not preclude profit-maximization, but neither does it imply maximization. A satisficing theory is of particular interest from the point of view of administering a particular firm, but it is difficult to use as a basis for generalizing and predicting.

From our viewpoint of trying to understand the role of the firm and the implications for the industry in a market economy, profit-maximizing remains the most important single motivation underlying the firm's behavior. The theory of the firm is most completely developed for the purely or "effectively" competitive market, in which case the firm may have no choice but to try to maximize profit.[2] In other market situations

---

[1] See Herbert A. Simon, "New Developments in the Theory of the Firm," *AER*, May 1962, 1–15. Also see R. M. Cyert and J. G. March, *A Behavioral Theory of the Firm*, Prentice-Hall, Englewood Cliffs, N.J., 1963.

[2] Professor Machlup suggests that competition is effective if its "effect" (whether because of conditions of entry or aggressive attitudes of existing firms) is to continually depress profits toward minimum tolerable levels. See Fritz Machlup, "Theories of the Firm: Marginalist, Behavioral, Managerial," *AER*, March 1967, Vol. LVII, No. 1, p. 18.

there may be obstacles to maximizing short-run profit, and the meaning of long-run profit-maximization may be illusive.[3]

The Meaning of Profit and Profit-Maximization

It is premature to argue about the normative aspect (*should* firms maximize profit) or the positive aspect (*do* firms maximize profit) of profit-maximization without first specifying exactly what is meant by profit or profit-maximization.

Economic profit can be identified as a residual remaining after all costs necessary to insure continuation of an enterprise have been met. These costs include imputed opportunity costs that may not require current outlay, for example, the opportunity cost of maintaining the owner's capital invested in his own enterprise.

The income foregone on any owned asset constitutes an opportunity cost that need not involve a cash outlay. On the other hand, any costs such as gifts or bonuses incurred for noneconomic reasons should be deducted from total cost if economic profit is to be estimated accurately. There may be considerable discrepancy between a profit-and-loss-statement measure of profit based on revenue and costs charged to a particular accounting period, and the concept of economic profit. Economic profit is a reasonable basis for business decisions, although it may be difficult to measure, particularly since it entails an estimate of what would be required for successful continuation of the enterprise. If economic profit is ignored, opportunities for increasing the firm's present or future earnings may be neglected. Negative economic profit is a signal that resources are not optimally allocated, and resources will tend to leave the firm or industry.

[3] R. Dorfman suggests a clarification of the question: Does business maximize profit? A businessman certainly does not try to maximize what he considers as profit: total revenue minus total money outlay currently charged to a given period, say, one year. The economist, on the other hand, may insist that businessmen typically do attempt to maximize profit but he means *economic* profit—a "future oriented" not easily measurable concept that includes more than current inflow and outlay of money. See Robert Dorfman, *The Price System,* Prentice-Hall, Englewood Cliffs. N.J., 1964, pp. 38–42. Prof. Machlup offers the following view of the firm under "effective" competition. "The model of the firm in (traditional price) theory is not . . . designed to serve to explain and predict the behavior of real firms; instead, it is designed to explain and predict changes in observed prices . . . as effects of particular changes in conditions (wage rates, interest rates, import duties, excise taxes, technology, etc.) In this causal connection the firm is only a theoretical link, a mental construct helping to explain how one gets from the cause to the effect." Ibid, p. 9.

The slightly different objectives of "trying to improve profit" or "trying to maximize profit" may not lead to the same position after some indefinite length of time; however, they could lead to equivalent positions if the time horizon chosen for maximizing is long enough.

Even if the firm strives to maximize economic profit, as we have defined it, there could be a conflict between maximizing in the short run (with fixed resources unchanged) and maximizing in the long run over an indefinite time horizon. A variety of current expenses (involving some sacrifice of short-run profit) are incurred to increase the firm's capacity to generate long-run profit; examples include training costs and research and development costs. In addition, there may be a conflict between investments that yield larger, more immediate cash flows and investments that generate smaller cash flows over a much longer period, particularly where the two types of investment are mutually exclusive or where resource limitations force a choice. Although economic profit strictly defined may favor the project with the longer time horizon if it promised a greater discounted earnings flow, there are very real complications such as time preference and the uncertainties associated with the longer investment horizon.[4]

The shorter period investment offers the advantage of re-evaluation with the possibility of renewal. The conflict is usually resolved by the entrepreneur or decision-maker in favor of the project or activity that in his judgment promises to best foster the growth in value of the enterprise (over an unlimited period in the case of a corporation with unlimited longevity).[5]

Maximizing Economic Profit: Short Run

Let us consider what short-run profit-maximizing implies in terms of total revenue and total cost functions.

In Fig. 8.1, total variable cost TVC, total fixed cost TFC, total cost

---

[4] Risk is sometimes distinguished from uncertainty. In the case of risk possible outcomes are known, and to each possible outcome a certain weight or probability can be assigned so that the expected value of the result is predictable; a risk is insurable and can usually be transformed into a known cost (a premium). Uncertainty cannot be treated in such a predictable fashion. The possible outcomes may be unknown and the situation unique. In practice the difference between risk and uncertainty is a question of degree; it may hinge on the distinction between subjective and objective estimates of probabilities.

[5] Finance literature tends to stress maximization of the net market value of stock. See Myron J. Gordon, *The Investment, Financing and Valuation of the Corporation*. Richard D. Irwin, Inc., Homewood, Ill., 1962.

TC, and total revenue TR functions are drawn. The vertical distance between TC and TVC represents total fixed or overhead costs (TFC) that do not vary with output.

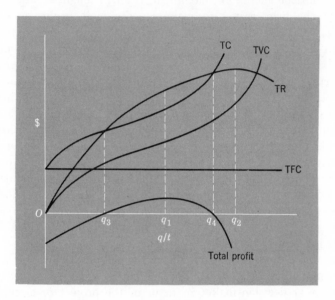

Fig. 8.1

Changes in fixed costs would cause parallel vertical shifts in the TC function but would leave TVC unchanged. The profit-maximizing firm will choose that rate of output that will maximize economic profit: the distance TR-TC. (The total profit function appears in Fig. 8.1.) Under normal conditions, which result in the expected shapes of the total revenue and total cost functions, profit will be greatest when the slopes of the two functions are equal: when marginal revenue equals marginal cost (MR = MC at q_1 in Figs. 8.1 and 8.2).[6]

The relationship between total revenue TR, marginal revenue MR, and the elasticity of demand e was examined in Chapter 2; recall Eq. 2.3, $MR = p(1 + 1/e)$. Beyond q_2 (in Fig. 8.1), where TR begins to

[6] For this to be strictly correct, a second-order condition must also be met. The second derivative of the profit function must be negative since it could be true that MC = MR at a rate of output that results in maximum loss, or at other outputs where profit is positive but not maximum—local maxima positions where the slopes of poorly behaved "bumpy" functions are zero at various points. These second-order conditions are met in Fig. 8.1, where there is a unique point of maximum profit at q_1.

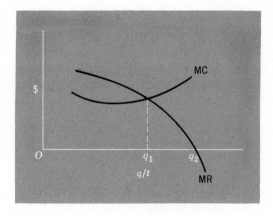

Fig. 8.2

decrease as output increases, the demand curve must be inelastic. If the firm's demand curve were horizontal (infinitely elastic as under perfectly competitive conditions), MR would be constant and equal to the given price. MR in Fig. 8.2 would be a horizontal line. MR is the slope of the TR curve, so where price is constant $(\bar{p}) =$ MR, the TR curve in Fig. 8.1 would be linear: $\bar{p} = $ AR $ = $ TR$/q$.

Figure 8.2 represents a situation with a well behaved MC function eventually increasing with output, due to the force of diminishing returns. MC crosses MR from below at a unique point as rate of output increases.

It should be noted that if a profit-maximizing firm is at its profit-maximizing position, an increase in fixed costs will not cause it to choose a different rate of output. This follows since a change in fixed costs does not affect marginal costs, so marginal cost will continue to equal marginal revenue at q_1. This is not to say that an increase in fixed costs will not be a source of concern to an enterprise. Its short-term rate of profitability will decrease, and unless the increase in fixed costs was incurred intentionally to increase future earnings, the value of the firm will decrease.

Suppose the gap between total cost and total revenue is zero (zero economic profit) and the firm is then confronted by an increase in fixed costs. The firm may consider the increase temporary and continue to operate at negative economic profit, providing total revenue covers total variable costs so that there is some contribution to fixed costs or overhead. The argument is simply that fixed costs are incurred whether or not the operation is temporarily interrupted. However, if negative economic profit is expected to continue as a result of the increase in fixed costs, this will induce some resources to seek a better return elsewhere. The result may be bankruptcy or perhaps the wearing down of capital without replacement.

Other Objectives

If a firm decided to pursue the objective of maximizing total sales revenue (or rate of growth of sales in a dynamic view), this would require operating at q_2 in Figs. 8.1 and 8.2, where total revenue is maximum and marginal revenue is zero. Such an objective, if followed in a very rigid fashion, would ignore cost information and might result in negative economic profit—the case illustrated in Fig. 8.1.

A more interesting suggestion[7] is "sales maximization subject to a profit constraint." Refer again to Fig. 8.1 and suppose the firm faces the profit constraint that economic profit be equal to or greater than zero; this would require operating as near as possible to q_4 but not exceeding it, even though sales revenue would be higher at q_2. This objective need not be inconsistent with maximizing total revenue if TC intersects with TR at or to the right of q_2. This rule appears more reasonable than simple sales maximization; it suggests pursuing activities or increasing operations, if marginal revenue remains positive and providing economic profit is not negative. "Sales-maximizing subject to a profit constraint" can explain what would seem to be, under a profit-maximizing objective, an irrational reaction to an increase in fixed costs; viz., raising price (cost-plus pricing) and cutting back output subject to market limitations described by the demand curve.

For such an objective to be prescribed in a normative sense, and not simply a mistake, it would be necessary to explain why trying to maximize economic profit would not be preferable or feasible, and why would the firm not try to reduce output and raise price prior to the increase in total cost?[8] This question will be considered later in the discussion of imperfect markets.

It has been suggested that the management of large firms is often occupied with the rate of growth of sales revenue. In this view, profit

---

[7] See William J. Baumol, *Economic Theory and Operations Analysis,* Prentice-Hall, Englewood Cliffs, N.J., 1961, pp. 198–199.

[8] An interesting empirical attempt to decide whether some form of profit-maximization theory is positivistically more accurate than a theory which allows for managerial discretion and more general utility maximization was made by O. E. Williamson, "Managerial Discretion and Business Behavior," *AER,* LIII, 5, Dec. 1963, pp. 1032–1057.

is not treated as a constraint but as an endogenous variable. Profit is necessary to obtain capital needed to finance expansion. An optimal profit stream would be one consistent with the largest rate of growth of sales revenue over the firm's lifetime. Profit may compete with sales; for example, low prices and high marketing outlays to promote sales may reduce net earnings.[9]

The Dynamics of a Firm's Profit-Maximizing Objective

We shall, in the discussion that follows, extend the meaning of profit-maximization in the context of the dynamics of a firm over time. Previously, economic profit was defined as a sum of money—the difference between total revenue and total cost (including implicit opportunity costs). This way of looking at profit was sufficient for the short run, since capital costs and overhead are fixed and therefore of little consequence in the short run. In the long run, the dollar amount of economic profit is less meaningful than the rate of profit. It is the attraction of a high rate of profit that lures new capital to an industry. Zero economic profit or a zero rate of profit is just sufficient to maintain resources in an enterprise.

In the short run with plant and equipment fixed, the firm that succeeds in maximizing profit will have equated marginal cost with marginal revenue. Whether or not a firm wants to maximize profit is another question, and whether or not a profit-maximizing firm employs easily identifiable marginal techniques is still another. In the short run, the firm's level of real capital is taken as given with certain costs fixed. It will pay to produce if total revenue exceeds total variable cost (and price is greater than average variable cost), even if total revenue is temporarily below total cost (and price is less than average cost). The firm may choose to operate with negative profit in the short run, providing the situation is considered temporary with improvement in the economic environment expected. If no improvement is in sight, then the firm must turn to a long-run solution involving a change in the level of real capital.

Funds are needed to finance current production; however, in discussion of the firm's short-run operation it is often implicitly assumed that revenue from sales is sufficient to cover operating costs, including working capital needed to finance current operations. We shall assume that the

[9] See W. J. Baumol, "On the Theory of Expansion of the Firm," *AER*, Vol. LII, 5, Dec. 1962, pp. 1079–1087.

cost of capital is not pertinent to the firm's short-run decisions, but is pertinent for long-run decisions.

In the long run the firm deals with decisions involving capital investment where time is an important factor. Investment requires a resource commitment and time lag before the cash inflow is sufficient to sustain current operation. Whether a capital project will be undertaken depends on comparison of the outlays with the stream of earnings generated by the project. Allowance must be made in such a decision for the cost of capital: the cost of "hiring" the funds needed to finance the project. In capital investment decisions, the cost of capital i and the time distribution of expected net cash inflows $\bar{Q}$ can be combined by discounting future incremental cash flows by the cost of capital to obtain the operationally useful concept of net present value PV. The net incremental flow or net quasi-rent is the expected difference between the net cash inflow if the project is undertaken and the net cash inflow if it is not undertaken.

$$\text{Net PV} = -C + \frac{\bar{Q}_1}{1+i} + \frac{\bar{Q}_2}{(1+i)^2} + \cdots + \frac{\bar{Q}_n}{(1+i)^n} + \frac{S_n}{(1+i)^n}$$

$$(8.1)$$

The single outlay C supposes that all investment costs are incurred at the beginning of the project. This is taken as some convenient point in time ($t = 0$) to which all money flows are discounted. (If capital costs are anticipated at other times, these outlays would have to be discounted, as are the net quasi-rents $\bar{Q}$, and the salvage value S, which may be expected at the end of the estimated useful life of the project.)

Net quasi-rent at the end of each period represents the expected after-tax net cash inflow generated by the fixed assets. This is the return or cash inflow above operating expenses and net of taxes. In Eq. 8.1 $\bar{Q}_n/(1+i)^n$ is the discounted value of the $\bar{Q}$ expected at the end of n periods from the initial point ($t = 0$). Depreciation D and interest on borrowed capital I_B enter only to enable us to correct quasi-rent Q by the amount of the tax. The tax is computed by applying the tax rate to Q after deducting depreciation and interest cost. Net quasi-rent $\bar{Q}$ in each period is Q minus the tax:

$$\bar{Q} = Q - \overbrace{\text{tax rate } (Q - D - I_B)}^{\text{tax}}$$

$$(8.2)$$

Let us look at the following example. Suppose a firm is considering a plant expansion involving a capital outlay of \$100,000. There is a tax rate of 50% and a depreciation charge of \$10,000 per year on a \$100,000 investment in fixed capital (using straight line depreciation over 10 years). The investment is expected to generate $20,000 per year Q over a 10-year period. Of the $100,000, $80,000 is borrowed at 5%, so yearly interest cost I_B is $4000.

From Eq. 8.2:

$$\bar{Q} = \$20,000 - 0.5(20,000 - 10,000 - 4000)$$
$$Q = \$20,000 - 0.5(6000)$$
$$\bar{Q} = \$20,000 - 3000$$
$$\bar{Q} = \$17,000$$

The net quasi-rent $\bar{Q} = \$17,000$ is expected to be earned every year for 10 years; the cost of capital i is given and equal to the borrowing rate of 5% (as it would be in a perfect market with no risk and no taxes), and there is no salvage value at the end of 10 years. Using Eq. 8.1, present value can be found to equal $131,410.[10]

If the net present value—the sum of the discounted net cash inflows and outlays—is positive, then the investment is worth undertaking. This statement of the investment criterion is a simplified and quite general statement. For such a general criterion to be of operational use to a firm, we must consider the appropriate cost of capital—the rate chosen to discount future money flows.

Whereas the cost of capital is only one of the variables involved in evaluating capital investment decisions, the choice of the proper discount rate to reflect the time value of future money flows may be crucial in the ranking of several alternative projects or in deciding whether or not to undertake an individual project. An examination of the elements of the net present value equation (8.1) reveals other variables involved in the firm's investment decision: investment costs (C), net quasi-rents (influenced by tax rates, expenses, sales volume and prices), length of useful life, and salvage value at the end of the expected useful life. All of these are estimates or expected values to which varying degrees of risk or uncertainty apply.

The present value concept is inextricably connected to opportunity cost. To take a very simple example: suppose a barrel of wine will net $105.00 one year from today. Its present value is the amount which, if invested at some rate of interest and compounded over the one year would be worth $105 at the end of the first year. The discount rate

---

[10] With a constant stream over a finite period, instead of discounting each period's $\bar{Q}_t$ separately (as in Eq. 8.1), we may use Eq. 8.4 to find the present value (in $1000's) of this constant stream of net quasi-rents:

$$PV = 17\left[\frac{(1 + 0.05)^{10} - 1}{0.05(1 + 0.05)^{10}}\right] = 17\left[\frac{1.63 - 1}{0.05(1.63)}\right] = 07\left[\frac{0.63}{0.0815}\right] = 17[7.73]$$

$$PV = 131.41$$

used in finding the present value depends on available investment opportunities. As originally defined, the present value of money was intended to reflect the time value of money, not the uncertainty value. It is desirable, when net present value is used as a criterion for evaluating investment, to add a "risk premium" to the riskless rate to reflect the extra risk or uncertainty of the project under consideration. The appropriate rate would then depend on opportunities available for investing in projects of equivalent risk. If the $105 to be received a year from now were a low-risk project, the best alternative rate of return on such a low-risk investment might be to invest in government bills offering 5% per annum. The present value of $105 would then be $100, since the $100 if invested at 5% would be worth 100 $(1.05)^1 = \$105$ at the end of the one year.

This result is easily generalized. If a certain amount P_o is invested at a certain rate of interest i per period compounded over n periods, the value of the investment at the end of n periods (P_n) is $P_n = P_o (1 + i)^n$. (This is the compound interest formula, an exponential function of a geometric progression.) The present value of P_n is $P_o = [P_n/(1 + i)^n]$; these are the terms in a general equation for present value PV,

$$\sum_{t=0}^{n} \left[\frac{P_t}{(1 + i)^t} \right] \tag{8.3}$$

where t is the number of periods that will have elapsed since the common point in time, 0. In Eq. 8.1 we subtracted the capital outlay from the present value of the expected stream of earnings to get net present value.

Where P_t is a constant $(\bar{P})$, where $t \rightarrow \infty$, and $1/(1 + i)$ is a constant ratio (< 1), the expression for present value reduces quite simply to $\bar{P}/i$ or $\bar{P}(1/i)$, where $1/i$ represents the sum of the diminishing geometric series:

$$\sum_{t=1}^{\infty} \left[\frac{1}{(1 + i)^t} \right] \text{ as } t \rightarrow \infty$$

This result can be used to quickly calculate the present value of a constant cash flow of infinite duration. The interest rate i relates the income flow to the value of the stock of capital. Equation 8.4 is useful where P_t is a constant $(\bar{P})$ and we want to compute the present value of a constant stream over some finite number of periods n.

$$\text{PV} = \bar{P} \left[\frac{(1 + i)^n - 1}{i(1 + i)^n} \right] \tag{8.4}$$

Cost of Capital

We do not discuss how interest rates are determined in financial markets; we are concerned here with the interest rate that is the appropriate cost of capital to the firm making a long-term capital investment decision. Choosing the appropriate discount rate would require consideration of the firm's objectives, and the special areas of finance that have to do with the firm's capital structure, sources of investment funds, and other factors that influence the firm's cost of capital.[11]

Whether the funds for financing capital projects are acquired from external sources (stocks and bonds) or internal sources (retained earnings or depreciation reserve), it is reasonable to suppose that some opportunity cost applies to committing the funds to a particular project. There exists the alternative of lending internally generated funds, or even lending borrowed funds, if the rate at which the firm can borrow is less than the lending rate (which would be the opportunity cost of capital). We shall assume that the lending and borrowing rates are the same as they tend to be in a perfect capital market.

There are circumstances where the firm is not necessarily willing to invest at the lending rate but may insist on some minimum acceptable rate of return above the lending rate. Management may have a. preference for additional leisure, or judge that there are diseconomies in further expansion due to stress on managerial capacity, or it may feel that there is a limited amount of capital to be rationed. There always exists the alternative of paying out internal cash reserves or unallocated earnings as dividends, whether or not the expected return on a project is above the lending rate. Used as a criterion for investment, a net present value greater than zero on a particular project implies that the ratio of estimated earnings per share (without the investment) to price per share will not be reduced as a result of the investment. This ratio is a reasonable estimate of the cost of capital to be used for discounting purposes if investment is undertaken to increase the value of existing owners' equity. The implication of this criterion—net present value greater than zero—is interpreted by Modigliani and Miller: "Will the

---

[11] See F. Modigliani and M. H. Miller, "The Cost of Capital, Corporation Finance and the Theory of Investment," *AER*, June, 1958. It also appears in an excellent collection of articles on capital theory: *The Management of Corporate Capital*, ed. by Ezra Solomon, Free Press, Glencoe, Ill. The authors argue that capital structure has no effect on cost of capital. The more traditional view is represented in J. Fred Weston and Eugene Brigham, *Managerial Finance*, rev. ed., Holt, Rinehart, and Winston, New York, 1966, Chap. 12.

project, as financed, raise the market value of the firm's shares? If so, it is worth undertaking; if not, its return is less than the marginal cost of capital to the firm."[12]

This formulation of the net present value criterion for undertaking an investment presumes that the goal of the decision-maker or decision-making group is to maximize earnings over time for the benefit of existing stockholders; the improved earnings per share of stock is likely to be reflected in the appreciation of the market price per share.

Where borrowed capital can be secured at rates below the cost of "equity" capital, there exists the possibility that a somewhat lower cost of capital may be used for discounting purposes. However, risk tends to increase with increases in the debt/equity ratio and this *may* be reflected in the market valuation of the per share price. There *may* be some optimal debt/equity ratio. Cost of capital *may* be taken as a weighted average of the cost of debt and equity capital as used in optimal proportion.[13]

Yield or Rate of Return on Investment

An alternative method of evaluating capital projects is to estimate the project's yield or internal rate of return or marginal efficiency of capital. The three concepts are synonymous; they describe the rate which, if used to discount the future flows, would make the net present value zero. We shall refer to this rate as the *yield*. It is the discount rate which equates discounted values of capital outlays and net cash inflows.

The criterion in terms of yield would be to accept the project if the yield is greater than the cost of capital. The yield minus the cost of capital gives us a workable definition for the *rate of profit* of a project. Where C is capital cost and the expected net quasi-rents $\bar{Q}$ are constant and expected over an infinite time horizon, the sum of an infinite geometric series applies. The yield r on such an investment is then simply $C = \bar{Q}/r$ or $r = \bar{Q}/C$.[14] The two criteria proposed for deciding whether to invest in a project may not always lead to the same decision, particularly with respect to the ranking of mutually exclusive projects with varying lengths

[12] Modigliani and Miller, *op. cit.*, p. 152.

[13] The several qualifying *mays* in this paragraph suggest the existing controversy over these issues. For a good introduction to the literature on this subject see, Ezra Soloman, "Measuring a Company's Cost of Capital," *Journal of Business*, Oct. 1955. (Also in "The Management of Corporate Capital," *op. cit.*)

[14] These conditions were assumed to apply in our discussion of the long-run average cost curve in Chapter 7.

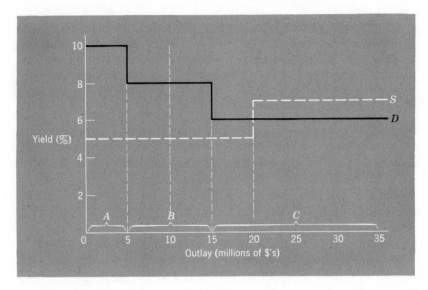

Fig. 8.3

of life and unequal time distribution of earnings. In fact, there may even be multiple yields on a project where inflows and outlays are intermixed over time. Although techniques exist for making the yield criterion consistent with net present value criterion, the net present value criterion is often simpler to apply. Using either criterion, the relevant cost of capital must be chosen prior to a rational decision to accept or reject a project requiring a capital outlay.[15]

The yield method, while the more likely to lead to ambiguous results in special cases, does provide a convenient basis for ranking several possible projects. It provides a neat schematic framework to conceptualize the firm's capital decisions in terms of profitability (see Fig. 8.3).

Suppose the firm is considering three nonmutually exclusive capital projects. Project *A* requires a $5 million outlay and yields 10%, project *B* requires a $10 million outlay and yields 8%, project *C* requires a $20 million outlay and yields 6%. All told, $35 million would be required to finance all three projects. If the appropriate cost of capital to the

---

[15] If mutually exclusive projects under consideration are of unequal lives, decisions based on the yield method implicitly assume that the cash inflows generated by the shorter-lived projects can be reinvested at the yield rate or internal rate of the project. The presumption using the net present value criterion, in evaluating projects of unequal life, is that the cash inflows can be reinvested at the firm's cost of capital.

firm were constant at 5%, all three projects would provide a positive rate of profit (yield minus cost of capital).

If we assume the cost of capital is independent of the particular project and its yield but (perhaps due to institutional restraints) not independent of the volume of investment funds required, the supply curve of money capital may be upward sloping beyond some point. (Or the supply of money might be a step function, proceeding by steps, as was the case with the demand for investment funds in our example.) If the supply of investment funds to the firm indicates that $20 million is attainable at a cost of capital of 5%, but additional funds would cost 7%, only *A* and *B* could be undertaken (assuming that project *C* is not divisible and its yield on a $20 million outlay would be less than the average cost of capital).[16]

Our discussion presumes a profit-maximizing objective stated in the language of dynamics; a burden is imposed on the choice of the appropriate "cost of capital" necessary for either method of evaluating capital projects. It should be apparent now that maximizing profit in dynamic terms involves considerably more than choosing the optimal rate of output or the optimal resource combination within a short-run period, taking certain resources as fixed. Long-run decisions are investment decisions that must contend with changes in technology and with the growth in and modification of the firm's real capital structure. Whether or not a capital project is undertaken depends on the firm's objectives and decision-making processes. We have outlined criteria for undertaking investment in terms of a profit-maximizing objective presented in dynamic terms. A project that promised a positive rate of economic profit would increase the earnings per share of common stock and add to the value of owners' equity.

---

[16] Sometimes a minimum acceptable cut-off rate of return is established by a firm above the "appropriate" cost of capital; such a criterion (as well as other "rules-of-thumb" methods of evaluating investments) is used to contend with imperfect data and uncertainty.

9

Monopoly

Monopoly refers to a market with a single (mono-) seller. Identification of a seller as a monopolist rests in part on the setting of relevant market boundaries—identifying gaps in the chain of substitute products. As a practical matter, the determination of whether a product is unique enough for its producer to be identified as a monopolist requires certain arbitrary judgments. Suppose the "overall" cross-elasticity between products is high, but the cross-elasticities in the various "end-use" markets are low. The cross-elasticity between cellophane and some other film, such as Saran Wrap, may be high, but for the specific purpose of packaging cigarettes it may be quite low. And what are the critical values of cross-elasticity for deciding whether a monopoly exists, even after the relevant market is identified? In 1956 after much litigation the U.S. Supreme Court decided that DuPont was not a monopolist in the cellophane market because the relevant market was the broader market for flexible packaging materials, where the "overall" cross-elasticity between cellophane and other flexible packaging materials was not low enough to constitute a monopoly.[1] Monopoly in a dynamic perspective takes on new characteristics, and the identification of the producer as a monopolist requires rather arbitrary judgments and qualifications.

A monopolist's position is based on some means of limiting and controlling the supply of the unique or "highly differentiated" product. As a practical matter, the means by which supply is controlled or entry barriers are erected may be crucial in determining whether the monopoly is given legal and social approval. If the monopoly position is temporary and based on a successful innovation, it may be, as under existing patent laws, condoned and encouraged as a necessary incentive for further technological progress.

[1] A review by economists Stocking and Mueller of "The Cellophane Case" can be found in the *A.E.R.*, XLV, 29, 48–49.

An important invention and its successful application—an innovation—are often given social approval. The government, in granting patent protection (17 years under present law) to a new product or process, gives legal sanction to an initial monopoly position resulting from the innovation. The inventor or the innovator receives an incentive equal to the present value of the temporary monopoly. The temporary monoplist's position can be undermined by new sellers entering the market with close substitutes.

Over the years the monopoly problem has been attacked by the U.S. Congress and reviewed by the courts many times. Under the Sherman Antitrust Act, passed in 1890, every contract, combination, or conspiracy in restraint of trade is illegal. Persons engaged in interstate commerce who "monopolize or attempt to monopolize . . . any part of trade" are guilty of a misdemeanor. The Sherman Act provides the original legal base for the enforcement of competition in the United States. The law emphasized behavior (monopolizing) rather than market structure (monopoly). It remained for the courts to interpret the law. In the years that followed, the courts found such acts as price fixing and market sharing illegal; and in 1911 in the Standard Oil Case, the Supreme Court restricted the Sherman Act to unreasonable behavior in "restraint of trade"; this decision has been called the "rule of reason."

In 1914 Congress passed the Clayton Antitrust Act, which prohibited specific kinds of behavior (e.g., price discrimination, tied sales, and interlocking directorates); the act also excluded labor unions from the antitrust laws. In the same year the Federal Trade Commission Act brought into being the Federal Trade Commission to investigate "unfair methods of competition" and to issue "cease and desist orders" against illegal practice, "where the effect may be substantially to lessen competition or tend to create monopoly." Again, the courts were to decide what was "unfair" and whether the effect of particular practices would be to substantially lessen competition or tend to create monopoly.

In 1936 the Robinson-Patman Act strengthened the Clayton Act's provisions against price discrimination; price differences had to be supported by cost differences, except where prices were lowered in good faith to meet competition in certain markets. In 1950 the Celler-Kefauver Act placed limitations on mergers, plugging another of the Clayton Act's loopholes.

The courts in the Alcoa Case (1945) at least temporarily abandoned the rule of reason and decided on the basis of size and market structure that Alcoa's monopoly position was illegal. The court recognized that Alcoa's control of 90% of the virgin aluminum market was based on normal, prudent, and not predatory business practices. The court nevertheless declared against Alcoa, even though it found no behavioral evidence of misuse of power. No longer was the "good" monopolist, whose position was legally acquired and in practice not abused, exonerated by the courts under the rule of reason. The court was becoming more concerned with potential power rather than with the use or abuse of past power. In this new interpretation of the Sherman Act, the court replaced a standard based on market behavior with one based on market structure.[2]

Pure Monopoly Contrasted with Pure Competition

In a purely competitive market there are many sellers, each one a price-taker. Under pure monopoly, there is a single seller in the market. The monopolist's demand is the market's demand. The monopolist is a price-maker. Pure monopoly suggests a no-substitute situation where the consumer has no options with respect to other products or with respect to other suppliers. In the limiting case there are no substitutes, and demand for, say, a certain drug may be so urgent that the seller can preempt the consumers' entire income at any price. The demand curve would then be a rectangular hyperbole ($e = -1$), and the seller could choose that output which minimized his costs. He could produce one unit and set the price high enough to absorb the consumers' entire income.

The pure monopoly model, while useful for analysis, is a fiction. In its pure form, it resembles nothing in the real world. The monopolist is never completely insulated from competition. He must compete with all other sellers for consumers' limited budget. Even poor substitutes threaten the monopolist's market if the price differential is large enough. Potential competition is also a threat to the monopolist's pricing policies. The market mechanism is often ingenious in finding ways to erode the monopolist's position.

A distinguishing characteristic of monopoly and of all other forms of imperfect competition is that price elasticity of demand is not infinitely elastic (as in the case of the purely competitive firm). The demand curve facing the monopolist (single seller) is the negatively sloping market demand. However, the fact that the monopolist is the sole seller gives him the power to determine the market price by regulating the quantity he decides to sell. The expected upper limit of the

[2] Concurrently with its vigil against monopoly, the government helped to establish "regulated" monopolies in public utilities, transportation, and communication. For an interesting discussion of the legal history of regulation, see Leonard W. Weiss, *Case Studies in American Industry,* John Wiley and Sons, New York, 1967.

rate of sales at given prices is described by the market demand curve. To sell an additional unit and move downward to the right along the negatively sloping demand curve requires decreasing the price of *all* units. This means that the marginal revenue from selling an *additional* unit must be less than the unit price of all units. All units including the additional unit are assumed homogeneous and a single market price is assumed to prevail at any time for all units. Facing a negatively sloping demand curve, the monopolist will find that marginal revenue will be less than price as long as the slope of the demand curve is less than zero.[3]

Where the demand is negatively sloping, $p > $ MR. As we have seen, the MR from a (negative) Δp and a (positive) Δq may be either positive or negative, depending on the price elasticity of demand. The change in total revenue (ΔTR) from a $(-\Delta p)$ and (Δq) may be viewed as a resultant of two components (see Fig. 9.1):

$$\text{TR} = pq$$
$$\Delta\text{TR} = (p + \Delta p)(q + \Delta q) - pq$$
$$= \underbrace{p\Delta q}_{\substack{\text{sales} \\ \text{gain}}} + \underbrace{q\Delta p}_{\substack{\text{price} \\ \text{loss}}} + \underbrace{\Delta p\Delta q}_{\substack{\text{interaction} \\ \text{of sales gain} \\ \text{and price loss}}}$$

(Under pure competition $\Delta p = 0$, so ΔTR $= p(\Delta q)$, or MR $= \Delta$TR$/\Delta q =$ p.)

Under the general profit-maximizing model for a purely competitive firm, facing a horizontal (infinitely elastic) demand curve with a constant unit price $P_c (= \text{MR})$, the firm produces to the point where the firm's MC equals $P_c (= \text{MR})$. The general profit-maximizing model for the monopolist, whose demand curve is negatively sloping, requires producing up to the rate of output Q where MC equals MR and substituting this rate of output into the demand function—$P_M = f(Q)$—to solve for the monopolist's profit-maximizing price $P_M (> \text{MR})$.

The quantity supplied under monopoly depends not only on MC, as under pure competition, but also on demand and price elasticity e. At the profit-maximizing output, MR = MC; at any output, MR = $P(1 +$

---

[3] Stated algebraically: since marginal revenue MR is the derivative of total revenue TR with respect to quantity,

$$\text{MR} = \frac{d(\text{TR})}{dq} = \frac{d(pq)}{dq} = p + q\frac{dp}{dq}$$

and since $dp/dq < 0$, price p must be greater than marginal revenue for the equality to hold.

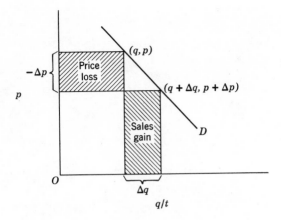

Fig. 9.1

$1/e)$. We cannot predict what the monopolist's quantity supplied will be, as a function of price, unless we know the price elasticity of demand e at various prices.[4]

[4] Let π be economic profit; total cost TC can be expressed as a function of output q, and the monopolist's demand price p can be expressed as a function of output q. Profit π can then be expressed as a function of total revenue TR and total cost TC, each of which can be written as a function of output q:

$$p = f(q), \quad TR = p \cdot q, \quad TR = f(q) \cdot q, \quad \text{and TC} = TC(q)$$

Thus

$$\pi = TR - TC$$
$$\pi(q) = p \cdot q - TC(q)$$
$$\pi(q) = f(q) \cdot q - TC(q)$$

To find the necessary condition for profit-maximization, we take the derivative of the profit function with respect to output, and set the derivative equal to zero:

$$\frac{d\pi}{dq} = f(q) + q\frac{d[f(q)]}{dq} - \frac{d[TC(q)]}{dq} = 0$$

$$\underbrace{p + q\frac{dp}{dq}} - \underbrace{\frac{d(TC)}{dq}} = 0$$

$$\left[MR \equiv \frac{d(TR)}{dq} \right] \left[MC \equiv \frac{d(TC)}{dq} \right]$$

or profit is maximized at an output where MC = MR, providing this criterion meets the sufficient condition for profit maximization. The second derivative of $\pi(q)$ must be negative: $d^2\pi/dq^2 < 0$ or $d(MR)/dq < d(MC)/dq$. This means that for profit to be maximum, output must be carried to that point where MC = MR, and that MC must cross MR from below as this output is approached.

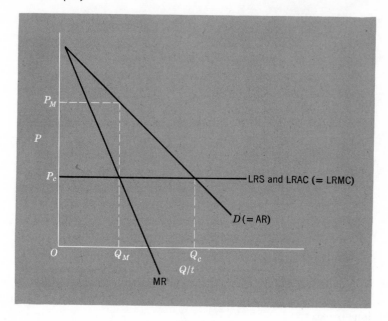

Fig. 9.2

To compare pure monopoly with pure competition, let us take the simplest case of a constant-cost industry. In such an industry, output can expand without affecting the long-run average costs of firms in the industry; this implies no external economies or diseconomies as the industry increases in size. Under the conditions specified, the long-run supply curve (LRS) in a constant-cost, purely competitive industry is horizontal (see Fig. 9.2). This horizontal LRS corresponds to the monopolist's long-run average cost curve (LRAC), still including rents that are presumed unaffected. If a purely competitive industry were reorganized under a unified management so that decision making in the industry were centralized without affecting the average cost of industry supply and without influencing industry demand, the LRS of the purely competitive industry would then, under a central management, be the LRAC of a monopoly. The monopoly's constant LRAC equals its LRMC in this simple constant-cost industry case. The market demand under pure competition is the monopolist's average revenue (AR) curve. Under pure competition the equilibrium price P_c tends to equal the minimum average cost (including rent) of firms in the industry (we have specified that minimum average cost is independent of industry size). Where the long-run supply curve (LRS) intersects market demand, we have the long-run equilibrium rate of output Q_c in the purely competitive industry. At this output, all firms in equilibrium have produced to that rate of output where MC $= P_c$.

The monopolist, since he has some control over price and output, considers that it is not in his interest to produce out to the point where marginal cost equals price—the purely competitive equilibrium position where the value of a unit of output is equal to the marginal cost of providing it. The monopolist realizes that the value of the extra output to him is the marginal revenue, which is less than the price or value on the market. The monopolist in pursuit of maximum profit will produce to the point where MC $=$ MR (as did the pure competitor who had no control over price, but whose unit price and marginal revenue were identical). This determines his profit-maximizing output Q_M, which he can sell at a price P_M.

For a variety of reasons the monopolist may choose a lower price and forego maximum profit in the period; perhaps he treats the lower price as an investment in good will or as a means of discouraging other firms from entering and undermining his position. Even at some lower than profit-maximizing price he would still tend to produce to the limit set by the demand curve, providing the price he chose was greater than his marginal costs. (If the monopolist chose to set the price equal to the purely competitive equilibrium price P_C and if he chose to produce Q_C, where $P =$ LRMC, he would be making zero economic profit.) The monopolist has a profit incentive and an opportunity to set the price P_M above P_C by restricting output below what it would have been in purely competitive equilibrium. Under monopoly, $MC[= f(Q)]$ is less than price. It is for this reason that resources are said to be underutilized under monopoly; at the margin of production the value of the product (price) is greater than the value of the resources employed (MC). Compared to the purely competitive output, the restrictive implications of monopoly are more pronounced the more inelastic the monopolist's demand function.

Under pure competition, the firm was in equilibrium only when its marginal cost curve was rising and intersected its horizontal demand curve from below. Equilibrium is possible under monopoly when MC is rising, constant, or even falling (as long as MR is falling more rapidly, so that it intersects the falling MC curve from above) as in Fig. 9.4. Where there are strong external economies of scale in a purely competitive industry, these economies may become internalized upon reorganization of the competitive industry into a monopoly. If the reorganization permits substantial technological or pecuniary savings, not available when the industry was structured competitively, the firm's costs would shift downward, and some qualification would have to be made regarding the comparison of industry output under conditions of pure competition with output under monopoly.

Resources are optimally allocated among markets if the ratios (P/MC) are equal in each market. If pure competition and monopoly exist side-by-side with $P = MC$ in the purely competitive markets but $P > MC$ in the monopoly market, resources are said to be misallocated (since $P_c/MC \neq P_M/MC$). A transfer of resources from the purely competitive market (where $P = MC$) to the monopoly market (where $P > MC$) will increase net output, since some resources are able to make a greater contribution in the monopoly market, where output is restricted below the point where $MC = P$.

Monopoly Output and Optimum Size

It is only in the very special case where the monopolist's MR function just happens to equal long-run marginal costs at a rate of output that coincides exactly with the minimum point on the monopolist's long-run average cost function that the monopolist would choose to use the most efficient-sized plant at its lowest cost of operation. This fortuitous set of circumstances ($MR = LRMC = SRMC = LRAC$) is illustrated in Fig. 9.3. Rarely would the monopolist's profit-maximizing size lie precisely at the minimum point of the LRAC curve. In general, there is no necessary relation between monopoly and efficiency of operation. Depending

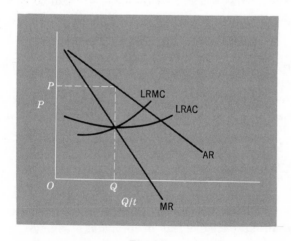

Fig. 9.3

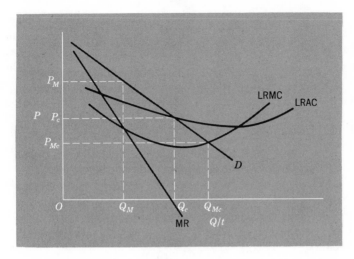

Fig. 9.4

on the size of market demand, the monopolist may be smaller or larger than the most efficient size.

Where on the LRAC curve the monopolist will choose to produce will depend largely on the size of the market. In Fig. 9.4, the market is so limited that MR intersects the monopolist's declining LRMC curve at an output smaller than the minimum point on the LRAC curve. A profit-maximizing monopolist in this case would choose to produce with a plant smaller than the most efficient-sized plant. Whenever the MR cuts MC in a region where AC is declining (internal economies of scale), producing at the lowest point on the LRAC curve would result in negative economic profit to the monopolist. In fact, where AC is declining (so that MC < AC), if output were carried to the point where MC intersects the demand curve (as under pure competition), AC > P(= MC) and the monopolist's economic profit would be negative.

Natural Monopoly and Regulation

Where economies of scale indicate that a given market could be served considerably more efficiently by a single producer than by many smaller firms, the situation is often identified as a natural monopoly. This situation occurs often in the public utility industry, where public regulating commissions may impose price ceilings as a substitute for the automatic control of the competitive market mechanism.

Usually a state regulating commission is appointed to decide what price would provide a "fair" return on some reasonable assessment of the value of the capital investment. Where there are internal economies of large-scale operation over the range of output permitted by the market, the rate regulating commission is unable to set a price equal to marginal cost (as in a purely competitive market) and still permit a "fair" return on capital. The reason can be seen by inspection of Fig. 9.4; as the average cost curve declines, marginal cost must lie below average cost. The size of the market demand is such that a price set equal to marginal cost (P_{MC}) must lie below the average cost of operation; the result is negative economic profit. Given the size of the market, the lowest price the commission can set and still permit a "fair" return (without a subsidy) would be P_C, where price equals average cost. In this case the regulated monopolist would earn zero economic profit (as would a purely competitive firm in long-run equilibrium) providing demand were stable and correctly estimated.

In the more common case where marginal costs are rising and at least equal to average costs, the regulating commission may set prices so that the monopolist will have an incentive to produce to the point where MC equals the regulated price (the regulated price ceiling would be the regulated monopolist's horizontal marginal revenue and demand curve up to the point where it is bounded by the monopolist's average

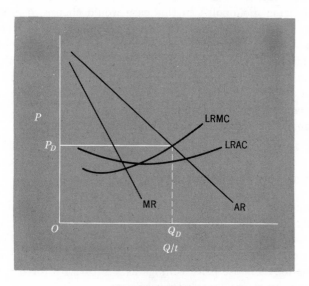

Fig. 9.5

revenue curve—AR in Fig. 9.5) and still earn a "fair" return on investment.

If the regulating commission set the price ceiling at P_D, where LRMC intersects AR at point D, the price P_D would in effect be the regulated monopolist's marginal revenue curve and he would be inclined to produce to Q_D—the maximum rate of output the market will buy at this price. The price P_D will equal the firm's LRMC, which is consistent with optimal resource utilization.[5]

Discriminating Monopoly

So far, we have assumed that a "simple" monopolist—whether temporary or permanent, regulated or unregulated—has offered its product at a uniform price. Suppose it were possible for a "discriminating" monopolist to segment his market, spatially or temporally, and charge different prices to different buyers of the uniform product (third-degree price discrimination) or, in the extreme (sometimes referred to as first-degree price discrimination), charge a given buyer a different price for each of the various units purchased.

To segment a larger market and to maintain different prices in each segment requires not only that the market segments be identifiable and separable, but also that there be no possibility of resale. If this were not the case there would be a strong tendency for prices to converge, since buyers in the low priced market would be able to undersell the monopolist in the high priced market. The monopolist would in effect lose his monopoly in the high priced market, since he would not be able to restrict supply into the high priced market. There are markets where resale would be extremely difficult, if not impossible; for example, the services of a physician or the sale of electric energy. Sometimes segmentation and price discrimination are made possible by physical separation coupled with high transport costs or import tariffs (in the case of foreign markets).

Let us suppose the monopolist is able to segment his market into submarkets. To maximize profit, he would try to produce to the point

---

[5] Where average costs were falling and MC < AC, setting price so that the rate of output would be carried to the point where price equals marginal cost yields negative economic profits. The difficulty (in this case) with marginal cost pricing is that a subsidy is then required to permit a "fair" return on investment. The welfare problems raised by this situation, including the problem of financing the subsidy, are summarized in Nancy Ruggles, "The Welfare Basis of Marginal Cost Pricing," *Review of Economic Studies,* Vol. 17, 1949–50, pp. 29–46.

where the marginal revenues in each market were equal to the marginal cost of producing the total product. The distribution of the total product among the markets should meet the condition that marginal revenue from the last items sold in each market be equal. If this condition were not met, a reapportionment of total output could increase total revenue. If a unit of output is taken from a market where the last item yields a marginal revenue of say $2 and added to a market where the last item yields a higher marginal revenue of say $3, total revenue would increase by $1.

If x_1 is output sold in market 1 and x_2 is output sold in market 2, and if $MC_{x_1+x_2}$ is the marginal cost of the total output (assuming no difference in the MC of supplying either market), then the profit-maximizing rule can be written

$$MC_{x_1+x_2} = MR_1 = MR_2{}^6$$

Diagrammatically we can represent the two separate markets in Figs. 9.6a and 9.6b; in Fig. 9.6c we represent the common marginal cost function of producing the total output and the horizontal addition of the two separate marginal revenue functions (indicating the total output

---

[6] The discriminating monopolist's profit function $(\pi = TR_1 + TR_2 - TC)$ may be written as a function of output in each market: $\pi = x_1D_1(x_1) + x_2D_2(x_2) - TC(x_1 + x_2)$, where $D_1(x_1)$ and $D_2(x_2)$ are the inverse forms of the demand curve in each market, and TC is a function of total output, whether sold in market 1 or market 2. To find the profit-maximizing output in each market, we may take the partial derivatives of the profit function with respect to x_1 and x_2, and set them equal to 0:

$$\frac{\partial \pi}{\partial x_1} = D_1(x_1) + x_1 \frac{d[D_1(x_1)]}{dx_1} - \frac{\partial (TC)}{\partial x_1} = 0$$

$$\frac{\partial \pi}{\partial x_2} = D_2(x_2) + x_2 \frac{d[D_2(x_2)]}{dx_2} - \frac{\partial (TC)}{\partial x_2} = 0$$

Assuming the marginal costs of supplying either market are identical, $\partial(TC)/\partial x_1 = \partial(TC)/\partial x_2$. Therefore

$$D_1(x_1) + x_1 \frac{d[D_1(x_1)]}{d(x_1)} = D_2(x_2) + x_2 \frac{d[D_2(x_2)]}{d(x_2)}$$

or

$$P_1 + x_1 \frac{dP_1}{d(x_1)} = P_2 + x_2 \frac{dP_2}{d(x_2)}$$

or

$$P_1\left(1 + \frac{1}{e_1}\right) = P_2\left(1 + \frac{1}{e_2}\right)$$

or

$$MR_1 = MR_2$$

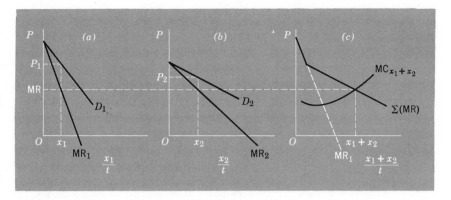

Fig. 9.6

that can be sold in the two separate markets under the condition that the marginal revenues of the last unit sold in each market are equated).

Equating the marginal revenue in the separate markets to the common MC of total output determines the quantity to be sold in each of the markets. In Fig. 9.6c the total output for the profit-maximizing "discriminating" monopolist is determined by the intersection of MC and Σ(MR). The horizontal summation here refers to the sum of the outputs at which the MRs are equal in both markets. The profit-maximizing values of x_1 and x_2 in the separate markets can then be determined by extending a horizontal line from this intersection and noting where it crosses MR_1 and MR_2. At these intersections of the horizontal line with MR_1 and MR_2, the MRs in each market are, of course, equal.[7]

The equality of marginal revenue in the two markets does not imply equality of price in the two markets. Having determined x_1 and x_2, we now substitute these values into the separate submarket demand functions to find the prices in the two markets at which these quantities may be sold. The discriminating monopolist's prices are indicated by P_1 and P_2 in Figs. 9.6a and 9.6b, respectively.

Referring back to the general algebraic relationship between marginal revenue MR, price P, and price elasticity of demand e—MR = $P(1 + 1/e)$— and relying on the discriminating monopolist's ability to equate the marginal revenues in the separate markets, it follows that

$$\left[\mathrm{MR}_1 = P_1 \left(1 + \frac{1}{e_1} \right) \right] = \left[P_2 \left(1 + \frac{1}{e_2} \right) = \mathrm{MR}_2 \right]$$

[7] If this were a multiplant operation, the producer would attempt to equate marginal costs in each plant, and derive an estimate of total output that could be produced at various common levels of marginal costs.

If the elasticities differ in the two markets, so must the prices differ in order to equate the marginal revenues—MR_1 and MR_2—in each market. Market elasticities numerically greater than one are required if the MRs are to be positive.

For a given level of marginal revenue ($= MC$), the more inelastic the demand, the higher the price that the discriminating monopolist will set. It will pay the simple monopolist to discriminate in price if the elasticities in the submarkets differ, and if the markets are separable.

Several extensions of this discussion should be noted. There are situations where it may not be profitable for a simple monopolist to produce at all, but a discriminating monopolist, by separating the market into submarkets, may be able to produce profitably. In certain cases involving declining marginal costs, the price under third-degree price discrimination may be below the simple monopolist's price, even in the less elastic market. Further, a discriminating monopolist may find it profitable to extend the total market into areas that would have been excluded under simple monopoly. An example of this might be a university which raises its tuition to nonscholarship students in order to offer more scholarships to poorer students, who could not otherwise have afforded a university education.

Examples of third-degree price discrimination are found in sales of electricity to domestic and business customers, pricing practices by doctors and other professional people (charging their affluent patients a higher fee than their impoverished patients), export and domestic price differences where demand abroad is relatively more elastic than demand at home.[8] (The price charged abroad by the profit-maximizing discriminating monopolist may be below the average cost of the total output, thus inviting cries of "dumping" by competitors in the foreign market).

In presenting the bare outline of the price discrimination model, we have taken the simple case where we assumed that the costs of producing and supplying the product in the separate markets were identical ($MC_{x_1} = MC_{x_2}$) and where price differences could persist in the separate markets. No ethical connotation was attributed to the practice of charging different prices for the same product where costs were assumed identical. The costs of supplying the separate markets may differ (contrary to the assumption in our analysis above). From the monopolist's viewpoint, cost differences arising from selling or distributing the product can often be handled by obtaining net marginal revenues (cor-

---

[8] Illustrations of these special cases look much more complicated than they really are. For further exploration into the interesting subject of price discrimination, see Joan Robinson, *The Economics of Imperfect Competition,* Macmillan and Co., London, 1934, Book V.

recting marginal revenue functions for cost differences). In practice, to distinguish between discriminating pricing practices (cases where price differences are not supported by cost differences) and nondiscriminating price differences (supported by cost differences) is a difficult task.

Multiple Products—Joint Costs

Commonly, the large firm is engaged in the production of multiple products, related in supply (and perhaps in demand). Hide and beef from a steer is a common example of complementary joint products. If more hides were produced, there would be more beef as a by-product; or if more beef were produced, there would be more hides as a by-product. Sometimes joint products may be substitutes: gasoline and kerosene are both processed from unrefined oil, and any increase in the amount of one, produced from a given amount of fuel oil, necessarily implies a decrease in the amount of the other. In general, if the demand curves for the various products are independent, the ordinary profit-maximizing rule—produce to the point where marginal cost intersects marginal revenue from below—still applies.

If the products can only be produced in fixed proportion, costs cannot be separated and allocated to each product. Product prices should be determined by the demand curve for each product. Suppose beef X and hides Y can only be produced from steers Z in fixed proportions. Steers should be produced to the point where MC_Z equals the vertical sum of the MR_X and MR_Y (the sum of marginal revenues at given outputs). At the profit-maximizing output, prices can be set up to the limits of the demand curves, D_X and D_Y. The analysis is illustrated in Figs. 9.7a and 9.7b.

In Fig. 9.7a, MC_Z cuts $(MR_X + MR_Y)$ at an output where MR_X and MR_Y are both positive (so that the sum $MR_X + MR_Y$ lies above either MR_X or MR_Y taken separately). At this rate of output $(\bar{Z} = \bar{X} + \bar{Y})$ X can be sold at P_X and Y can be sold at P_Y. Figure 9.7b illustrates a situation where MC_Z intersects $(MR_X + MR_Y)$ at an output where MR_X is negative so that $(MR_X + MR_Y)$ is less than MR_Y (Y is still making a positive contribution to revenue). In this case, output should be carried to the point $(\bar{Z} = \bar{X} + \bar{Y})$, where MC_Z intersects MR_Y. $\bar{Y}$ is sold at a price P_Y', but only $\bar{X}'$ (of the total $\bar{X}$) should be sold at a price P_X'. The remainder of X should be destroyed or withheld from the market by a profit-maximizing monopolist, since it makes a negative contribution to the firm's revenue. (Society would gain if this leftover supply were sold, instead of destroyed.) As long as the sum of the prices $(P_X + P_Y)$

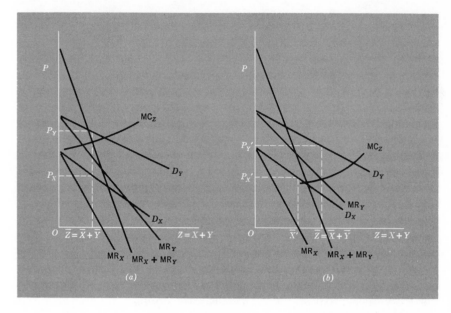

Fig. 9.7

exceeds AC_Z, the monopolist will earn better than positive economic profit and will have an incentive to produce.[9]

Often multiple products can be produced in variable proportions. In the variable proportion case, it is usually possible to derive an estimate of the separate marginal costs of producing each product, say gasoline G and kerosene K from fuel oil F. In neither the fixed proportion nor the variable proportion case is it possible to allocate common costs among the joint products. Any allocational scheme (whether based on sales, labor time, variable costs, etc.) is arbitrary and incorrect, if the allocation of common costs leads to outputs that differ from outputs determined on a marginal cost basis.

Where demand curves for the various products are independent, the ordinary $MC = MR$ rule applies for each product. For a two-product case the profit-maximizing rule can be illustrated with the device of iso-cost and isorevenue curve, as in Fig. 9.8. Total outlay is constant for all combinations of products X and Y along the isocost curve— $\Delta X(MC_X) + \Delta Y(MC_Y) = 0$. The isorevenue curve traces all com-

---

[9] Under pure competition, a firm's output would be carried to the point where the marginal cost of producing the joint output (in fixed proportion) equals $(P_X + P_Y)$—the sum of two horizontal demand curves facing the firm.

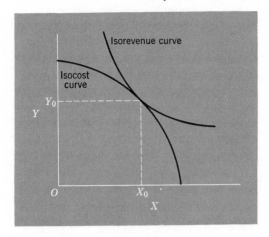

Fig. 9.8

binations of products X and Y that yield equal revenue—$\Delta X(MR_X) +$ $\Delta Y(MR_Y) = 0$. The slope of the isorevenue curve is $-MR_X/MR_Y$, and the slope of the isocost curve is $-MC_X/MC_Y$. As long as MC rises as output increases, and MR falls as output increases, we would expect the isocost curve to be concave to the origin, and the isorevenue curve to be convex to the origin (as illustrated).

The monopolist, for a given outlay (isocost curve), would try to select the combination that yields maximum revenue—this would be the point of tangency (X_0, Y_0) where the concave isocost curve touches the highest convex isorevenue curve. At this profit-maximizing point, the slopes of the two curves are equal:

$$\frac{MC_X}{MC_Y} = \frac{MR_X}{MR_Y} \quad \text{or} \quad \frac{MR_X}{MC_X} = \frac{MR_Y}{MC_Y}^{10}$$

If the demand curves of the separate joint products are not independent, the monopolist would have to take account of the change

[10] Under pure competition (where $P = MR$), the isorevenue curve would be linear, since the product price would not be effected by the firm's output decision. This special case of the profit-maximizing rule would be

$$\frac{P_X}{MC_X} = \frac{P_Y}{MC_Y}$$

and the output would be carried to the point where marginal cost equals price for each product.

in the rate of output of X on other product prices and outputs (e.g., on Y and P_Y).[11]

Summary

Monopoly is the antithesis of pure competition. In equilibrium, purely competitive markets achieve optimal resource allocation with price equal to marginal cost. Monopoly results in misallocation of resources since price exceeds marginal cost.[12] The persistence of monopoly profit tends to concentrate income in monopoly industries, unless prevented by regulation. Monopoly has also been criticized in terms of the financial and political power that may reside in concentration.

Arguments in favor of monopoly rest on economies of scale (natural monopoly), countervailing power (to offset existing monopsony power), achievement of adequate rates of growth, and provision of a cushion against economic shocks. In the real world there are competitive elements in any monopoly situation; e.g., competition from other products, competition from other places (imports), potential competition from new producers or new products, threat of public control or regulation, technological innovation, and countervailing power to reduce monopoly power. The theory of monopoly ordinarily assumes away these competitive elements.

In this chapter and the following one, our interest centers not in how firms may exercise their monopoly power and achieve profit-maximizing positions, but rather on the implications of monopoly power. We shall be concerned, too, with various models of how firms behave in imperfect markets.

---

[11] Where the multiple products are not independent in demand, the equilibrium condition for joint production would be

$$P_X + X\frac{\partial P_X}{\partial X} + Y\frac{\partial P_Y}{\partial X} = MC_X$$

A separate relation could be written for each product. If the separate functions are known, the equations could be solved simultaneously for equilibrium values of X and Y. See J. R. Hicks, "Annual Survey of Economic Theory: The Theory of Monopoly," *Econometrica*, 1935. Also in *AEA Readings in Price Theory*, eds. George J. Stigler and Kenneth Boulding, Richard D. Irwin, Homewood, Ill., 1952.
[12] Arnold C. Harberger, "Monopoly and Resource Allocation," *AER*, Vol. XLIV, No. 2, May 1954, pp. 77–79. Professor Harberger finds the malallocative effects of monopoly to be relatively small.

10

Imperfect Markets: Monopolistic
Competition, Duopoly, Oligopoly

When we relax the assumptions that underlie pure competition and monopoly, we sacrifice the determinateness of models with predictable equilibrium prices and outputs in exchange for greater descriptive realism. The analysis of imperfect markets does not yield pat answers; it does yield insight into the problems faced by firms operating in this middle ground, and it does bring us closer to being able to predict and understand industrial behavior.

The organization of product markets may differ in several dimensions: number of sellers, degree of product differentiation, conditions of entry, degree of (recognized or unrecognized) interdependence, and degree of uncertainty. Various combinations of these dimensions are possible, although some combinations are unlikely to occur in practice. For example, where few sellers produce a standardized product, it is unlikely that each will act independently without regard to the effect of the action on rivals. (Mutual awareness and interdependence of action are the major characteristics of oligopoly markets.)

Any given dimension can be broken down in any number of ways. Depending on the intent of the analysis, the number of sellers could be classified in various ways but is most often restricted to one (monopoly), two (duopoly), few (oligopoly), and many (pure or monopolistic competition). The many-seller case (where each seller acts independently and has little if any effect on market price) is a purely competitive market when the product is completely standardized (units indistinguishable to buyer). When the product is slightly differentiated (high cross-elasticity among products) the many-seller case becomes one of monopolistic competition; in both cases independence among sellers and easy entry or exit are assumed.

Certain market structures (or combinations of dimensions) have been singled out either because of the realism of their assumptions—their similarity to actual market conditions, as in the case of monopolistic competition—or because analytically they lead to interesting and significant results, as in the case of the purely competitive model.

Monopolistic Competition

E. H. Chamberlain and Joan Robinson independently became interested in markets which do not conform to the assumptions of the extreme cases of pure competition and monopoly (or perfect competition and pure monopoly). Their separate works, dealing with the large middle ground that encompasses the majority of real world markets, came out in 1933.[1]

We shall be principally concerned with Chamberlain's analysis of monopolistic competition—his "large-group" case. The reference to large group rather than industry arises from the fact that the group consists of a large number of competitors, each one selling a differentiated (non-homogeneous) product. New firms may enter the group with similar but not identical products. Under pure competition, new firms could enter the industry by selling products identical to those of the firms in the industry.

Monopolistic competition differs in several respects from the purely competitive model. Most of the differences can be traced to the relaxing of the homogeneous product assumption. In Chamberlain's large-group case, the variations among the products do not cause differences in cost among the firms in the large group. Some recognizable degree of product differentiation modifies the results of pure competition in the direction of greater descriptive realism. The departure from homogeneity of product gives the horizontal demand curve facing the purely competitive firm a slight tilt; in monopolistic competition the demand curve slopes *slightly* in a negative direction. (The products are only slightly differentiated.)

If the products of firms under monopolistic competition were distinct (with low cross-elasticity among products) each seller might be cast as a separate monopolist rather than one of a large group of firms selling similar products. In the monopolistic competition model, a symmetry assumption, intended to simplify the analysis, stipulates that whereas

[1] Joan Robinson, *The Economics of Imperfect Competition*, Macmillan Co., London, 1933; and E. H. Chamberlain, *The Theory of Monopolistic Competition*, Harvard University Press, Cambridge, Mass., 1933.

firms' products are differentiated, each firm's costs and demand curve are identical. The demand for each firm's slightly differentiated product at any time is assumed the same for all firms. After new firms enter and the total market is divided among more firms, perhaps producing even closer substitutes, each firm's anticipated demand will have shrunk in size and is likely to become more elastic as compared to the situation before entry.

A negatively sloping demand curve affords the firm some pricing discretion not available to the purely competitive firm. Where the product is differentiated and the firm has even limited price discretion, the purely competitive model no longer accurately describes the market. Competition under monopolistic competition remains impersonal with many firms acting independently.

The monopolistically competitive firm is essentially a minor monopolist. In fact, the short-run analysis of the monopolistically competitive firm is identical to the short-run analysis of the profit-maximizing monopolist. In the short run, the number of firms in the large group and their products are assumed constant.

The principal distinction between monopoly and monopolistic competition becomes apparent in the long run. Under monopolistic competition we assume free entry into the large group of firms producing similar close-substitute products. Under monopoly, there is a single-product market without any close substitutes; the monopolist is able to maintain his monopoly position in the market (entry into the market is denied potential competitors).

Figure 10.1 shows the firm initially in short-run equilibrium at (q_1, P_1), and eventually in long-run equilibrium at (q_0, P_0), where its anticipated demand (d_{F_0})—assuming other firms in the group do not vary their prices—becomes tangent to the LRAC curve. The zero profit tangency solution is the result of new firms entering the group with similar products (so that d_{F_0} is likely to be more elastic than d_{F_1}) and of the existing firms expanding their output (since in short-run equilibrium LRMC < MR < P, and each firm sees its demand as quite elastic).[2]

In the long run, assuming positive economic profit and free entry, the number of firms and the number of slightly differentiated products

[2] In fact, if every firm responds by lowering price, each firm's actual demand —with all firms lowering price—will be much more inelastic than d_{F_0}. See the dashed demand curves $\overline{d_1}$ and $\overline{d_0}$. The dashed lines drawn through the firm's short-run and long-run equilibrium positions represent the proportionate demand curves facing each firm, where all firms always charge the same price (avoid price competition) and share the market equally. The shift to the left from $\overline{d_1}$ and $\overline{d_0}$ is due to new firms entering.

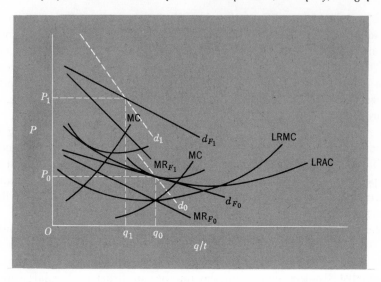

Fig. 10.1

will increase; we can expect some erosion of the firm's demand over time, even with constant "industry" demand. A similar phenomenon was present under pure competition, except that products were assumed homogeneous, and the firm's demand curve was infinitely elastic. Markets that conform to the assumptions of monopolistic competition include retailing (grocery stores, cigar stores, restaurants, barber shops), repair and other services (shoe and auto repair), and light manufacturing (printing and women's clothing). Remember that for these examples to be completely valid, there must be large numbers of independent producers in the same market.

Let us compare the long-run equilibrium positions in Figs. 10.2*a* and 10.2*b*. Both cases involve the tangency of the firm's demand curve with average cost; however, in Fig. 10.2*a* the purely competitive firm in long-run equilibrium finds product price just covering average cost at its most efficient rate of operation—the output rate where average costs are at a minimum (a measure of engineering efficiency) and where $P_c = MC$ (a measure of economic efficiency). In Fig. 10.2*b* the tangency (long-run equilibrium) position finds the monopolistically competitive firm just covering average costs but at a price slightly higher than in the purely competitive case, where the firm faced a horizontal demand curve (no product differentiation). Just how much higher will be the monopolistic competitor's price will depend on the elasticity of the seller's imagined or subjective demand curve, which is largely dependent on

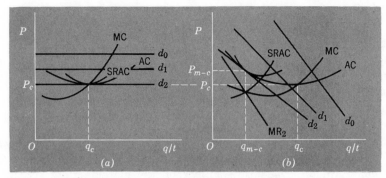

Fig. 10.2. (*a*) Firm under pure competition. (*b*) Firm under monopolistic competition.

the degree of product differentiation (it would be less elastic if he thought other firms would meet any price change). In addition to the higher equilibrium price, the monopolistically competitive firm is underutilizing its facilities. There is excess capacity in that it operates its existing plant somewhat short of the most efficient rate of operation (inefficient allocation of existing resources), and it operates with a plant that is somewhat smaller than the optimal-sized plant (insufficient use of resources): $P > \text{SRMC} > \text{LRMC}$.

As the total market demand is carved into smaller portions, as new firms enter and industry capacity expands, a monopolistic competitive firm has an incentive to further distinguish or differentiate its product by real or apparent improvements, for example, superior quality, longer-lasting materials, better wrapping, more effective advertising, or any device to prevent a diminishing of its market as new products become available. Enterprise in these directions was not required of the purely competitive firm. If the total market expands at a rate sufficient to offset the erosion resulting from new firms and new product proliferation, the firm may be able to continue earning positive economic profit (although it may have to contend with a more elastic demand curve, causing the firm to lose some of its discretionary control over price). As attempts are made to actually or apparently differentiate its product, through technological improvements, advertising, better distribution, promotional schemes, etc., each firm's average costs may increase. Equilibrium (perhaps a rather unstable one) may be approached at some higher price, reflecting these new costs.[3]

[3] The relation between elasticity of demand and advertising (and other forms of product differentiation) for profit-maximizing firms has been formally demonstrated by R. Dorfman and P. O. Steiner, "Optimal Advertising and Optimal Quality," *AER,* Vol. 44, December, 1954, pp. 826–836.

Even if costs remained the same for firms in both market situations, the consumer under monopolistic competition pays a slight premium (higher price) and society sustains a slight loss in the efficiency with which resources are utilized $(P = AC > MC)$. In exchange, there is a gain in product variety; we do not compare the prices of identical products.

In the monopolistic competition case, the emphasis is on the firm's reaction to market signals—the shifting demand and loss of market at prices set by the firm within the limits established by the firm's anticipated demand curve. Firms are assumed to be numerous enough so that the impact of any *one* firm's actions on the market is not recognized by any other firm; each firm continues to act independently without trying to predict rivals' reactions.

The sellers in the monopolistic competitive case do not sell a homogeneous product but many similar products. It is therefore not quite correct to compare the market price under pure competition with a single market price under monopolistic competition. The industry price and output under this larger group case (a cluster of substitute products, each of which exhibits high cross-elasticity of demand with respect to any other) would have to be characterized by a price and quantity index rather than by a single price or aggregation of homogeneous quantities.

Two additional criticisms of the monopolistic competition model should be mentioned. Professor Harrod has criticized the excess capacity equilibrium, which he feels results from an inconsistency in the concept of the "rational" firm. Harrod points out that the tangency solution in monopolistic competition requires that a very "short-sighted firm" follow a *short-run* marginal revenue function and a *long-run* marginal cost function in determining optimal plant size and output. Allowing for entry, the long-run marginal revenue curve is more elastic than the short-sighted firm thinks it is. A far-sighted rational firm would, according to Harrod, charge a lower than short-run profit-maximizing price to inhibit entry. The far-sighted firm's more elastic demand (allowing for entry) would be tangent to average costs at a higher output, closer to the purely competitive output and beyond the long-run equilibrium output in the large group case we have considered. The far-sighted firm would, in effect, set an entry-limiting price, sacrificing short-run profit. In fact, Chamberlain's large group case rests on the independence assumption; the short-sighted firm is an important part of the monopolistically competitive model.[4]

---

[4] See R. F. Harrod, *Economic Essays, Harcourt, Brace, New York,* 1952.

There is a related problem pertaining to the realism of the independence assumption. Do monopolistic competitors really ignore each other's actions? In many markets, where interdependence is recognized, one of the many oligopolistic models may yield more accurate predictions than does the monopolistic competition model.

"Classical" Duopoly Models

An early "classical" solution to the duopoly (two seller) problem was given by Cournot.[5] He took the case of two sellers (duopolists), perfectly substitutable products, identical costs, no entry, and no recognized interdependence—a rather unlikely set of dimensions (perhaps an empty set or empty box since the "no recognized interdependence" assumption is not compatible with the other conditions). In the original presentation, both rivals operate identical mineral springs. To simplify the analysis, there are zero costs—customers bring their own containers to the spring to get mineral water.

Each duopolist knows the total market demand curve, and he knows his rival's current output. Each chooses his profit-maximizing output on the assumption that his rival's output will remain unchanged. Both duopolists (A and B) may be said to assume that conjectural variation with respect to output is zero. A assumes that B will not react to a change in A's output, so A takes the total market demand and B's output as given. Under these conditions, each duopolist can calculate the demand price and net revenue (= net profit with zero costs) that will result from whichever rate of output he chooses.

Suppose market demand were the linear demand curve D-D in Fig. 10.3a, and at the start, B's output were zero. A would, in effect, be a monopolist and would choose to produce at q_A, where the marginal revenue curve MR_A (whose slope is twice as steep as the linear demand curve) bisects the X-axis (which is also the marginal cost curve—$MC = 0$).[6] OD would correspond to the purely competitive output with price = MC (= 0). As a monopolist, A chooses to sell q_A, which is one-half of the competitive output, at a price P_A, which is determined by the known

[5] Augustin Cournot, *Researches into the Mathematical Principles of the Theory of Wealth* (1838), English trans. by N. T. Bacon, Macmillan, New York, 1897.
[6] If the demand curve is linear—$P = a - bQ$—the total revenue curve is $TR = PQ = aQ - bQ^2$, and the marginal revenue curve is $MR = d(TR)/dQ = a - (2b)Q$. The slope of the marginal revenue curve is twice as steep as the slope of the linear demand curve, and cuts any horizontal line from the vertical price axis to the demand curve into two equal parts.

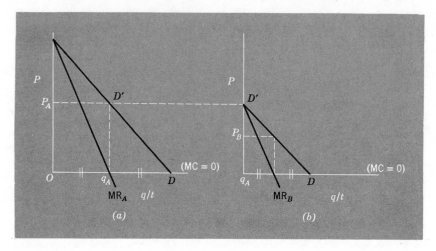

Fig. 10.3

market demand. *A* estimates his maximum net profit to be $q_A \cdot P_A$ (he could easily estimate his profit for any other output he might choose). If *B* enters the market, he assumes *A*'s output will remain at q_A and takes his demand curve to be that section of the market demand to the right of D'. *B*'s demand curve is represented in Fig. 10.3*b*; *B* will choose to sell to one-half of the remaining market where MR_B bisects the *X*-axis ($MC = 0$) at q_B. As a result of *B*'s choice of output at q_B,

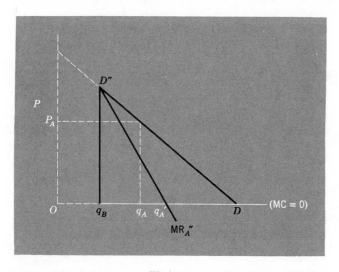

Fig. 10.4

the market price will fall to P_B. This will be a surprise to A since he had assumed B's output would remain at zero.

Let us follow the process a little further. In Fig. 10.4, A takes B's output to remain fixed at q_B, and D''-D becomes A's effective demand. A will now choose to sell q_A' ($\frac{3}{8}$ or $\frac{1}{2}$ of the remaining $\frac{3}{4}$ of the market where $\mathrm{MR}_A'' = \mathrm{MC} = 0$). If each continues to set output on the assumption that the other's output will stay put, the process will continue until an equilibrium is reached with each selling $\frac{1}{3}$ (OD), where OD is the competitive output. This result can easily be generalized to more than two sellers. If there were n sellers, the equilibrium output of all n sellers would be $n/(n+1)$ times the competitive output, with the market equally divided among the n sellers.

The approach to equilibrium can perhaps be more readily understood using reaction curves, as in Fig. 10.5. Each point on a reaction curve yields maximum profit, on the assumption that the rival will not respond by adjusting his output in turn.[7] A's reaction curve passes through the maximum point of A's isoprofit curves (A_1 A_2, A_3 . . .). All points on one of A's isoprofit curves represent combinations of A's output and B's output that yield equal profit for A. The reaction curves are linear (with linear demand and constant costs). The points q_A and D—the monopoly and competitive outputs, respectively—are the same as in Fig. 10.4 in our previous analysis. Note that if A sold OD—the

---

[7] The mathematical argument of Cournot's duopoly model follows.

Given: Duopolists i and j; their outputs q_i and q_j; and market price P.

Market demand function: $P = f(q_i + q_j)$ or $q_i + q_j = h(P)$

Duopolist's total cost function: $\phi(q_i) = \phi(q_j)$

Duopolist i's profit function: $\pi_i = q_i P - \phi(q_i) = q_i f(q_i + q_j) - \phi(q_i)$

Maximizing profit: $\partial\pi_i/\partial q_i = q_i[f' + f'(dq_j/dq_i)] + f(q_i + q_j) - \phi'(q_i) = 0$

Duopolist i will choose his output, q_i, which will maximize π_i for given q_j, market demand, and costs.

Assuming zero conjectural variation with respect to rival's output: $dq_j/dq_i = 0$, i's reaction curve would be: $q_i f'(q_i + q_j) + f(q_i + q_j) = \phi'(q_i)$. With marginal cost $\phi'(q_i)$ assumed equal to zero, i's reaction curve reduces to:

$$q_i f'(q_i + q_j) + f(q_i + q_j) = 0 \quad \text{or} \quad q_i \frac{dP}{dq_i} + P = 0$$

With marginal cost $\phi'(q_j)$ assumed equal to zero, j's reaction function (derived in a similar manner) is

$$q_j f'(q_i + q_j) + f(q_i + q_j) = 0 \quad \text{or} \quad q_j \frac{dP}{dq_j} + P = 0$$

The two reaction functions can be solved simultaneously for the equilibrium values of q_i and q_j. (Note that q_j is taken as given in i's reaction function and q_i is taken as given in j's reaction function.

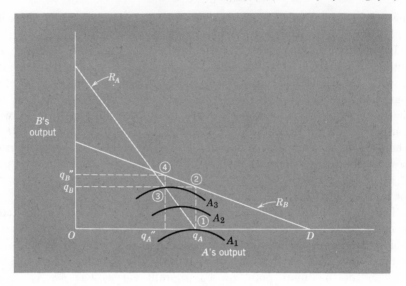

Fig. 10.5

competitive output—where price = MC, *B*'s reaction would be to sell zero output. If *B*'s output were zero, *A* takes this as given and would react by choosing q_A—the maximum point on his highest isoprofit curve A_1. The lower the output of *B*, the higher the profit level that *A* can achieve. *B*'s reaction curve, R_B, is also drawn, although without the supporting isoprofit curves. If *A* chooses q_A, *B* will react along his reaction curve at the point 2—q_B, as in our previous analysis. *A* will then react by choosing point 3—q_A'' along his (*A*'s) reaction curve (still on the assumption that *B* will *not react* to *A*'s change of output). *B* reacts by moving to point 4. The convergence along the path—1, 2, 3, 4, and so on—continues until equilibrium is reached at the intersection of the reaction curves. The distribution of output at the point of equilibrium has been discussed previously.

So much for the workings of the Cournot model with its conjectural variation of zero with respect to output. The main question is whether the model is likely to conform to observed behavior. The answer is that it is quite unlikely to correspond to duopoly behavior since, as was suggested earlier, the set of assumptions underlying the model do not appear compatible. Under the assumptions of the model, there is a unique and stable equilibrium at the intersection of the two reaction curves; in practice, it is doubtful that this equilibrium position would ever be reached, unless both parties should choose this position initially.

If B did initially choose to produce the equilibrium output at q_B'' (in Fig. 10.5)—one-third of the total competitive market—then A would choose the same output—also one-third of the total competitive output (assuming that B's output does not change). They would be in equilibrium at the intersection of the two reaction curves. The assumption of "no change in rival's output" would be correct only at this equilibrium output, since, in equilibrium, each produces one-third of the competitive output and one-half of the remaining two-thirds of the market equals one-third, which is the profit-maximizing amount both parties would choose to sell at the point of intersection of the reaction curves.

If the parties do not initially choose to sell to one-third of the competitive market, in the process of converging to equilibrium they may realize that the assumptions underlying the reaction curves are never realized. After all, it is not realistic to continue to assume that your rival's output will stay put when, in fact, your rival's output does change repeatedly in response to your own change in output. If, contrary to experience, neither rival makes an attempt to anticipate the other's reaction and, instead, continues to ignore the rival's behavior, then, as the model implies, the rather passive reactors may eventually reach equilibrium. There is the possibility that, in a changing economy, each may attribute the rival's output changes to changes in market conditions and so fail to suspect any functional relationship between their own output and their rival's output. It is likely, however, that eventually they will awaken to the fact of interdependence and begin to doubt the validity of acting on the basis of an assumption continually demonstrated to be false (except at the equilibrium position).

Indeed, even if the duopolists were at equilibrium with each selling one-third of total demand, it is doubtful whether they would remain there. Suppose A thought he could improve his profit position by taking the initiative and increasing his output from one-third to one-half the total competitive market, hoping (contrary to the assumption of the Cournot model) that B's output would not remain fixed at one-third. A could remain at one-half the market as long as B were willing to take A's new output as fixed and decide to sell half the remaining market. If B tried the same aggressive tactic and both produced one-half, the market price would fall to zero ($=$ MC).

An optimal decision for both (or all) parties would be to restrict their combined output to one-half of the competitive output, and share the profit. This would be the monopoly profit-maximizing solution under conditions of linear market demand. The difficulties in agreeing to a basis for profit-sharing, as well as the problems of enforcing such an agreement, not to mention the questionable legality of collusion, can obstruct such a solution, even though both parties may benefit by colluding and restricting output to one-half the competitive market.

Perhaps the main significance of the original Cournot model lay in its vulnerability to criticism. It was the model's very restrictive and unrealistic assumptions that yielded a unique determinate equilibrium. The stability of the equilibrium depended on the adjustment process assumed in the model—each rival successively adjusting his own output, taking his rival's output as given. Others tried to improve on the model by offering alternative (but often equally restrictive and unrealistic) assumptions. Surprisingly, it was not until 1883 (45 years after the appearance of the Cournot model) that Joseph Bertrand, a French mathematician, reviewed Cournot's model, and suggested that price was a more appropriate decision-variable. Bertrand posited a model where each duopolist, in setting his own profit-maximizing price, believed that his rival would not vary his present price (zero conjectural variation with respect to price). With homogeneous product and unlimited capacity, Bertrand believed that the purely competitive market solution was the most likely solution to the duopoly problem.

Each duopolist, by slightly undercutting his rival's price, could capture the entire market or, alternatively, he could sell up to the point where his marginal cost of producing additional output equalled price. At prices below the rival's price, each duopolist's demand would be the market demand. With perfectly substituable products and identical prices, each duopolist would hope to face a demand curve one-half the size of total market demand, sharing the market equally. But each hopes to gain by undercutting his rival's price, thus greatly expanding his sales. Bertrand believed an equilibrium would be reached (after rapid price-undercutting) at a price equal to MC (= AC), and only then would they be content to share the market equally. There are possible variations to this solution: if one seller has lower costs than the other, he might desist from the final price-undercut and, by simply meeting his rival's lower price, gain the extra profit (or rent) equal to the differential cost advantage; alternatively, the low cost seller could make the final undercut and take the entire market (or that part of the market up to the point where his rising marginal costs equal his rival's marginal costs). In this "duel-to-the-end" type of rivalry, there is some question whether the firm with a cost advantage can out-survive the firm with greater financial resources.

Edgeworth[8] developed Bertrand's suggestion, agreeing that firms in

[8] F. Y. Edgeworth, *"The Pure Theory of Monopoly,"* reprinted in *Edgeworth Papers Relating to Political Economy*, Macmillan, London, 1925, Vol. 1, pp. 111–142.

imperfect markets are more likely to set price than output. As in the Bertrand model, output would be a function of the price chosen to maximize profit, taking the rival's price as given. Edgeworth introduced the assumption that each seller's capacity was fixed (in the short run). If price declines (via Bertrand-undercutting) to the level of marginal cost or to some price above marginal cost if the firm's capacity is so limited, and if one seller then sells his entire output at this lower pricing limit, the other seller (if he has the foresight to abstain from selling at the lower price limit) can view the remaining leftover demand as a captive market[9] and, for a time, charge a monopoly price. The rival, aware that he had been duped into selling out at the low price limit, could then capture (at the first opportunity) as much of the market as he likes by just undercutting his sneaky rival. And so the process continues, each setting price on the assumption that his rival's price will remain unchanged, and price will move up and down between the upper and lower limit—a perpetual oscillation without any necessary equilibrium. It strains the imagination (even more than in the Cournot model) to believe that in the midst of continual price-cutting and price fluctuation, each seller would continue to operate on the assumption that his rival's price will stay put, and that his own undercut will be the last. Of course, he may have no option but to continue to undercut, but eventually the assumption of zero conjectural variation with respect to price would be replaced by some more viable pricing policy, as sellers become aware of their interdependence.[10]

It is likely that the "classical" duopoly models of Cournot and Bertrand would trigger unstable situations before reaching a stable equilibrium under the assumption of independent action.

Spatial Competition

Hotelling[11] demonstrated that the Bertrand-Edgeworth assumption of zero conjectural variation with respect to price could lead to a stable equilibrium, where there are locational (or product) differences. In Hotel-

[9] In the case of storable commodities, questions of inventory and production time are likely to cast some doubt on the duopolist's control over the leftover demand.

[10] For a more complete discussion of the Bertrand-Edgeworth case, see William Fellner, *Competition Among the Few*, Alfred A. Knopf, New York, 1949. Fellner emphasizes that in "competition among the few" firms will seek group stability by agreement, whether explicit or tacit.

[11] Harold Hotelling, "Stability in Competition," Economic Journal, XXXIX, 1929, pp. 41-57.

ling's model, two sellers (*A* and *B*) produce identical products with one important exception. Each seller has a locational advantage over some segment of the market distributed uniformly among buyers over a straight line. The locational advantage (which gives each seller a "sheltered" portion of the market) may be taken to represent product difference.

Hotelling assumed that (refer to Fig. 10.6) (1) there are two producers, *A* and *B*, with identical costs (2) buyers are uniformly distributed along a straight line from *O* to *E*, (3) buyers' demand is completely inelastic—they do not vary their rate of purchase as the delivered price varies, (4) transportation costs vary in proportion to distance but the rate per unit of distance is the same to both rivals, (5) each seller sets his factory price on the assumption that his rival will hold his price fixed, (6) the buyers will buy from either seller, whichever offers the lower delivered price (factory price plus transportation cost).

If *A* charged a price P_A and *B* charged a price P_B and the sloping lines from P_A and P_B represent factory price plus transport costs, the delivered price at any point along the road can be represented by the line segments $P_A S$ and $P_A T$ (for *A*'s customers) and $P_B T$ and $P_B U$ (for *B*'s customers). Buyers to the left of *M* will find it cheaper to buy from *A*, and those to the right if *M* will find it cheaper to buy from *B*. The position of *M* is determined by the intersection of the delivered price lines at *T*. The delivered price depends on factory price, transport costs per mile, and location.

If each seller were located one-fourth of the total distance (*O* to *E*) from the ends of the road (or from the middle), transportation costs would be minimized. Located symmetrically along the road, each seller would set the same factory price. If the sellers' locations were fixed

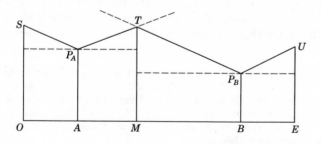

Fig. 10.6

but not at equal distances from the center, the equilibrium factory prices would differ. The closer either seller is to the center, the higher the price he is likely to charge and the greater the profit he is likely to receive.

Hotelling argued that if choice of location were open, and if each seller chose his location on the assumption that the other's location (but not his price) were fixed, each would move closer to the other in order to maximize the length of the market segment he could control. Eventually they would converge at the middle, where transportation costs would be a maximum. By analogy, Hotelling extended his theory of convergence to differentiated product markets, politics, and religion.

Smithies and others have demonstrated that some of the force of Hotelling's convergence theory arises from his restrictive assumptions: completely inelastic demand, two rivals, identical costs, etc.[12]

Oligopoly: Interdependence Recognized

If, instead of assuming that his rival will hold price constant (as in the Bertrand-Edgeworth model), each duopolist recognizes interdependence and tries to anticipate the other's reaction pattern (perhaps trying to discover it by exploratory trials), each would choose a price such that his rival's price response (along his rival's reaction curve) would lead to his own maximum profit. Given their price reaction curves, R_A and R_B, A would choose P_A, where B's reaction curve R_B is tangent to A's highest isoprofit curve (see Fig. 10.7). A anticipates that B will react to P_A by setting a price P_B' according to B's reaction curve (as estimated by A). If B reacts as A anticipates, we have an equilibrium under this price leadership situation. A sets price P_A with knowledge of B's reaction curve, and B complies by choosing P_B' along his reaction curve.

However, suppose B does not wish to follow A's lead, but thinks he can improve his profit position by estimating A's reaction pattern; B sets price accordingly (where A's reaction curve is tangent to B's highest isoprofit curve). If both parties, acting independently, think that they know each other's reaction pattern and set price to maximize profit, they will be surprised and disappointed. The combination of prices will be (P_A,P_B), which is not on either rival's reaction curve, and yields a lower profit than either anticipated. Both "leaders" were misinformed

[12] See Arthur Smithies, "Optimum Location in Spatial Competition," *JPE*, 49, June 1941, pp. 423–39.

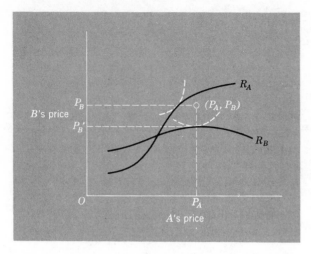

Fig. 10.7

about each other's reaction pattern. There is no reason to expect that this double-leadership case will lead to a stable equilibrium.[13]

Oligopoly

Where sellers are few enough and some at least are dominant enough, we have an oligopoly situation characterized by a strong sense of inter-dependence and rivalry. With few sellers, each is likely to be aware that his own action will have an impact on his rivals and on the common environment.

Implicit in all economic models are elements of uncertainty; however, under oligopoly, uncertainty is magnified by the lack of knowledge of rivals' reactions. Limited barriers to entry apply to most oligopoly situations. The degree of product differentiation is not always specified in models of oligopoly markets, but a distinction is sometimes made between pure oligopoly (among firms with homogeneous products) and differen-

[13] If both leaders happened to choose prices that corresponded to the intersection of R_A and R_B, presumably this would be a stable equilibrium. With homogeneous products, the prices at the intersection will be identical. (The intersection might correspond to the monopoly solution.) If each rival were a Bertrand duopolist, so that each ignoring his rival's reaction, followed his own reaction curve based on the assumption that the other's price remains fixed, the intersection might be a Bertrand equilibrium with price = AC.

tiated oligopoly (among firms with differentiated products). The less differentiated the products, the more a sense of interdependence is likely to manifest itself among the few firms producing similar products.

The organization of an oligopoly industry may vary from a formal cartel, where all parties agree to act in unity for the "group" benefit, to the other extreme of independent action. The most likely situation is somewhere in between where a tacit collusion is recognized—where there exists "conscious parallelism," and firms implicitly accept the fact that they must act together if at all, but without any explicit agreement.

Oligopoly covers a wide spectrum of cases, including (1) independence of action (the sense of mutual interdependence does not preclude oligopolists from "acting" independently with or without regard to rivals' reactions), (2) implicit agreement (leadership), and (3) explicit agreement (cartel).

Barriers to Entry

Oligopoly presupposes limited entry. Without barriers to entry the industry would tend to approach pure competition (where products are homogeneous) or monopolistic competition (where products are heterogeneous). Barriers to entry under oligopoly are likely to be similar to those that sustain monopolies. Barriers include (1) market control over supply (limited supplies of raw materials or control over transportation), (2) government legal sanctions (patent, franchise, quota), (3) shortage of capital or technical knowledge, (4) limited size of market demand and internal economies of scale (only one or a few firms may be able to produce profitably in a limited market), and (5) limit-pricing. We shall elaborate here on (4) and (5).

Internal Economies of Scale and a Limited Market

In Fig. 10.8 total market demand is represented by the demand curve D and the firm's long-run average cost is represented by the LRAC curve. Two firms, sharing the market between them, would be able to charge a price greater than average cost. Each firm, facing $\frac{1}{2}D$, could cover costs by operating between Q_1 and Q_2. However, the market would not be sufficiently large to permit a third firm to enter. A three-way division of the market, so that each firm faced one-third the market demand ($\frac{1}{3}D$) would allow none of the three to earn positive economic

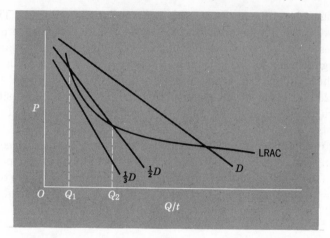

Fig. 10.8

profit. The market will not accept a price high enough to cover average costs at any output.

With a decreasing LRAC curve, one firm would be able to charge a low enough price (taking advantage of economies of scale) to capture the entire market in the case illustrated—a natural monopoly situation (refer back to the Bertrand duopoly model).

Limit Pricing

There are situations where the dominant firm(s)—whether a price leader under oligopoly, an insecure monopolist, or a cartel—may keep price below the short-run profit-maximizing price in order to discourage entry. In Fig. 10.9, the entry-limiting price P_L may be chosen in preference to the short-run profit-maximizing price P_M. The entry-limiting price happens to fall in the inelastic section of the demand curve in this figure. The marginal revenue curve would be the discontinuous segments $P_L L$ (identical to the established entry-limiting price up to the limit set by the demand curve) and the line segment NG. Marginal cost will equal the (entry-limiting) marginal revenue curve in the area of the discontinuity.[14]

---

[14] For an argument on the dynamics of limit-pricing under public pressure, see Allan J. Braff and Roger F. Miller, "Wage-Price Policies Under Public Pressure," *SEJ*, Vol. 28, No. 2 1961.

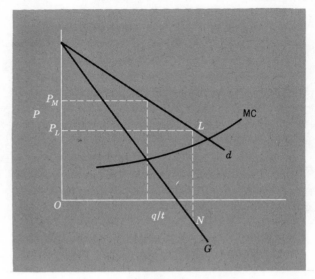

Fig. 10.9

The entry-limiting price can be explained in terms of maximizing profit over several time periods. The firm(s) may choose P_L, sacrificing some short-run profit in order to maximize the present value of the stream of earnings over future periods. If potential entrants are excluded by the price P_L, the present value of future earnings may be higher at a price P_L than if P_M were set (and higher short-run profit earned in the early periods).

The interdependency and uncertainty concerning rivals' actions are apparent when the *theory of games* is used to analyze an oligopolist's market behavior. Game theory focuses on a finite number of possible strategies where the outcome or payoff of "our" firm's strategy is dependent on our rival's (or all other firms taken together) strategy or counterstrategy (if our rival has knowledge of our strategy).[15] The strategies in oligopoly situations may be quite complex. They may involve nonprice dimensions such as advertising outlays, product differences, location, or combinations of these and other forms of competitive behavior.

If we were to take the strategies to be various pricing decisions by us and our rival, the outcome (or payoffs) might be the rates of output derived from selected points on the demand curves in Fig. 10.10 (where

---

[15] We direct our attention here to a two-person game between our firm and a rival; n-person games are undoubtedly more realistic with respect to most oligopoly situations, but as yet no very satisfactory solution to the n-person game exists.

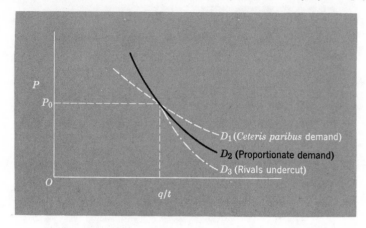

Fig. 10.10

each demand curve is based on a possible reaction on the part of our rival). The payoffs of our possible strategies and those of our rivals (selected points on the demand curves) can be easily presented in matrix form. (Probability estimates or weights could be employed to represent our estimate of the likelihood of our rival's reaction—will D_1, D_2, or D_3 apply?)

Game Theory

Game theory proposes a solution to oligopoly (or duopoly) behavior where the player acts independently, but with full awareness of interdependency. He recognizes that the outcome will depend not only on his strategy choice, but also on his rival's strategy choice. He considers the various possibilities, and tries to make a "rational" or reasonable decision, not by ignoring his rivals' reaction nor by making a rigid assumption (or conjectural variation) regarding his rivals' policy, but by hedging against the worst possible occurrence.

The "payoff" in the game theory example that follows is the share of the market. The total market is 100%, and both parties through pricing strategies attempt to obtain as large a share of the market as they can. This is a *constant-sum* (or zero-sum) game between us and our rival. (A zero-sum game is really a special case of a constant-sum game where the gain to one party equals the loss to the other: the sum of both parties' payoff is zero.) A constant-sum game implies a highly competitive game with direct and absolute conflict of interest.

Our gain is our rival's loss. In a constant-sum game, whatever the pair of strategies chosen, the total amount at stake (the payoff) is always constant; so that if our payoff is known, our rival's payoff is simply what remains from the constant sum. Each cell in Matrix 1 represents our payoff—our share of the market—that results from a combination of price strategy choices, ours and our rival's. The outcomes of payoffs from various combinations of pricing strategies are assumed to be known to both parties

Matrix 1

(Our Price Strategy) / (Rival's Price Strategy)	Substantial Price Reduction 1'	Lower Price 2'	Leave Price Unchanged 3'	Raise Price 4'
1/Lower Price	10	40	45	60
2/Leave Price Unchanged	20	30	40	55
3/Raise Price	5	10	25	50

Since our objective is to maximize our market share, we need not consider our third strategy (raise price); independent of what our rival does, our payoffs resulting from this third strategy are clearly "dominated" by the other two—all of the market shares in row 3 are the smallest in their column. Only our price strategies 1 and 2 are relevant, so we can simplify our payoff matrix (Matrix 2).

Matrix 2

		Rival's Price Strategy				
		1'	2'	3'	4'	Row Minima
Our Price Strategy	1	10	40	45	60	10
	2	20	30	40	55	(20)
	Column Maxima	(20)	40	45	60	

The choice between strategy 1 and strategy 2 is not an obvious one; some reasonable decision-criterion must be accepted prior to selection. (If the payoffs had represented net profit, the meaning of profit-maximizing would have to be clarified.) Strategy 1 offers us the possibility of the worst (10) and the best payoff (60), while strategy 2 is a little safer in that under the most unfavorable (to us) of our rival's strategy choices, we would be guaranteed a minimum of 20. For any rival's strategy other than 1', we would be better off choosing strategy 1 (lower price).

The game theory solution bases the decision on a *maximin* criterion, taking a rather defensive and pessimistic view of what our rivals will do. For any choice we may make, the game theory solution for this two-person zero-sum game requires that we disregard all but the worst of the payoffs that could befall us (the row minima in the last column of Matrix 2 is 10 if we choose strategy 1, and 20 if we choose strategy 2). Whichever strategy we choose, we expect our rival to make the choice that will do us the most damage. With no prior knowledge of what our rival does, we base our decision on the best (for us) of the worst possibilities, and choose the maximum of the row minima—the *maximin* solution. The maximin (best-of-worst) strategy choice in our example would be strategy 2. For each of our rival's strategies, our largest payoff is his smallest. He will choose that strategy that assures him the highest floor or the highest of his minimum market shares—the smallest of our possible maxima. Our rival would choose his *minimax* solution—the minimum of the column maxima or his strategy 1'. In this case, with each of us choosing a unique or pure strategy, our maximin value (20) equals our rival's minimax value (20), and a stable determinate solution or saddle-point exists. Where a saddle-point does exist, neither party can gain by changing strategy unilaterally. If our rival chooses 1', the best we can do is stay with our original choice, strategy 2. If we choose strategy 2, our rival's best choice remains strategy 1'. If a saddle-point exists, we have a stationary position with no incentive to change strategies. (Note that the "classical" duopoly models are easily considered within the game theory framework. We would simply assume that our rival had fixed on one of his strategies, as if we had prior knowledge of his choice, and make our own choice accordingly.)

Under oligopoly there are many interesting strategy choices involving decision-variables where the outcomes are not constant-sum. In nonconstant-sum games, there is often the possibility that each party may gain by collusion (or coalition in the case of *n*-person games). Both parties may gain by agreeing to a common price instead of acting independently; their combined revenue may be greater if they acted jointly than if they acted separately in a nonconstant-sum game.[16]

It is easy to construct a constant-sum game where the maximum of the row minima (our maximin value) is not equal to the minimum of the column maxima (rival's minimax), that is, there is no saddle-point. There is no reason to expect that a constant-sum game, with each party pursuing a pure strategy (choosing a unique course of action), will contain a saddle-point or determinate, stable solution. (Recall the Edgeworth model where price continually fluctuated between some upper and lower limit.) [17]

In the nonconstant-sum game, the players may cooperate to maximize their combined payoff, providing they can agree on a basis for sharing the total. Bargaining theory has contributed several possible bases for sharing the total payoff.[18]

Where the parties do not cooperate or agree to maximize their joint payoff, many interesting solutions or dynamic sequences of solutions are possible. A "game tree"[19] has been employed to catalog all possible sequences of strategies, including the separate payoffs from each combination of strategies as well as the transition probabilities of moving from one combination of strategies to another. Recently the game tree approach has been coupled with learning theory and applied experimentally to duopoly situations.

A duopoly game (with certain strategies, payoffs, and simple restrictions) is described to two subjects in a laboratory situation. Their response patterns have been observed to follow a mathematical learning

[16] This was the case in the collusion variation of the Cournot duopoly model, where setting a monopoly output offered the possibility of more profit to each than either could get acting independently.

[17] Von Neumann and Morgenstern proved that by using mixed strategies, a stable solution exists. A mixed strategy involves making a choice with the aid of some chance device and assigning probabilities to each pure strategy in such a manner that the expected value of the game will be maximized. To choose the most favorable probabilities in an optimal mixed strategy, Von Neumann and Morgenstern employed a special kind of "cardinal" utility rather than the original payoff. John von Neumann and Oskar Morgenstern, *Theory of Games and Economic Behavior,* Princeton University Press, Princeton, N.J., 1953.

[18] See John C. Harsanyi, "Approaches to the Bargaining Problem," *Econometrica,* Vol. 24, April, 1956; and T. C. Schelling, *The Strategy of Conflict,* Harvard University Press, Cambridge, Mass., 1960.

[19] The game tree is described in Martin Shubik, *Strategy of Market Structure: Competition, Oligopoly, and the Theory of Games,* John Wiley and Sons, New York, 1959. The book provides an interesting discussion of the applicability of game theory to economics.

curve, rather than a fluctuating response pattern (as in Edgeworth), or some pure strategy (as in Cournot), or a collusive solution (maximizing joint profit). The learning theory approach to oligopoly behavior is formulated in terms of stimulus, response, and reinforcement. It concentrates on the decision process rather than on a "rational" profit-maximizing solution. It is too early to predict whether this approach to the duopoly-oligopoly problem will be successful when applied to the "real" world; but it is an interesting attempt to use laboratory experiments to learn about complex economic phenomena, and to use a psychological learning process coupled with mathematical learning theory to solve a complicated economic problem—the behavior of firms in imperfect markets.[20]

Expected Value Criterion

Other criteria for rational solutions are possible. The maximin criterion is employed in the theory of games. Let us consider one more contribution to rational decisions—the "expected value" criterion. Suppose we assign probabilities to each of four possible rival's choices (if we are uncertain, we can invoke the "equal ignorance" rule and assign equal weights (.25) to each), and choose that strategy with the highest expected value. For example, if the (subjective) probabilities or likelihood weights applied to our rival's strategies were .4, .3, .2, and .1, respectively (the sum of the weights should equal 1.0), then the expected values of our strategies 1 and 2 would be:

$$EV(1) = .4(10) + .3(40) + .2(45) + .1(60) = 31$$
$$EV(2) = .4(20) + .3(30) + .2(40) + .1(55) = 30.5$$

So, although they are not far apart, we would choose strategy 1 (lower price). (Note that the maximin criterion previously discussed amounts to assigning a probability weight of 1.0 to our rival's potentially most damaging strategy choice and a weight of 0 to his other strategy choices.)[21]

The choice of strategy made on the basis of expected value may differ from the choice made on the basis of the maximin criterion (as in the preceding example). The possibility of more than one rational solution,

[20] See Patrick Suppes and J. Marrill Carlsmith, "Experimental Analysis of a Duopoly Situation from the Standpoint of Mathematical Learning Theory," *International Economic Review*, Vol. 3, No. 1, 1962, pp. 60–78.

[21] For those interested in exploring the intricacies of decision theory, see R. D. Luce and Howard Raiffa, *Games and Decisions*, John Wiley and Sons, New York, 1957.

depending on the decision criterion chosen, may require firms to reassess and sharpen their objectives, particularly in oligopoly markets characterized by interdependence, risk, and uncertainty.

Kinked Demand

Recognized interdependence and uncertainty of rival's reactions have often combined to make oligopoly prices insensitive to market forces. An interesting explanation of the "stickiness" or relative stability of price in an oligopoly market is the kinked demand curve (Fig. 10.11).[22] It should be emphasized that this is not a price determination model. It does not pretend to explain how or why the existing price came to be, only why the existing price may be somewhat insensitive to changes in market conditions.

If the few dominant firms in the industry acted jointly, each would face a "proportionate" demand curve such as D-D in Fig. 10.11. This represents the firm's demand as a fixed proportion of the total industry demand at various prices, assuming joint pricing by all firms in the industry. Or, if the firm in question were a price leader in the industry, it might expect that its decision to raise price along the dashed section of D-D would be supported by a similar action by other firms in the industry.

If, however, the firm in question acted independently on the assumption that other firms would not respond and follow its price change, then the firm might view its demand function as d-d (the *ceteris paribus* demand curve in the monopolistic competitive model).[23] The degree of elasticity would vary with the degree of product differentiation. The more standardized the product, the more elastic the firm's anticipated (*ceteris paribus*) demand curve, d-d.

Recall that one of the salient features of oligopoly is that the impact of the activities (particularly pricing) of any one firm is likely to be felt by other firms; if, acting independently, one firm lowered price, some price reaction by rivals might be expected, so d-d is not likely to apply for prices below the existing price in an oligopoly situation.

The kinked demand curve. d-K-D, arises from the assumption that

---

[22] P. M. Sweezy, "Demand Under Conditions of Oligopoly," *JPE*, Vol. XLVII, August, 1939, pp. 568–573. Also reprinted in Stigler and Boulding, eds., *Readings in Price Theory*, Richard D. Irwin, Chicago, Ill. 1952. pp. 404–409.

[23] The two demand curves, D-D and d-d, were discussed in E. H. Chamberlin, *The Theory of Monopolistic Competition*, 7th ed., Harvard University Press, Cambridge, Mass., 1956.

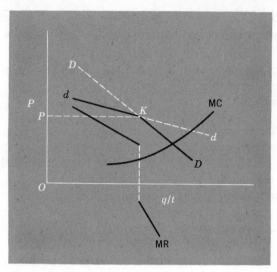

Fig. 10.11

a single firm, acting independently under normal economic conditions and uncertain about rivals' reaction, might expect rivals *not* to match the firm's decision to *raise* price above P_A (the existing price), but will expect rivals to match a decision to *lower* price. The kinked demand rests on an asymmetry in "conjectural variation" with respect to a price increase and to a price decrease. Under certain conditions, rivals are expected not to react to a price increase, but to at least match a price decrease. The firm would view its demand curve as highly elastic for prices above the prevailing price, but for prices below the kink K at the prevailing price P, the firm would expect the more inelastic demand segment KD to apply (KD is presumed inelastic in Fig. 10.11, so MR for downward price adjustments is negative).

It is possible that price cutting by the firm in question would trigger a price war where rivals decide on punitive measures such as continued price-undercutting by rivals. (Conceivably this could cause the firm's demand curve to slope in a positive direction—downward to the left from the original prevailing price.)

If a firm, acting independently, did view its demand curve as kinked with different elasticities prevailing for price changes in an upward and downward direction, there would be a discontinuity in the firm's anticipated marginal revenue function. Neither the shape of the demand function nor the marginal revenue function is known to the firm with cer-

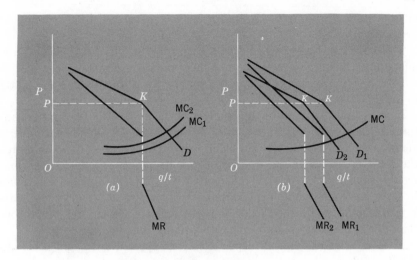

Fig. 10.12

tainty. With little knowledge of what rivals will do, the firm can only guess whether demand curve *d-d* or *D-D* applies.[24] In the Bertrand-Edgeworth duopoly model and under monopolistic competition, the firm assumed the more elastic demand *d-d* applies

If the conventional kink (*d-K-D*) applies, a firm acting independently may be discouraged from revising its price in response to changes in costs or demand, if its marginal cost continues to cut its marginal revenue in the area of the discontinuity (see Figs. 10.12*a* and 10.12*b*). The area of discontinuity may become even larger if the market weakens, since under these conditions the relevant upper section of *d-d* may be even more elastic (and the likelihood of joint action for revision of price in an upward direction is lessened). Under weak market conditions there is an increased likelihood that rivals will meet any downward price adjustment. In fact, *K-D* may be more inelastic in a weakening market, widening the area of discontinuity and discouraging any single firm from independent price cutting.

It is not unlikely, however, that some firms would attempt to sell below nominal or list prices by offering special services, discounts, freight absorption, etc., allowing *net* price to respond to a weakening market. They offer secret price decreases so that *K-d* may prevail. Even an

---

[24] It has been suggested that in a period when market demand is strong and expanding rapidly, a reverse kink (the dashed line *D-K-d* in Fig. 10.11) might be more accurate. See C. W. Efroymson, "Note on Kinked Demand Curves," *A.E.R.*, Vol. 33, March, 1943, pp. 98–109.

open price reduction by a minor firm may be permitted by the dominant firm without retaliation.

The kink itself may respond to changes in costs that are general and affect all firms; for example, an industry-wide excise tax or wage increase may move the kink upward for all firms (and perhaps slightly to the left if industry sales decrease at the higher industry price).

In an empirical study of oligopoly pricing in gasoline, cigarettes, anthracite coal, steel, and automobiles, Professor Stigler found that various versions of a price leadership model, where rivals were willing to match the leader's price increases (as well as his decreases), applied more commonly than did the kinked demand.[25] The kinked demand continues to serve as a reasonable explanation of why prices are "sticky" in markets where no established leadership pattern has arisen, and where considerable uncertainty remains regarding rivals' reaction.

The existence of the kink depends on the expected or imagined discontinuity in demand resulting from an estimation of rivals' reaction. Where the kink applies, we would expect some firms to be unwilling to revise prices upward. A firm that does go ahead and raises its price presumes that there is no kink. The kink may not apply if there is a leadership pattern, collusion, a very buoyant market, or a "shifting kink" where all react to changing conditions. The kink reveals a pattern of behavior if rivals act independently. Price rigidity in the face of changing market conditions is partial evidence of an absence of collusion. Of course, fear of public reprisal, competition from abroad, or potential entrants into the industry may also explain price rigidity. It is difficult to prove the existence of the kink, or to estimate how commonly it applies.

Average Cost Pricing

In our theory of the behavior of firms operating under various market conditions, we have concentrated on marginal analysis. We have supposed that profit-maximizing firms, while not necessarily actually employing marginal calculations in their attempt to maximize profit, would on the whole be sufficiently "rational" to achieve the results or responses implied by marginal decision rules. The outcomes of firms' (not any particular firm but the greater number) decisions would approximate the results indicated by marginal analysis—as if the industry response were the result of following marginal profit-maximizing rules.

Whether to make price behavior more stable and uniform, whether

[25] George J. Stigler, "The Kinky Oligopoly Demand Curve and Rigid Prices," *JPE*, 55, 1947, pp. 432–449.

to "justify" pricing behavior, or whether to use as a rule-of-thumb guide to pricing (lacking the additional information required of marginal analysis), oligopoly firms have often resorted to average-cost pricing. (Variations of the same technique also go by the name of full-cost pricing, cost-plus pricing, target pricing.)

Basically, average-cost pricing involves a mark-up above an estimated average cost or average variable (direct) cost.[26] The mark-up is intended to cover full costs. In multiple product situations, full-costs include the variable costs directly related to the particular product, plus the common costs that are somehow (whether on the basis of machine time, hours of direct labor costs, sales, etc.) allocated among the various products, plus some target rate of return at expected or standard output (per cent of capacity).

Average-cost pricing is sometimes used to explain the existing price at the kink in the kinked-demand analysis. Practice varies with respect to the rigidity of average-cost pricing—whether the per cent mark-up varies with fluctuation in demand or whether it is geared to average output or standard volume over several years. If demand does not support the full-cost price, or if expected output changes, then the average cost price must be varied.

It should be pointed out that average-cost pricing does not necessarily lead to results inconsistent with marginal pricing. MR = MC at the profit-maximizing output. Since $MR = P(1 + 1/e)$ and therefore $P = [e/(e+1)]MR$, a price equal to $e/(e+1)$ times MC need not differ from the profit-maximizing price. The price setter would simply have to estimate e and MC at the profit-maximizing output and apply the mark-up at this output. This is an easy task if the elasticity of demand is a constant $(\bar{e})$ and if marginal costs are constant and therefore equal to average variable costs (a not uncommon situation over a wide range of output); a fixed mark-up $[\bar{e}/(\bar{e}+1)$ times $AVC(= MC)]$ is then consistent with the (marginal) profit-maximizing price. The market will just support this price at that output where MC = MR.

Implicit Agreement: Price Leadership

Informal pricing arrangements are commonplace under oligopoly. A common industry price (however arrived at or maintained) may be the only viable alternative, under conditions of uncertainty and recognized

---

[26] See A. D. H. Kaplan, J. B. Dirlam, and R. F. Lanzillotti, *Pricing in Big Business,* Brookings, Washington, D.C., 1958; also see James S. Earley, "Marginal Policies of Excellently Managed Companies," *AER,* No. 1, March 1956.

interdependence, to continual price warfare. In some situations where markets are weak or knowledge is imperfect, considerable variation from the nominal or listed market price may be tolerated without triggering a price war. Price leadership is an informal (and often permissible) way of achieving price uniformity and stability.[27]

Any firm may play the leader's role in revising prices downward, but not necessarily with impunity if such an act is so contrary to rivals' interests that they retaliate by undercutting the price. If the kinked demand model were always a correct description of oligopoly behavior, any firm could revise prices downward and rivals would follow; however, they would not follow the independent firm's price increases. But this then would not be a leadership situation. In fact, unless there is some agreement that a price cut is in the interests of the few dominant firms, there is often great risk in attempting a downward price revision. An upward revision is likely to be profitable only if other firms follow; that is, if the leadership is accepted.[28]

There are several reasons why a firm under oligopoly may attempt price leadership and why rivals may choose to follow. Where the firm simply responds to market forces, for example, a cost increase common to all firms, and where a price increase is obviously advantageous to all, then rivals may choose to follow any firm's increase. Which firm goes first and takes the lead is not particularly important.

Let us look at two cases where a firm has an incentive to attempt price leadership. First, in Fig. 10.13a, firm 1 with a smaller, more elastic market (assume identical constant marginal costs) will prefer a lower price than firm 2 with a larger, more inelastic demand. (The "larger-smaller" qualification is only necessary if MC's are rising.) A downward price adjustment may be forced on an unwilling industry, whereas an upward price adjustment by the firm with a more inelastic market may have to be rescinded if some indefinite number of rivals facing more elastic demand curves refuses to follow. Second, in Fig. 10.13b, firm 1 with lower marginal costs will prefer a lower price than firm 2 with higher marginal costs (assume identical market demand).

Oligopoly situations tend to be much more complicated than these simple models suggest. It is easy to conceive of a situation where the

---

[27] If firms react similarly but not simultaneously to market conditions, outside observers have difficulty determining whether the similarity in price is the result of independent planning or mutual agreement; however, the continued similarity of price adjustments over time is likely to reinforce a judgement of collusion.

[28] In 1962 the initial price increase by several dominant firms in the steel industry had to be reversed when a few firms did not follow. The kink applies here, although it remains hypothetical whether the leadership situation broke down in response to economic or political pressure, or a combination of the two.

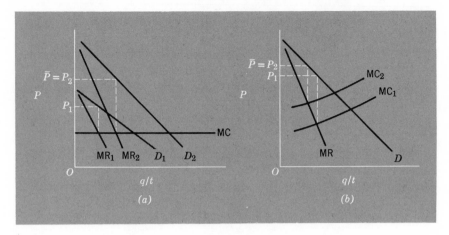

Fig. 10.13

high cost firm faces the smaller, more elastic market, and where its most advantageous price may be identical to that of the low cost firm facing the more inelastic market.

Price Leadership by a Dominant Firm

There are situations where a dominant low cost firm may set price higher than its own profit-maximizing price for noneconomic reasons. To avoid public scrutiny and possible antimonopoly regulation, the price leader may price high enough to provide a "price umbrella" over higher cost firms in order to prevent the industry from dwindling in number, perhaps becoming a duopoly or monopoly.

When a single dominant firm operates in a market with many small firms, the dominant firm may view its market as a residual, after minor firms have produced as much as they like at each price (up to the point where their $\Sigma(\text{MC}) = P$). The minor firms' supply curve would be $\Sigma(\text{MC})$ in Fig. 10.14. The dominant firm's demand curve d would be the total market demand D less the minor firm's supply $\Sigma(\text{MC})$ at any given price. The leader or dominant firm, if he chooses to view his own demand as a residual and if the minor firms are willing to react passively to the dominant leader's price, would choose to produce q_d, where his marginal costs MC_d equal his marginal revenue MR_d. Acting as a monopolist with respect to the residual demand, he would choose to produce q_d, where his marginal revenue MR_d derived from his residual demand curve equals his marginal costs, and set the

/

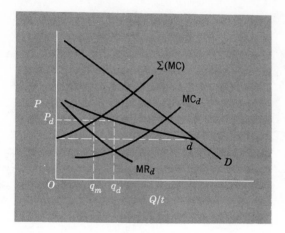

Fig. 10.14

price P_d. The minor firms would take P_d as their marginal revenue and produce q_m where $\Sigma(MC) = P_d$, which is their marginal revenue.[29]

Formal Agreements (Cartels)

Occasionally a "monopoly" solution to the oligopoly problem is possible, if the separate firms can agree to operate as a monopoly. This requires setting the monopoly price and output for the industry, and, in addition, agreeing to some basis for distributing the industry output and profit among the firms. Usually this requires collusion (often a formal agreement—a cartel), and some form of sanction or punitive measure that may be instigated against any firm that tries to break the agreement. There are numerous difficulties that may arise before formal agreement or joint action can be reached (or enforced), particularly where cartels are illegal, as they have been in the United States since the Sherman Antitrust Act of 1890.[30]

[29] A model almost identical to this was discussed using reaction curves in a duopoly situation, where one firm, knowing his rival's reaction curve (in the dominant firm case this would correspond to the minor's supply curve), acted as leader and the other firm chose to respond as expected.

[30] Cartels have been illegal except for a brief period in the depression of the 1930s when, under the National Recovery Act (1933), industrial price codes were encouraged, and except in special cirumstances such as competing in international markets, labor unions negotiating in factor markets, agricultural marketing co-operatives, and international air transport.

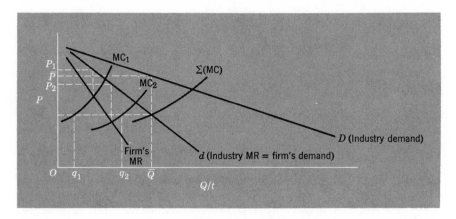

Fig. 10.15

The monopoly solution under a cartel requires that the cost of total output be minimized by allocating total output among firms (or among plants in a multiplant monopoly or merger situation) in such a manner that firms' marginal costs be equal. Total output $\bar{Q}$ would be determined at the point where the horizontal summation of firms' MC curves intersects industry MR, and a profit-maximizing price would be set at $\bar{P}$ (see Fig. 10.15.) Cost minimization would require output quotas such that firm 1 produce q_1 and firm 2 produce q_2 (where their MCs are equal). If the market demand D were divided equally between the two firms, so that each faced a demand curve, d ($= \frac{1}{2}D$ = industry MR), the two firms with different costs would prefer different prices (firm 1 would prefer P_1 and firm 2 would prefer P_2).[31]

If firms had identical costs and identical products, output could be equally divided, and all would receive an equal share of profit without redistribution. Where costs (or products) differ, there is likely to be considerable difficulty in reaching agreement on price and/or market share. If the cartel's profit is to be maximized, output quotas and market share would have to be controlled, and some redistribution of profit might be necessary.

Cartels may also face the problem of the outsider. Some firms may

[31] If the market could be segmented into separate submarkets, and if price discrimination were possible and advantageous, total output would be set where $\Sigma(\text{MR}) = \Sigma(\text{MC})$. Output quotas would be unchanged (q_1 and q_2), but sales would be allocated to equate MR in each submarket. A separate price would be set in each submarket, depending on the elasticities. Submarket prices and sales are likely to differ from those in Fig. 10.15.

find it profitable to remain outside the cartel (unless the cartel can exert some form of coercion against the outsider). The outsider may sell at the cartel's monopoly (or near monopoly) price without being restricted to any market share.[32] It would be in the members' interest to bring the outsider into the cartel. If entry into the industry is not restricted, members' market share will tend to dwindle. Where the cartel's control is partial (perhaps limited to pricing), there is often considerable rivalry among cartel members. Operating costs tend to rise as members advertise, differentiate their product, and in general explore new ways to increase their market share. If the cartel controls market share as well as price, members may attempt to increase their capacity (if output quotas are assigned on the basis of capacity). Each cartel member's market share and profit will tend to decrease, unless the cartel enjoys a strong monopoly and unless the cartel has the legal and economic power to punish the recalcitrant firm who has an incentive to price independently (perhaps because of lower marginal costs or more elastic market).

Merger is a more efficient means of reducing competition in a market. The analysis is similar to that of a cartel with the combined organization attempting to allocate output and to set price in order to approach monopoly profit.[33] Although mergers eliminate many of the cartel's problems relating to agreement among members (now merged into a single firm), there is still the problem of entry and the outsider. The merged firms may be able to effect certain economies (or diseconomies) of scale.

Summary

None of the oligopoly models just considered has been general enough to apply under any set of conditions. Unless all firms face identical demand and cost conditions, the existing price (assumed in the kinked-demand analysis) is not likely to be the most advantageous one for every firm involved. We have considered some of the economic reasons

---

[32] The analysis would be similar to the model of the dominant firm facing a residual demand. The cartel's demand would be reduced by the outsider's MC curve.

[33] We are concerned with horizontal merger here among firms selling in the same market. Other forms of merger are possible. Vertical merger involves merger between buyer and seller involved in different stages of the production process. Recently, conglomerate mergers have been more common than the other two types combined. A conglomerate merer takes place when firms in different industries combine and reorganize into a single enterprise. See D. Patinkin, "Multiple-Plant Firms, Cartels, and Imperfect Competition," *QJE*, 66, Feb. 1947, pp. 173–205.

for accepting an existing price, for preferring an alternative price, and for implementing a price revision.

The kinked-demand analysis is usually applied to a firm considering independent action. Price leadership models are examples of informal pricing procedures to avoid charges of overt collusion. There is no sharp distinction between the various forms of organization found in oligopoly industries. In fact, except for the possibility of strong punitive measures or government sanction, even a formal cartel-like organizational structure faces problems similar to those that apply in informal leadership situations.

It is very likely that oligopoly firms under conditions of interdependency and uncertainty will engage in rivalry far more intense than the impersonal kind of competition under purely (or monopolistically) competitive conditions. On the other hand, particularly where barriers to entry into the industry are substantial and firms have developed informal agreements or operating rules satisfactory to all, price competition is often "out-of-bounds" and price quite insensitive to market forces under oligopoly. Cartels and mergers were considered as formal methods of organizing to reduce competition and rivalry. Even when permitted or encouraged, they were not always able to completely insulate themselves from competitive forces.

Oligopoly tends to be the dominant market structure in manufacturing industries. Concentration of industry output among a few firms is high in automobiles, flat glass, aluminum, cigarettes, and rubber tires, among many others.

Just how far pricing and output under oligopoly differ from pure competition depends largely on how restrictive are the barriers to entry, and on how successful the firms are in reaching agreements (informal or formal) that permit the firms to approach the monopoly price-output solution. Entry-limiting pricing (to cope with potential competition) may keep oligopoly pricing closer to competitive levels than would be the case where no threat of potential forms of competition existed. Technology (internal economies) and limited market may prevent the formation or continuation of a purely competitive market. Where there are strong economies of scale, a few large firms may be able to produce at lower costs than many less-than-optimal-sized small firms. Whether or not the lower costs will be passed on to consumers in the form of lower price will depend on which oligopoly model applies—whether the large few manage to contain price rivalry. Pricing under oligopoly, because of the dangers and uncertainty involved, is likely to be more insensitive to market forces (changes in conditions underlying supply and demand) than under purely competitive conditions. It is output rather than price which is more likely to fluctuate with changes in market demand. Price is likely to be responsive to general changes in supply.

Nonprice competition is likely to replace price competition under oligopoly, at least to the extent that the rivals are successful in stifling price competition. Behavior under oligopoly may vary; we have looked at only a partial sample of the models advanced to explain some facets of oligopoly behavior. In general, firms under oligopoly have greater discretion and compete over a broader spectrum (price, quality, advertising, multiple-products, market share, etc.,) than do firms under pure competition.

11

Income Distribution and Factor Markets

Most of the income distributed in this society results from payments for the use of resources. In the private sector of the economy, the earnings of resource owners are costs of production to business firms. The theory of resource pricing and allocation is fundamental to a complete understanding of how income is distributed.

Let us look then at markets for resources. On the demand side the firm is the buyer of resources, whereas on the supply side the resource owner is the seller of resources. If the supplier of the resource is another firm at some lower stage in the production process, such as a coal mining company supplying coke for a steel-making operation, the analysis on the supply side is identical to that of the firm supplying or selling some final product. In the final product market, the firm is the supplier trying to maximize profit from the sale of its product, while the buyer of the product is the consumer, trying to maximize satisfaction; in the resource market, the buyer is the firm hiring the productive services of resources for their contribution to the firm's product.

The Demand Side: Marginal Productivity Theory as an Explanation of Income Distribution

We shall examine the demand for resources in terms of marginal productivity theory. Marginal productivity theory is not intended as a complete explanation of income distribution; it has nothing to offer regarding the supply of a primary resource, where the resource owner is a household attempting to maximize utility.

Marginal productivity theory is principally an explanation of the demand for resources by a profit-maximizing firm. In a short period, where resource supply can be considered fixed and thus resource pricing may

209

be viewed as demand determined, marginal productivity theory can be taken as an explanation of income distribution. Its predictive accuracy depends on the realism of the profit-maximizing objective, on the ability of firms to measure the marginal physical (and value) contributions of resource units, or on their ability to implement profit-maximizing objectives in some other way (perhaps using a rule-of-thumb leading to a profit-maximizing outcome).[1]

In the case of the profit-maximizing firm, we assumed that the firm was combining resources as efficiently as possible. Subject to the constraints of time and technology, we concluded that the firm would produce its product up to that rate at which $MR_x = MC_x$. The assumption that the firm is maximizing profit implies that all variable resources will be combined in such a manner that they are equally efficient at the margin of use. For maximum efficiency at any output, the last dollar outlay on any one resource makes the same contribution to production as does the last dollar spent on any other resource. We discussed this condition for maximum efficiency in an earlier chapter; it is called the principle of substitution. The equality of the ratios of marginal product to price of the variable resources employed by the firm, $MP_a/P_a = MP_b/P_b$, is a condition for the least cost of production for any given output. (It is also a condition for achieving maximum output for a given outlay.) At various rates of production, average variable cost will be a minimum if this equality condition is met. In the long run all resources are variable and average cost will be minimized if the equality condition holds with respect to all resources used by the firm.

Firm's Optimum Input Purchases

At the firm's profit-maximizing output where $MR_x = MC_x$, each variable resource will be employed up to the point where its contribution to the firm's total revenue—the marginal revenue product (MRP)—equals the addition to the total cost of hiring an additional unit of the resource or factor—the marginal factor cost (MFC); in equilibrium, $MR_x = MC_x$ and $MRP_a = MFC_a$, where the subscript a is any variable input and the subscript x is the output of the production process.

Marginal revenue product is defined generally as the addition to total revenue as an additional factor unit is hired, $\Delta TR/\Delta_a$. This ad-

[1] See R. L. Hall and C. J. Hitch, "Price Theory and Business Behavior," *Oxford Economic Papers*, No. 2, 1939; Richard A. Lester, "Shortcomings of Marginal Analysis for Wage-Employment Problems," *American Economic Review*, Vol. XXXVI, March 1946; and Fritz Machlup, "Marginal Analysis and Empirical Research," *American Economic Review*, Vol. XXXVI, September 1946.

dition to total revenue is the product of two components: the marginal product in physical terms of an additional input unit ($MP_a = \Delta x/\Delta a$) and the marginal revenue from an additional unit of output ($MR_x = \Delta TR/\Delta x$). $MRP_a = MP_a \cdot MR_x = \Delta x/\Delta a \cdot \Delta TR/\Delta x = \Delta TR/\Delta a$.[2]

Under purely competitive conditions in the product market where the firm cannot affect product price, marginal revenue MR_x and price P_x are

Table 1

A. Pure Competition

Unit of Factor A	Physical Output	MP	Product Price	VMP
9	180	—	$10	
10	200	20	10	$200
11	210	10	10	100
12	215	5	10	50

B. Monopoly

Unit of Factor A	Physical Output	MP	Product Price	$MRP\left(\dfrac{\Delta TR}{\Delta a}\right)$ *
9	180	—	$10.5	
10	200	20	10	$+110
11	210	10	9.50	−5
12	215	5	9	−60

---

* The computation of the MRP values is illustrated below:

$200 \times 10 \ = \ \$2000$	$200 \times \$10 \ = \$2000$	$210 \times \$9.50 = \$1995.00$
$180 \times 10.5 = \underline{\quad 1890}$	$210 \times \quad 9.50 = \underline{\quad 1995}$	$215 \times \quad 9.00 = \underline{\quad 1935.00}$
$+\$110$	$-\$5$	$-\$60$

[2] Proof that $MRP_a = MP_a \cdot MR_x$. By definition, $MRP_a = \Delta TR/\Delta a$ and $MP_a = \Delta x/\Delta a$. Recall the relationship betweeen marginal revenue, price, and price elasticity of demand: $MR_x = P(1 + 1/e)$. Now

$$\Delta TR = (P + \Delta P)(x + \Delta x) - Px = P\Delta x + x\Delta P + \Delta P\Delta x$$

We assume the last term ($\Delta P \cdot \Delta x$) is negligible. Thus

$$MRP_a = \frac{\Delta TR}{\Delta a} = \frac{\Delta x}{\Delta a}P + \frac{x\Delta P}{\Delta a} = \frac{\Delta x}{\Delta a}\left(P + x\frac{\Delta P}{\Delta x}\right) = \frac{\Delta x}{\Delta a}\left(P + \frac{P \cdot x \cdot \Delta P}{P \cdot \Delta x}\right)$$

$$= \frac{\Delta x}{\Delta a} \cdot P\left(1 + \frac{1}{e}\right) = MP_a \cdot MR_x$$

identical. Where $MR_x = P_x$, marginal revenue product MRP_a is usually referred to as the value of the marginal product VMP_a.

If $MR_x = MC_x$ in the product market, each variable resource must be employed up to the point where $MRP_a = MFC_a$. This follows since, whatever the rate of output, the least cost combination of resources requires that the ratios (MP_a/P_a) be equal for all variable resources. If resources are not employed according to this principle of substitution, costs can be reduced by substituting a resource that makes a greater contribution per dollar for one that makes a lesser contribution per dollar, until the ratios—marginal product to resource price—are equal for all variable resources, and resources are again employed in optimal proportion. If $MP_a/P_a = MP_b/P_b$, the equality will also hold true for the inverse of the ratios, $P_a/MP_a = P_b/MP_b$. If output is increased by varying a single variable input, the inverse form of the ratio, P_a/MP_a, represents the marginal cost of producing an additional unit of output, MC_x:

$$\frac{P_a}{MP_a} = \frac{P_a}{\Delta x/\Delta a} = \frac{\Delta a \cdot P_a}{\Delta x} = \frac{\Delta TC}{\Delta x} = MC_x{}^2$$

Even in the more general case with more than one variable input, the least cost condition that holds everywhere along the firm's equilibrium

---

[2] More generally with at least two variable inputs, the marginal cost of an expansion in output may be defined as:

$$\frac{\partial a}{\partial x} P_a + \frac{\partial b}{\partial x} P_b + \cdots = MC_x.$$

The necessary equilibrium condition for the least cost combination of inputs for a given output may be derived by minimizing the Lagrangian function: $L = C + \lambda [\bar{x} - x(a,b)]$, where $C = P_a \cdot a + P_b \cdot b$ is the cost function, $x = x(a,b)$ is the production function, $\bar{x}$ is a given output, and λ is the constant Lagrangian multiplier. Cost is minimized subject to the constraint of the production function.

The necessary cost-minimizing conditions are:

$$\frac{\partial L}{\partial a} = P_a - \lambda \left(\frac{\partial x}{\partial a} \right) = 0; \lambda = \frac{P_a}{\partial x/\partial a}; \text{ or } P_a = \lambda \left(\frac{\partial x}{\partial a} \right)$$

$$\frac{\partial L}{\partial a} = P_b - \lambda \left(\frac{\partial x}{\partial b} \right) = 0; \lambda = \frac{P_b}{\partial x/\partial b}; \text{ or } P_b = \lambda \left(\frac{\partial x}{\partial b} \right)$$

Substituting the expression for P_a and P_b into our definition of marginal cost:

$$MC_x = \frac{\partial a}{\partial x} \left(\lambda \frac{\partial x}{\partial a} \right) + \frac{\partial b}{\partial x} \left(\lambda \frac{\partial x}{\partial b} \right) = \lambda \left(\frac{\partial a}{\partial x} \cdot \frac{\partial x}{\partial a} + \frac{\partial b}{\partial x} \cdot \frac{\partial x}{\partial b} \right) = \lambda$$

We see that in equilibrium the constant λ equals marginal cost and equals each of the ratios: input price/marginal product.

$$\lambda = MC = \frac{P_a}{\partial x/\partial a} = \frac{P_b}{\partial x/\partial b}$$

where $\partial x/\sigma a$ and $\partial x/\sigma b$ are the marginal products of a and b.

expansion path can now be written as follows (see argument in footnote 2): $P_a/\text{MP}_a = P_b/\text{MP}_b = \text{MC}_x$. This extended statement of the principle of substitution implies that, at the margin, the addition to total cost of making a small addition to total product will be about the same, no matter which factor or combination of factors is used more intensively to achieve the incremental addition to total product. The equilibrium conditions for both the product and factor markets are combined in Eq. 11.1:

$$\left[\frac{P_a}{\text{MP}_a} = \frac{P_b}{\text{MP}_b} = \text{MC}_x\right] = \text{MR}_x \qquad (11.1)$$

If the least cost condition in the brackets holds, resources will be employed in optimal proportions to minimize cost at any output; if, in addition, $\text{MC}_x = \text{MR}_x$, the profit-maximizing rate of input purchase will be achieved—inputs will be hired in optimal amounts. Since the equilibrium condition, $P_a/\text{MP}_a = P_b/\text{MP}_b$, is equivalent to MC_x, and since $\text{MC}_x = \text{MR}_x$, multiplying through $(P_a/\text{MP}_a = \text{MR}_x)$ by MP_a yields $P_a = \text{MP}_a \cdot \text{MR}_x = \text{MRP}_a$; or multiplying $P_b/\text{MP}_b = \text{MR}_x$ by MP_b yields $P_b = \text{MP}_b \cdot \text{MR}_x = \text{MRP}_b$. Where firms purchase resources under purely competitive conditions, $P_a(= \text{AFC}_a) = \text{MFC}_a$. The extra cost of hiring an additional unit of the factor is then simply the constant factor price.

When we presented the argument for the least cost condition, we assumed that factor prices were constant and not affected by the quantity of the factor purchased by the firm. This is equivalent to assuming that the firm is a purely competitive buyer of the factor. In general, when $\text{MC}_x = \text{MR}_x$, $\text{MFC} = \text{MRP}$ for all variable factors employed by the firm.

The Firm's Demand for Labor or Any Factor

In purely competitive markets the firm views factor price(s) and product price as constants (factor supply and product demand curves are infinitely elastic to the purely competitive firm). The value of the marginal product (VMP_a) from employing an additional unit of input A is the marginal physical product MP_a multiplied by the price of the output P_x:

$$\text{VMP}_a = \text{MP}_a \cdot P_x = \frac{\Delta \text{Total Revenue}[3]}{\Delta a}$$

[3] This is quite different from the value of the average product of the input, which would be computed by taking the total physical product, dividing by the number of input units involved, and multiplying the quotient (the average physical product) by the product price.

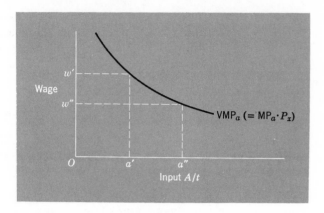

Fig. 11.1

Our emphasis is on the marginal decision—the value of an input's contribution at the margin. As additional units of some variable input (in this case labor) are added to existing (fixed) inputs, we expect that the law of diminishing returns will eventually apply, and MP_a will eventually decrease. In our discussion of production theory, we concluded that the marginal product function will be negatively sloping in the region in which input A can be profitably employed. With P_x constant, the VMP_a ($= P_x \cdot MP_a$) function, too, will be negatively sloping, as in Fig. 11.1. An increase in either the marginal product curve MP_a or in the product price P_x will cause the VMP_a function to shift to the right.

Given the VMP function for a variable resource whose wage rate is at a certain level w', it will pay the employer to hire a' units of this variable input A. If the wage rate that the firm must pay were somehow lowered from w' to w'', it would pay the firm to hire additional units, since the value of their marginal product would be greater than the marginal factor cost—the extra revenue to the firm would exceed the extra cost of hiring the additional units. Under pure competition in the product market, the VMP_a function is a first-order approximation of the firm's demand curve for the input.[4] In general, under any market structure, the demand curve for an input is the marginal revenue product function, $MRP_a = MP_a \cdot MR_x$.

The firm's demand curve for a resource MRP tends to be more inelas-

---

[4] We qualify this later when we consider that input A may be related (substitute or complement) to other inputs; the marginal products of other inputs may shift as more of A is used and this may induce a shift in MP_A (and in VMP_A). Also, if all firms expand output in response to a change in resource price, the product price P_x may decrease.

tic, (1) the more inelastic is the demand for the product, (2) the more inelastic is the supply of substitute (or cooperant) factors, and (3) the more limited are the opportunities for substitution among factors. The first condition relates to the product market, the second to the supply curve of other factors, and the third to the shape of the production function. The most relevant characteristic of the production function for the purpose of considering the derived demand for factors of production is the substitutability between factors, which may be measured by the elasticity of substitution (σ).[5]

The elasticity of substitution between factors 1 and 2 (σ_{12}) can be defined as the relative change in factor proportion with respect to a relative change in the factor price ratio:

$$\sigma_{12} = \frac{\Delta(X_1/X_2)}{(X_1/X_2)} \Big/ \frac{\Delta(P_2/P_1)}{(P_2/P_1)}$$

(The inversion of subscripts permits a positive value for σ_{12}.)

A decrease in P_2/P_1 will induce an increase in X_2/X_1, but to consider the relation between the distributive shares of two factors and the elasticity of substitution between two factors, let us consider the absolute or numerical value of σ. If $\sigma < 1$ (inelastic), a relative decrease in P_2/P_1 will induce a less than proportionate increase in X_2/X_1, and X_2's distributive share—$P_2X_2/(P_1X_1 + P_2X_2)$—will decrease. If $\sigma > 1$ (elastic), where X_2/X_1 is responsive to a relative decrease in P_2/P_1, X's share of the total pie would increase. In the unit elastic case, where $\sigma = 1$, the relative changes in the price and quantity ratios would just counterbalance each other. With the elasticity of substitution equal to unity, there would be no change in relative distributive shares of the two factors.[6]

---

[5] See M. Bronfenbrenner, "Notes on the Elasticity of Derived Demand," pp. 254–261, and J. R. Hicks, "Marshall's Third Rule: A Further Comment," pp. 262–265, *Oxford Economic Papers*, Oct. 1961.

Professor Bronfenbrenner makes explicit the complicated and uncertain effect of k—the share of a particular factor's cost in total cost—on the elasticity of the derived demand for a factor. Marshall's controversial third law of derived demand stipulated that the smaller a factor's share in total cost, the less elastic would be the derived demand for the factor. Although this may very well hold true in the short run, the direction and magnitude of k's impact on the elasticity of derived demand depends on the relative signs and magnitudes of the elasticities of product demand, substitution, and factor supply.

[6] The elasticity of substitution can be expressed in terms of X_2/X_1 and the rate of technical substitution—$RTS = MP_2/MP_1$. Refer back to the discussion of isoquants and price lines, and recall that in equilibrium the cost at any output (along any isoquant) is minimized at the points of tangency between the isoquants and the price lines where the slopes are equal $(P_2/P_1 = MP_2/MP_1)$.

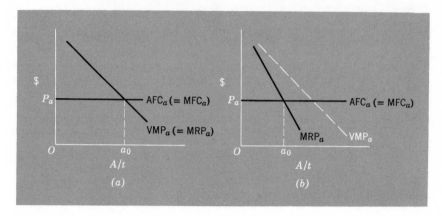

Fig. 11.2

Value to Firm versus Value to Society

The price of the product P_x is a measure of the product's value to society. The value of the marginal product VMP_a is a measure of an input's value to society—its marginal physical contribution MP_a times product price P_x. The marginal revenue product MRP_a is, in general, the input's value to the firm—the addition to the firm's total revenue from an additional input unit: $MRP_a = MP_a \cdot MR_x = \Delta TR/\Delta a$. Since the product demand curve facing the firm has a negative slope (and a finite negative elasticity) under imperfect conditions in the product market, MR_x is less than P_x as additional units of output are sold. Under purely competitive conditions, where $P_x = MR_x$, $MRP_a = VMP_a$ ($= MP_a \cdot P_x$).[7] In an imperfect product market, the value to the firm of the contribution of an additional input unit—MRP_a ($= MP_a \cdot MR_x$)—would be something less than VMP_a ($= MP_a \cdot P_x$). (Remember P_x is a uniform price that applies to all units, so when P_x decreases, $MR_x < P_x$.) Under imperfect competition the change in total revenue attributable to the input is MRP_a, which is less than VMP_a, since $MR_x < P_x$; so the value of an input to a hiring firm MRP cannot be expected to equal its value to society VMP in an imperfectly competitive market. Under purely competitive conditions, $MRP = VMP$.

[7] Under conditions of pure competition in the product market, $P_x = MR_x$, since the demand curve facing the firm is infinitely elastic. $MR_x = P_x + P_x/e$ reduces to $MR_x = P_x$, since $e = -\infty$ and $P_x/e = 0$. Under imperfect market conditions where e is some finite negative value, $P_x > MR_x$, since P_x/e is negative.

The marginal revenue product is the firm's demand curve for the input—the value of the input to the firm. The factor supply P_a, where the firm is a perfectly competitive buyer, is constant—$AFC_a = MFC_a$. Fig. 11.2a shows the demand for input A in a purely competitive market (where $MRP_a = VMP_a$), and Fig. 11.2b shows the demand in an imperfectly competitive market (where $VMP_a > MRP_a$).[8]

Qualifications on Demand for a Factor

Where several variable factors are involved and are not independent in production, a single VMP (or MRP) will not suffice to describe the firm's demand for the resource. Adjustments in other resources employed will be required as more of resource A is used. If other resources, whether they be substitutes or complements of A, are to be used in optimal proportion with A ($MP_a/P_a = MP_b/P_b$), higher-order adjustments with respect to A and the other resources must be made.[9]

[8] If VMP_a is reserved for the purely competitive situation where P is constant, then in an imperfectly competitive market there would be no VMP_a. Where P_x changes with an increase in inputs hired and output sold, $P_x \cdot MP_a$ is sometimes called "marginal value product"—the change in the VMP due to changes in MP_a *and* in P_x as an additional output unit is hired.

[9] Suppose A and B are complements. As P_a decreases, more of A is used; as more of A is used, the marginal product of the complementary factor B will increase and MP_b will shift to the right. If P_b remains constant, more of B will be used, leading to a shift to the right of MP_a (and a corresponding shift in VMP_a). If A and B were substitutes, MP_b would shift to the left as more units of A were used, and MP_a would still shift to the right when the second-order response is made to fewer units of B. In the diagram in this footnote, A and B are complements.

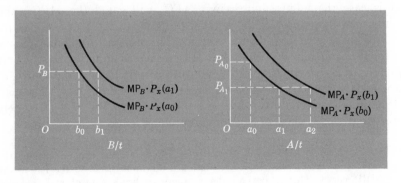

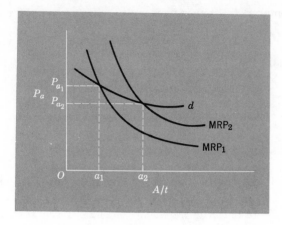

Fig. 11.3

The firm's demand for input A, where other factors are not independent of input A, is illustrated in Fig. 11.3. As P_a falls and more of A is employed, it is likely that the MRP_a will shift to the right, and the firm's demand for A will not lie along the initial MRP_a function but will lie along points connecting MRP_a functions.[10]

Pure Competition in Buying and Selling Inputs

If the firm purchases the services of the input in a purely competitive market where there are many buyers, the firm will not be able to affect the market price of the input by varying the number of units hired. In this case the input supply curve AFC_a will equal the MFC_a, and the marginal factor cost of the input will appear to the firm as a parameter—the unvarying unit factor cost w_0. The general profit-maximizing rule for hiring resources still applies. Hire resources up to the point where $MFC = MRP$—where the additional cost of purchasing a resource or factor equals the extra revenue that results from the purchase. The general marginal productivity principle is illustrated in Fig. 11.4 for purely competitive conditions in the factor and product market.

[10] If as a result of a decrease in factor price, all user firms expand output, the price of the product P_x may decrease, causing a downward shift to the left in the firm's MRP curve. This is beyond the competitive firm's control and is called an "external effect" of a change in factor price.

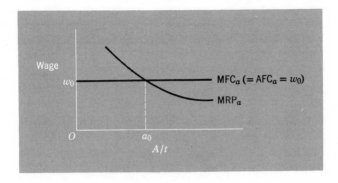

Fig. 11.4

Monopsony Buyer

Monopsony exists where a single employer can influence input price. A single buyer (monopsonist), by employing fewer units of the input, can effect a reduction in the input supply price. The argument is analogous to that of a single seller (monopolist), able to influence product price by varying output.

In an imperfectly competitive market, where the firm is able to affect the input price by varying its rate of purchase, the input supply curve AFC_a slopes upward, as in Fig. 11.5. By the same reasoning that applied to demand and marginal revenue in the product market, the MFC_a

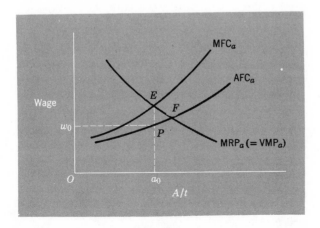

Fig. 11.5

will lie above the upward sloping input supply curve AFC_a. $MFC = AFC(1 + 1/e_s)$, where e_s is the positive elasticity of supply; therefore $MFC\text{-}AFC = AFC/e_s$, which is a positive number. The monopsonist's resource supply curve is the market supply—there is no other buyer in the market. Resources may be specialized or lack mobility, thus affording the monopsonist some control over resource price. Resource hiring and pricing by a single buyer (a monopsonist) is illustrated in Fig. 11.5, where the monopsonist is also a purely competitive seller (no *one* seller is able to affect the single product price that applies to all). All input units are homogeneous and paid at a uniform rate.

Suppose the buyer is an employer who wishes to decide the most favorable rate of employment for his enterprise. The sellers are individual unorganized labor units. The supply curve of labor—the number of hours work that laborers are willing to supply at given prices w—is the monopsonist's average factor cost. The monopsonist's ability to keep the wage rate low by restricting the rate of hire depends on a positively sloping market supply curve. If the average factor cost curve AFC is rising, the marginal factor cost MFC must be greater than the average factor cost AFC. The rising AFC reflects the willingness of additional labor units to work only if the wage rate is increased.[11]

It will not pay the monopsonist to hire beyond a_0, where the MFC—the addition to total cost—begins to exceed the marginal revenue product MRP. The profit-maximizing rate of purchase is at a_0, where $MFC_a = MRP_a$. If all inputs were hired according to this simple but reasonable rule, maximum profit could be achieved by the hiring firm.[12]

The profit-maximizing factor price at this rate of hire is w_0 on the resource supply curve AFC_a. This would be the minimum wage that must be paid by the monopsonist to secure the services of a_0 units of labor.

The triangular area EPF in Fig. 11.5 is a measure of the social loss due to monopsony. At a_0 the resource's contribution to the firm is greater than its opportunity cost (the value of its contribution in some best alternative use). Hiring is restricted to a_0, where $MRP_a > w_0$.[13]

[11] The cost of an additional input unit to a monopsonist is MFC_a, not AFC_a. We therefore must generalize our rule for obtaining the least-cost combination of resources at any given output. Instead of using factor price, which equalled MFC_a under purely competitive buying conditions, our rule now is: $MP_a/MFC_a = MP_b/MFC_b$. MP/MFC is now marginal product per additional dollar expenditure at the margin of purchase.

[12] It may not be simple in application. It may be quite difficult to determine, even in physical terms, the marginal product (the addition to total output) that would result from hiring an additional unit.

[13] See M. Bronfenbrenner, "Potential Monopsony in Labor Markets," *ILRR*, 9, July 1956, pp. 577–588.

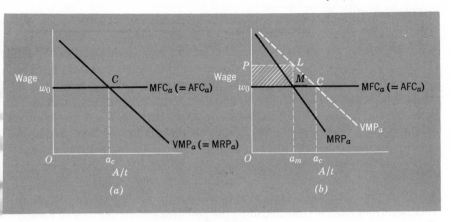

Fig. 11.6

Monopoly Seller

Now let us take the case of a firm that sells in a monopoly product market, but buys in a purely competitive market (see Fig. 11.6). As a buyer, the firm faces an infinitely elastic resource supply curve—the firm cannot affect the resource price by varying its rate of purchase (MFC = AFC, as in Fig. 11.4). When the hiring firm sells in a monopoly product market, the value of an additional man to the firm depends on the additional revenue that accrues from the sale of the MP_a—this is the value of the additional man's contribution to the firm (MRP_a). We know that when a firm sells in a monopolistic market where the product demand curve has a negative slope ($P_x > MR_x$), the firm's demand curve for the resource is the $MRP_a (= MP_a \cdot MR_x)$ curve, which lies below the $VMP_a (= MP_a \cdot P_x)$ curve—the resource's contribution to society.

Earlier we concluded that the profit-maximizing monopolist has an incentive to restrict product output to the point where $MC_x = MR_x$, short of the socially optimal output where $MC_x = P_x$. This restrictive tendency applies, as well, to the factor market, where the monopolist has an incentive to restrict his rate of input hire to the point where MFC = MRP, where the additional cost of hiring an additional input unit equals the additional revenue to the firm. If $P_x > MR_x$, $VMP_x > MRP_x$; society would gain if hiring were carried to a_c (in Fig. 11.6b), where $MFC_a = VMP_a$ instead of restricted to a_m, where $MFC_a = MRP_a$.

Comparing the monopoly seller to the purely competitive seller in Fig. 11.6, we can see the sense in which underemployment of resources exists under monopoly. It would not pay the monopolist to hire an additional input unit beyond a_m, where $MFC_a = MRP_a$, even through

$VMP_a > MRP_a$ at that rate of hire. The purely competitive seller will tend to hire up to a_c, where $MFC_a = VMP_a(= MRP_a)$—where input price w_0 equals the society's valuation of the input's contribution VMP. When a purely competitive seller and monopoly seller employ the same resource, the resource would be misallocated. Society would gain, that is, the value of the net social product would increase, if an input unit were transferred (reallocated) from the competitive firm (in Fig. 11.6a) to the monopoly firm (in Fig. 11.6b), since at the margin of hire VMP_a is greater in the monopoly market than in the purely competitive market. Whenever a resource transfers from a use where it is making a smaller contribution to one where it can make a larger contribution, there will be a net gain in output. The value of the total product would continue to increase from such a transfer, until the resource's contributions to society (VMP) were equal in all uses. The triangular area LMC in Fig. 11.6b is a measure of the net social loss attributable to monopoly.

The shaded area Pw_0LM in Fig. 11.6b has been called "monopolistic exploitation." It is a rent that accrues to the firm due to firm's monopoly power in the product market. The value of the resource's contribution to society VMP is greater than its value to the monopolist MRP at a_m, where $w_0 = MRP (< VMP)$.

In Fig. 11.7, the firm is a monopsonist buyer, in addition to being a monopolist seller: $AFC < MFC$, and $MRP < VMP$. The shaded area Tw_1EP is a rent that accrues to the firm; it has been called "monopsonistic exploitation." Monopsonistic exploitation exists if, at the margin of purchase, the wage rate is below the MRP—the value of the resource's

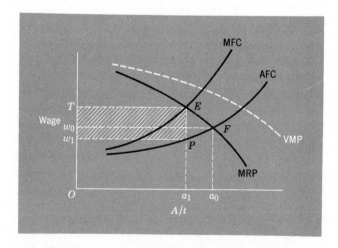

Fig. 11.7

contribution to the firm. At a_1 (in Fig. 11.7), $w_1 <$ MRP. The resource, in this monopsonistic situation, earns less than its value to the firm. Resources are paid less than they contribute to the firm's receipts. In this sense resources are "exploited"—a rather "value loaded" term. The monopsonistic power of the firm has its source in the positively sloping input supply curve AFC. The positive slope is due to immobility of resources, and to the absence of real or known alternatives—the result of ignorance, specialization, or insecurity. Because the input supply curve is positively sloping, and the elasticity of supply e_s is positive, the cost to the firm of the marginal unit MFC lies above the average factor cost AFC: MFC $=$ AFC$(1 + 1/e_s)$. MFC $-$ AFC $=$ AFC$/e_s$ is a measure of the firm's monopsony power.

In this situation the firm, by hiring a_1 units of labor (or any other factor) instead of a_0, is able to keep the wage rate at w_1. If it expands its operation by hiring additional workers $(a_1$-$a_0)$, a higher rate w_0 must be paid not only to the additional workers hired, but to all those previously employed at a lower wage. If a_0 are hired, even those workers who evidently were willing to work for wage rate w_1 must now be paid w_0 (unless the monopsonist discriminates and pays different rates to different people for the same work). In a monopsony situation, the firm finds it profitable to restrict output to a_1—the profit-maximizing hiring point where MFC $=$ MRP. At this rate of hire, the wage rate is kept at w_1 rather than allowed to rise to w_0. Measures to counteract monopsony power include affecting the structure of the buying market (increasing the number of sellers), directly influencing the resource price (a minimum wage), opposing monopsony power by some countervailing power (unionization), and reducing monopsony power by increasing resource mobility. Increasing mobility means providing more effective alternatives through improvement in the dissemination of job information, increasing the opportunities for job training, and assisting in relocation.

Suppose monopsony power were neutralized by a public minimum wage law or by unionization, so that the lower section of the input supply curve appeared to the firm as a horizontal line. For the section of the supply affected (up to the point where MFC$_a$ reaches the limit set by the demand curve MRP$_a$), the MFC$_a$ to the firm would equal the AFC$_a$, the authorized wage (w_0 in Fig. 11.7). The result would be an increase in the wage paid by the firm (w_1 to w_0) and, in addition, an increase in the number of input units hired. At a fixed minimum wage, w_0, output would be carried to a_0, where $w_0 =$ MRP$_a$—monopsony power would be negated. If the minimum wage is increased above w_0 (where the original positively sloping supply curve AFC crosses the

MRP function), then the inverse relation between the wage rate and the quantity hired would hold.[14] We may note, too, that same monopsonists, whose competitive position depended on exploitation, may be driven out of business as a result of the neutralization of their monopsony power.

Bilateral Monopoly

In the case illustrated in Fig. 11.7, the monopsony buyer had things his own way. Facing a positively sloping input supply curve, he was able to restrict the rate of purchase in order to buy at a lower price. Now suppose the sellers were to combine. For example, suppose workers organize to form a union. In effect, they become a single seller—a monopolist to "countervail" the power of the single buyer, the monopsonist. When a single seller faces a single buyer, we have what is called bilateral monopoly.

The monopsony buyer (B) would still like to hire up to the point where his marginal factor cost equals his marginal revenue product $(MFC_B = MRP_B)$. At this rate of purchase a_B he would like to set an input price w_B along the input supply curve AFC_B—as it appears to him, the buyer. This part of the analysis of bilateral monopoly (illustrated in Fig. 11.8) does not differ from our previous analysis of the monopsony case (refer to Fig. 11.7).

We shall take the monopoly seller's supply curve $(AFC_B$ to the buyer) to be the marginal cost of supplying labor services (MC_S).[15] This seller's supply curve represents the rate at which the monopoly seller is willing to supply labor as a function of various given prices (or wages). The buyer's demand curve MRP_B is viewed by the monopoly seller as a demand or average revenue curve (AR_S). The seller's marginal revenue curve (MR_S) represents the additional revenue derived from the sale of additional labor service.

The monopoly seller would like to sell units of labor service up to the point a_S where the marginal revenue from the sale of the input equals

[14] Of course, as the wage rate increases, the *ceteris paribus* condition that underlies partial equilibrium analysis may have to be relaxed if we are to examine the implications of the wage change beyond the first-order effects. As the wage increases, more of other factors may be substituted for labor and, since MC will increase, there is an incentive to reduce output. One or both of the components of MRP (MP and MR_x) may be affected. (Refer back to Fig. 11.3.)

[15] In Fig. 11.8, the monopoly seller's supply (MC_S), demand (AR_S), and marginal revenue (MR_S) curves are set in( ) with a subscript, S, to distinguish them from the monopsony buyer's curves. The unit bought or sold is a unit of labor service.

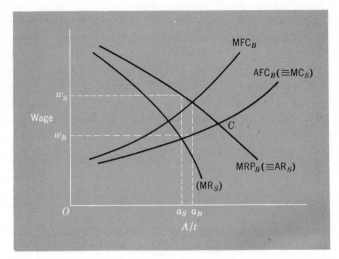

Fig. 11.8

the marginal cost of supplying the input ($MR_S = MC_S$).[16] At this rate of sale, the monopolist would like to set the price of its product (labor service) at w_S along the demand curve—$MRP_B(\equiv AR_S)$.

It should be evident from the analysis that there is a gap or area of indeterminacy between the preferred selling price of the monopoly seller (w_S) and the monopsony buyer's preferred purchase price w_B. (As the curves are drawn in Fig. 11.8, there is also a discrepancy between the preferred rates of sale and purchase, a_S and a_B.) Whether the final agreement will lie closer to w_S or w_B depends on the many factors that determine whether buyer or seller will have the upper hand. These factors—market power, financial strength, attitude toward risk, utilities of gains and losses inherent in the particular bargaining situation, and skill in negotiations—if known and specified, can lead to a determinate solution. Apart from this formal possibility, it is fair to say that the solution, within the framework of our simple, two-variable supply and demand analysis, is indeterminate.

In addition to the indeterminacy of the solution, we may also question

---

[16] Note that the MR_S curve is the only additional curve needed in the bilateral monopoly analysis, as compared to the case of a single firm who purchased in a monopsony market and sold its product in a monopoly market (illustrated in Fig. 11.7). Whether or not the monopsonist sells in a competitive or monopoly product market is of secondary importance to the bilateral monopoly model. The degree of monopoly power in the product market is, however, likely to influence the strength of its bargaining position as a monopsony buyer.

the stability of the bilateral monopoly situation. Because of the difficulty of reaching agreement and because the agreement once reached may not be entirely satisfactory to either party, buyer and seller may tire of bilateral negotiations. If buyer and seller were able to effect a vertical merger (or agree to combine against the rest of the world) they could increase their combined profit by setting a rate of purchase and purchase price at point C (in Fig. 11.8) where $MC_S = MRP_B$. The bilateral monopoly and merger solutions are both likely to be closer to the purely competitive solution (where $MC_S = VMP_B$) than is the "unopposed monopsony" solution (in Fig. 11.7).

Resource Supply

Resource supply is often taken as given and not explained. Since marginal productivity theory does not explain supply of primary resources, it is not a complete theory of resource pricing. The exception is the special case where market supply is taken as given and completely inelastic. Marginal productivity does explain the quantities that would profitably be demanded at various prices. To explain the equilibrium resource price, we must be able to derive market supply.

Where the resource or factor is produced at some lower stage in the production process, the analysis of factor supply is similar to the analysis of supply of the final product by the firm. The distinction between marginal cost (MC) of the output unit and marginal factor cost (MFC) of the input unit still serves to clarify the difference between the input and output unit. The demand for a resource is the firm's demand (MRP), in contrast to the demand by households for consumer products. Under purely competitive conditions, the firm's supply curve for the produced resource would be its marginal cost function.[17] The short-run market supply for the produced resource would be the sum of the supply curves of those firms that produce the resource and supply the market's requirements.

Where retaining the resource offers utility to the owner, the amount of the resource offered for sale by the owner is not necessarily the amount available. The owner may retain part of the total supply. This is sometimes referred to as a reservation demand. Where the owner's reservation demand for the resource is responsive to price, resource supply is not necessarily a positively sloping function of price.

[17] There are pricing limits. In the short run, firms would not be willing to supply the resource at prices below average variable cost. In the long run, firms would require that price be at least equal to average cost.

Backward-Bending Supply Curve for Labor (or Other Inputs)

Let us take the case of a primary resource (labor) supplied by house-holds. Suppose there is a given number of hours of labor time an indi-vidual can supply per day—24 hours, which can be divided between work and leisure. We equate leisure with time not worked: eating, sleeping, recreation, etc. If the price (wage rate) of an hour's labor rises, the price (opportunity cost) of leisure (not-working) will have risen—there is an increased loss of purchasing power from hours not worked. As the price of leisure rises, the individual may or may not retain more hours for leisure and so offer fewer hours for work. The individual, reacting to the substitution effect of the price increase, will tend to substitute income for the more expensive leisure time. An increase in the wage rate can be expected to have a direct and substantial income effect.[18] If leisure is a superior good, with income elasticity > 1, the positive income effect may be strong enough with respect to leisure to dominate and offset the negative substitution effect.[19]

Indifference Curve Analysis of the Supply of a Primary Resource

In Fig. 11.9a, the indifference curve represents points of indifference be-tween income and hours of leisure (hours not worked). The slope of the indifference curve is the marginal rate of substitution between income and leisure. The slope of the linear price lines equals money income divided by 24 hours. The slope represents the wage rate or the price paid for an hour of work (which is equivalent to the opportunity cost of an hour of leisure). If the wage rate increase from w_1 to w_2, a given number of hours of work (or leisure) will yield more income. At a given wage rate, a rational individual will move along the price line to some point where the slope of the price line (income/hour = wage rate) equals the slope of the indifference curve $(\text{MRS} = \text{MU}_{\text{leisure}}/\text{MU}_{\text{income}})$. The equilibrium may be expressed in terms of balancing the disutility of

---

[18] In the theory of consumer choice it was suggested that the income effect of a change in the price of a single commodity is not likely to be as powerful as the substitution effect; however, in the case of leisure, an increase in the price of leisure (the wage rate) will have a strong, direct income effect, which may be stronger than the substitution effect.

[19] The shape of the supply curve of loanable funds as a function of "the" interest rate is subject to the same uncertainty. As interest rate rises, so does income tend to rise (?). The income effect may or may not offset the substitution effect of a rise in interest rate.

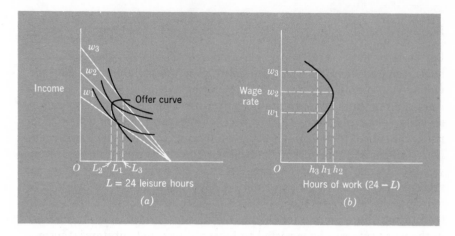

Fig. 11.9

additional effort (utility of leisure) against the utility of income from additional effort. For various wage rates, the points of equilibrium, where the slopes of the price lines and indifference curves are equal, trace the individual's price-consumption (or offer) curve.

The individual's supply curve for work is the relationship between the hours he is willing to work $h(= 24 - L)$ and the wage rate w. The slope of the supply curve depends on the individual's preference map, that is, the indifference curves representing relative preference for income and leisure.[20] Figure 11.9b is the backward-bending supply curve derived from Fig. 11.9a. Each of the points on the supply curve in Fig. 11.9b is a reflection of points on the offer curve in Fig. 11.9a.

The aggregate supply of a particular type of labor in a particular market can be derived by summing individual supply curves of the kind considered previously. The equilibrium price is that price which clears the market for the resource: the price w_0 at which the quantity supplied equals the quantity demanded (A_0 in Fig. 11.10). The income per period to this resource would be the amount employed A_0 multiplied by its average market price w_0 over the period.

---

[20] Note some individuals may have more leisure than they desire so that after some point, the indifference curve may become horizontal to the x-axis, indicating an unwillingness to exchange any additional hours of leisure for income. At high levels of income and leisure, the indifference curve may even begin to slope positively, indicating that an additional hour of leisure may be a discommodity. The individual in such an extreme situation would be willing to work an additional hour for a negative wage (pay to work).

Even where individual supply curves are backward-bending, the market supply of a specialized resource is likely to be positively sloping in the long run, since at higher rates of pay, more individuals may be attracted to the market either from other occupations or from outside the work force. The time and cost of training, the scarcity of the required talent or skill, the amount of unemployed resources, and the level of real income will affect the shape of the market supply.

Classical Economics and the Marginal Productivity Theory of Wages

Historically, wage theory developed from the simplest, most general theory and has been continually modified in the direction of greater realism.

Adam Smith contended that if labor units were homogeneous (in his time most people who worked for wages were unskilled agricultural laborers) and if the market for labor were perfectly competitive, in the long run a single wage rate would tend to prevail in all markets. The equilibrium wage rate (w_o in Fig. 11.10) would be established where the aggregate supply of labor equalled the aggregate demand for labor. In fact, even in 1776 when Adam Smith published his great work, *An Inquiry into the Nature and Causes of the Wealth of Nations*, there were continuing differences in wage rates. He thought these continuing differences were due not to temporary shifts in local market conditions, but to compensating or "equalizing differences" in the conditions of employment. The willingness to transfer from a more favorable to a less favorable occupation (horizontal mobility) would be less than perfect.

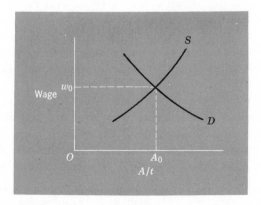

Fig. 11.10

Particularly hazardous or unpleasant work would tend to require a relatively higher wage, whereas for extremely pleasant work, a wage lower than the long-run competitive wage might suffice. Classical economists dwelled on the painful or unpleasant aspects of work.

Later political economists modified Smith's view. In 1848, J. S. Mill pointed out that certain prevailing wage differences could not be adequately explained as simply "equalizing differences." Mill noted that some apparently attractive jobs seemed to be continually higher paying. He enlarged upon Smith's theory by pointing out that the labor market was not a single perfectly competitive market with homogeneous and mobile labor units. There were, he said, several separate markets—"noncompeting groups" with separate and separable supply. There is a lack of vertical mobility; supply in certain markets was restricted due to special talent or ability, lack of equal educational opportunities, social advantages, etc. Some of these restrictions were due to natural advantages and some to artificial causes.

Early classicists were particularly concerned with the aggregate supply of a resource. Rev. T. H. Malthus noted that population and supply of labor tended to increase geometrically, whereas ability to provide food for the expanding population would at best increase arithmetically. His gloomy prediction was a subsistence level of living, with eventual checks on population from war, pestilence, famine.[21]

David Ricardo, a contemporary of Malthus—they disagreed on many issues—accepted the Malthusian "law of population," and propounded his own pessimistic "Iron Law of Wages." Ricardo thought it was inevitable that the competition for jobs by the expanding labor force would tend to force the equilibrium wage rate down to a level just sufficient to sustain the survival of the population.

Neither Malthus nor Ricardo were very hopeful that any permanent improvement in real wages was likely; inexorably, supply would increase to drive the equilibrium level down again to the subsistence level. A better than subsistence level of living in one generation would undo itself in the next. The long-run supply of labor would, they thought, be infinitely elastic at the subsistence level of living.

The demand for labor depends basically on the productivity of labor and value of the output; but the wage level depends on demand and supply. Predictions of the direction of the average wage level were continually modified by conditions of the time. In the late eighteenth and early nineteenth centuries, Ricardo's pessimistic Iron Law of Wages

[21] In a revised edition of his Essay, Malthus added "natural restraint" as a check in his "law of population." See T. R. Malthus, *An Essay on Population*, Everyman Library, No. 692, London: J. M. Dent & Sons Ltd., 1914.

prevailed; it was questioned as the industrial revolution, with its rapid advances in technology, took hold. Real wages improved as the increases in the productivity of labor began to exceed the rate of increase in the labor supply. The slowly improving conditions were supported by certain humane laws (e.g., child labor laws) that tended to restrict the supply of labor.

Today, in some industrially developed parts of the world, it is taken for granted that the wage rate will tend to rise over long periods—that demand will increase more rapidly than supply—however, many parts of the world are still plagued by the specter of the Malthusian Law of Population.

The analysis of the demand for labor, viewed quite generally by the classicists in terms of the productivity of the larborer and the value of his product, was refined by neoclassical and contemporary economists in terms of the marginal productivity theory, discussed previously. The market demand for a particular type of input is derived from the horizontal sum of the marginal revenue product functions of all users of that input (allowing for shifts in MRP functions due to dependency relationships with other inputs and allowing for changes in product price).

Resource Supply and Market Price

Resource supply was developed historically in the context of a perfectly competitive market. The equilibrium market price for the resource is the price that equates quantity supplied and quantity demanded in the market. The perfectly competitive buyer (the hiring firm) will face a horizontal input supply function (a constant input price), since acting independently the firm will be unable to affect the price of the input.[22] A price below the equilibrium price (w_0 in Fig. 11.11) will result in a shortage, and will induce employers to bid up the price. At a resource price above w_0, there will be a surplus—some input units will be unemployed. Competition for the limited number of jobs by those without work who are willing to work at a lower price will force the price back down to the equilibrium level w_0. If the resource price is below w_0, competition by buyers with job vacancies will, in this shortage situation, pull the price back up to the market-clearing price w_0. In the long run, differential prices will tend to disappear as resources withdraw from

[22] The analysis is analogous to the firm selling in a perfectly competitive product market where the firm's demand curve is infinitely elastic. Here the competitive firm's factor supply curve is infinitely elastic.

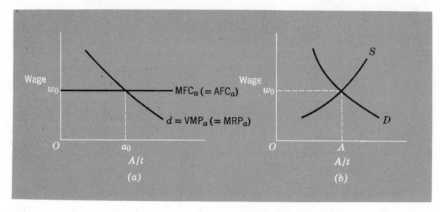

Fig. 11.11. (*a*) Firm. (*b*) Market.

the lower-priced occupation or area and move to the higher-priced employ (supply shifts in each market). The long run will vary in different occupations depending on the required training time.

Rent

Differentials may persist where the supply of heterogeneous resources is inelastic, as is often the case with people of special ability, fertile land, and scarce natural resources. Classical economists viewed rent as a permanent differential to a specialized resource whose supply is zero-elastic. A distinction is sometimes made between rent—where the scarcity is due to natural causes such as talent or natural fertility of land—and monopoly profit—where the scarcity is artificially maintained or is the result of imperfections in the market such as immobility, imperfect knowledge, and monopolistic market restrictions.

Rent, viewed as a differential to factors in fixed supply, has a long historical tradition. Originally, rent applied principally to land or natural resources. Consider several grades of land in Fig. 11.12. Grade 1 is superior land, grade 2 is average land, and grade 3 is inferior land. Combined capital-and-labor units in fixed proportions (C-L) are applied to an acre of each of the three grades of land. All three grades of land are used to produce bushels of wheat (X) of a given quality to be sold at a price P_x, and land is assumed to have no alternative use—zero opportunity cost. The differences in the $\text{VMP}_{C-L}(= \text{MP}_{C-L} \cdot P_x)$ curves are attributed to the differences in productivity of the three grades of

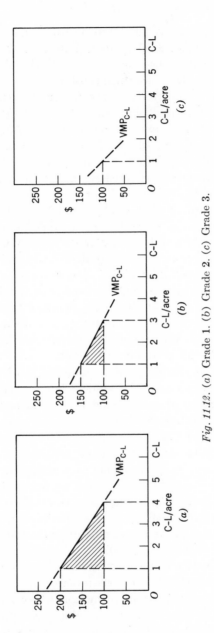

Fig. 11.12. (a) Grade 1. (b) Grade 2. (c) Grade 3.

land. The value of the marginal product of 1 unit of C-L is \$200 if applied to grade 1 land, \$150 if applied to grade 2 land, and \$100 if applied to grade 3 land. The shape of the VMP follows from the law of diminishing returns (P_x is assumed constant).

We assume pure competition in the factor market, so that units of C-L will be hired up to the points where $P_{C\text{-}L} = \text{VMP}_{C\text{-}L}$. On each grade of land, capital-and-labor units will be added up to the intensive margin where the opportunity cost of a unit of C-L equals the value of the marginal product of an additional unit. If the cost of a combined capital-and-labor unit were \$100, the intensive margin on grade 1 land would be 4 units (where the $\text{VMP}_{C\text{-}L} = P_{C\text{-}L}$), the intensive margin on grade 2 land would be 3 units, and on grade 3 land it would be 1 unit. Grade 3 land is just fertile enough to pay for cultivating—applying a single unit of C-L. On less productive land, say grade 4, the VMP of a single unit of C-L would be less than its cost. Grade 3 land is the extensive margin of cultivation (if the cost of a unit of C-L equals \$100).

There is zero rent (no residual) derived from land at the extensive margin after paying the variable costs required to work the land. If capital-and-labor are employed up to the value of their intensive margins and are paid the value of their marginal products, the residual (shaded areas in Fig. 11.12) on grades 1 and 2 land is rent to the landowner. The rent may be attributed to the productivity of the better grades of land. Given the productivity of grade 3 land at the extensive margin and given the product price, the land at the extensive margin has no rental value. The positive residual on superior grades of land is due to their greater productivity.

It is not difficult to turn the example around and suppose that the rental price of an acre of grade 2 land in a particular use is a constant, say \$50/acre, whereas capital and labor are in fixed supply (see Fig. 11.13). Land is cultivated up to the intensive margin ($= 5$ acres), where $\text{VMP}_{\text{land}} = P_{\text{land}}$ ($=$ rent per acre). The shaded area in Fig. 11.13 is a residual now accruing to labor and capital, while the owner of the land receives a return of \$250 ($= 5 \times \$50$).

Ricardian (classical) rent theory viewed rent as a differential accruing to owners of a superior heterogeneous resource in fixed supply, as compared to zero rent on the extensive margin where no residual accrued to owners of inferior land after all variable costs were met. Reversing the situation, we found that the return to land of superior productivity could be explained in terms of marginal productivity theory, where the price of a particular resource reflects the value of its contribution at the margin of use. There is no inconsistency between the two approaches.

The distinguishing characteristic of economic rent, as a return to a

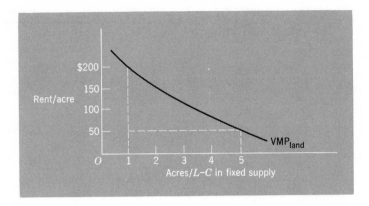

Fig. 11.13

specialized resource in fixed supply, is that the return to its owner does not influence supply. The resource is in fixed supply and has no alternative use, no opportunity cost to the user. The classicists took land in the aggregate to be in fixed supply with only one use—the growing of wheat. A given grade of land was either used in entirety or not used at all. The return, which can be attributed to the superior productivity of the specialized resource, is a residual. This residual (or surplus) could be appropriated (taxed away) without affecting the supply.[23] Since supply is zero-elastic, rent is said to be demand determined. From society's viewpoint, rent serves an essential allocational function, directing the resource to its most productive use. The user pays for the superior productivity of the resource—an explicit or imputed opportunity cost. However, since the resource is available in fixed supply, its opportunity cost to society is zero. The earnings to the resource owner could be taxed away without the supply in the aggregate being diminished or withdrawn.

The return to a resource which is temporarily fixed in supply is called a quasi-rent. It is a residual in the same sense that rent to land or to a natural resource permanently fixed in supply is a residual. Quasi-rent per period is what remains of total revenue after all variable costs of production are paid. It is the positive (or negative) amount remaining for the owners of the fixed factors. Unless the quasi-rent over the life

[23] Where supply is not zero-elastic, there is some ambiguity in the concept of economic rent, as in the concept of consumer surplus. See E. J. Mishan, "Rent as a Measure of Welfare Change," *AER,* Vol. XLIX, No. 3, June 1959, pp. 386–395.

of the capital asset is sufficient to cover its cost, including a competitive rate of return on the investment, the rate of economic profit on the investment will have been negative. Quasi-rent includes both a competitive return on the investment and economic profit.

There are elements of rent in the earnings of labor and capital, where they are at least temporarily in limited supply and at least temporarily specialized in a particular use. Since land is considered a part of the stock of capital, and since it is difficult is determine precisely what part of the earnings of labor and land are due to natural causes—not reproducible by the application of capital—it is no longer common practice to treat economic rent as a separate category.

Resource Allocation—Normative Implications

In a perfect competitive market there would be a single price for a homogeneous input. If resources are differentiated or if there are barriers preventing mobility, factor price differentials may persist. Wherever resources respond to price differentials, there will be a tendency toward the equalization of factor price among submarkets. Within a factor market, firms must pay the prevailing market price for a given resource or risk losing the resource. If the time horizon is sufficiently short and the market sufficiently imperfect, supply in the various submarkets may temporarily support different submarket prices—w_1 and w_2 in Fig. 11.14.

In the long-run, supply will tend to shift to the left in submarket 2 as resources move to the higher wage area, submarket 1. Supply will

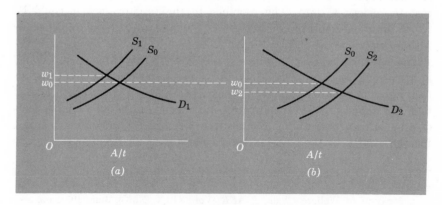

Fig. 11.14. (*a*) Submarket 1. (*b*) Submarket 2.

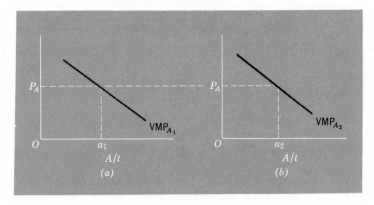

Fig. 11.15. (*a*) Submarket 1. (*b*) Submarket 2.

move to the right in submarket 1 as resources move into the area. The equalizing process will be hastened if capital moves out of submarket 1 into submarket 2, where marginal product per dollar spent on labor yields higher returns than in the high wage area. The movement of capital will be in the opposite direction to the transfer of labor.

In a purely competitive factor market, a single factor price will tend to prevail. In equilibrium, $P_A = \text{VMP}_A$ for all firms in the market, and net social product will be maximized (see Fig. 11.15).

A resource is optimally allocated when its VMP is equal in every use. The price system will not necessarily contribute to this ideal condition unless pure competition prevails. Suppose all users of a given resource are competitive buyers, but varying degrees of monopoly apply

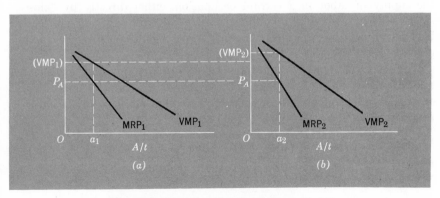

Fig. 11.16. (*a*) Submarket 1. (*b*) Submarket 2.

in the product markets. Firms will hire resources up to the point where $MRP_A = P_A$. The price system will tend to allocate a given resource so that its MRP will be everywhere equal, but this condition will not insure the equalization of its VMP in every use (unless the elasticities of product demand are equal in every use at the margin of purchase). This is illustrated in Fig. 11.16.[24]

Differences in Earnings among Occupations and Locations

We may look to the supply side of factor markets to explain long-standing differences in earnings. Differences in the long-run equilibrium earnings per year among occupations or areas may reflect net advantage, including occupational or locational preferences. The attractiveness of a given employment may influence supply and account for continuing differences in earnings. The employee receives certain nonpecuniary benefits from a particularly favorable location. Such a location may permit an employer to attract resources at relatively low cost. The location is worth something to the firm. If the firm owns the land, there is an imputed rental cost of operating at the favorable location. If the land is leased by the firm, presumably rental payments will reflect the benefit of the desirable location to the firm.

If both pecuniary and nonpecuniary advantages are taken into account when net earnings are compared, some (but not all) of the differences in earnings among locations or occupations would be explained.

Remaining differences in earnings among occupations, which require roughly the same training and ability, may be due to monopoly or artificial restrictions. For example, a strong union may be able to restrict the supply of labor in a certain occupation, either directly by "closed shop" practices (as in the building construction industry), or indirectly by controlling educational opportunities (an accusation directed to the practice of the American Medical Association).

Persisting differences in earnings among occupations may be due to natural scarcity—the rather inelastic supplies of certain natural talents or ability. Such differences in earnings are rents—returns to specialized resources in fixed supply—as discussed above.

Differences in average annual earnings among occupations may also

---

[24] $VMP_A = MP_A \cdot P_x$ and $MRP_A = MP_A \cdot MR_x$. The difference between VMP and MRP in each use will depend on the familiar relationship

$$MR_x = P_x\left(1 + \frac{1}{e}\right) \quad \text{or} \quad MRP_A = VMP_A\left(1 + \frac{1}{e}\right)$$

reflect: (1) occupational expenses—a carpenter may be required to bring his own tools or a soldier to buy his own uniform; (2) the differences in the certainty and stability of earnings in various occupations; and (3) the hazards or hardships or prestige of certain occupations, as suggested by Adam Smith in discussing the single wage and equalizing differences. If people generally prefer safe occupations, then hazardous employment such as mountain climbing guide or space explorer would require greater compensation than would postman or bank teller. The greater prestige attached to a particular occupation may permit relatively lower average compensation. There is some circularity involved here, however, in a society which usually attaches the greater prestige to the higher paying occupation. If low compensation persists in a historically high-prestige occupation, the prestige of that occupation is likely to dwindle.

Differences in earnings among occupations, which result from differences in the time and cost of training, reflect differences in the rate of return on investment in human capital.

The Distribution of Income among Households

Each household's annual income depends on the amounts and market price of productive services it provides. Wages and salaries comprise more than two-thirds of the personal income earned by households. The remainder of personal income can be considered a return to capital.

In measuring the functional distribution of income among resource categories, the sources of income are listed in the national accounting system as: compensation of employees, corporate profit, rent, interest, noncorporate and professional proprietors' income, and farm proprietors' income.

The personal distribution of income is the size distribution of income among households. The factors that account for occupational differences in earnings apply here; choice of occupation depends on people's preferences, abilities, educational and employment opportunities, and unforeseen random factors over which the individual has little control.

It may be useful to group the factors that account for differences in people's income from labor service, and match these factors with the income category that best explains the difference (see p. 240).

If we had considered lifetime earnings rather than the distribution of income among persons at any given time, factor I would not contribute much to an explanation of differences; however, accumulated experience might still vary among people. Income differences due to sex, race, re-

Factors That Account for Differences in Labor Income	*Components of Labor Income*
I. Age-experience factor	Wage
II. Natural ability, talent and energy	Rent
III. Formal education and training	Interest on human-capital
IV. Market imperfection (monopoly power, discrimination, ignorance of opportunities and immobility)	Monopoly profit
V. Random factors (unforeseen events such as changes in taste, technology, health)	Quasi-rent

ligion, and nationality are included in factor IV. If education were available to all who seek it, the present value of the earnings that result from the investment in human capital would reflect not only a return on capital invested, but also a rent to natural intelligence or learning ability.

Preferences have an important role in explaining the size distribution of labor income. We have discussed the role of preferences in the context of equalizing differences, pecuniary and nonpecuniary advantages of various employments, and preference for income and leisure. Preferences with respect to education, gambling, responsibility, and urban living also influence supply and contribute to the explanation of individual differences in labor income.

The earnings to nonlabor resources or property (capital assets) from savings, accumulated in one's own lifetime or inherited, account for the remainder of aggregate personal income (less than one-third). Property income tends to be more unequally distributed in the United States than is earnings from labor services.

12

General Equilibrium

The interdependence of economic relationships can be appreciated by examining the Walrasian system of equations. The system of equations represents consumers striving to maximize their utility (satisfaction) within the limitations of their budget constraints, and producers organizing factors of production to produce commodities subject to the constraints of production functions.

Households sell productive services in factor markets and buy commodities in product markets. A general equilibrium solution to this system of equations involves a simultaneous clearing of all markets. The emphasis is on the mutual interdependencies—the feedbacks and reactions—that are a part of economic processes.

In partial equilibrium many things are taken as given and unaffected by change in a particular causal agent. We consider only the first-order effect of a change in some variable on a particular market taken in isolation. The decision-making units treat part of their environment as beyond control. In static analysis certain variables are treated as parameters. The consumer takes as given his preferences, his income, and the prices and availability of all other goods. The firm takes as given its demand function, resource supply functions, and production possibilities within the bounds of available technological knowledge.

A general equilibrium analysis is not necessarily a complete analysis. It may involve a very few variables, but its great merit is to make explicit the network of mutual interrelationships. The interrelationships among economic phenomena may cause inaccuracies when the simplifying assumptions of partial equilibrium analysis are employed. For many problems the magnitude of error using partial equilibrium is quite tolerable in lieu of the much greater complexity involved when simultaneous solutions are sought for all markets, when many (but not all) of the "fixity" assumptions in the *ceteris paribus* condition are relaxed. It

241

is, after all, reasonable that the price level determined in a particular market may immediately affect the price in closely related markets for substitute or complementary goods. By taking all other prices as fixed, partial equilibrium assumes the relationship among economic goods is that of independence, when in reality even distantly related goods compete for the consumers' income and for limited resources.

In response to a change in supply or in tastes there may occur a change in the equilibrium price of hogs (the first-order effect that partial equilibrium analysis focuses on). This change in the equilibrium price of hogs is likely to cause a change in the price of cattle. Cattle is a substitute commodity, so a fall in the price of hogs will induce a shift in purchases from cattle to hogs. The weakened demand for cattle will result in a decrease in the price of cattle. This in turn may induce a correction—a second-order effect—in the equilibrium price in the hog market.

The principal methodology of price theory has always been partial (or particular) equilibrium analysis where prices in all markets except the one under consideration are assumed fixed at some level. The equilibrium price in the particular market is discovered, but subject to the *ceteris paribus* condition. In theory, this could be done for market after market until one tired of the task and searched out the answer to the more general question: Under what conditions is there a unique multimarket solution whereby there exists a set of prices that would result in a simultaneous solution in all markets without the artificial *ceteris paribus* condition? The level of abstraction involved and the very remote possibility of such a general equilibrium solution ever existing should not deter us from our investigation. There are significant insights to be gained.

We consider first the pure exchange case where consumers may exchange or barter already existing commodities, assuming some initial allocation of these pre-existing commodities has been made. Later we shall consider the more general case where production is possible. In the pure exchange case, the consumers' real income depends on the initial allocation of commodities. When production is included, the sale of the consumers' initial factor endowment provides the basis for purchasing power or real income.

Pure Exchange: General Case

Each consumer's satisfaction depends on the quantities of final commodities he consumes. We suppose the consumers' utility functions are known and that consumers will maximize their utility. We temporarily bypass the interesting problems regarding the distribution of real income, for example, how does "who" come to get "what"? The initial distribution is completely arbitrary here. You might imagine such solutions as an equal dole or commodities all stacked up and a division based on a contest of one kind or another, or a "free for all"—take all you can carry. It is highly likely that if trade is permitted, following an initial arbitrary allocation of commodities, some or all individuals will be able to increase their utility through trade or barter.

The time period for the pure exchange (no production) case corresponds to the market period or very short run in the partial equilibrium analysis of single markets where supply is fixed. Supply is fixed (zero supply elasticity) and, depending on the market price, each individual i may wish to buy or sell commodity j given his initial endowment and demand function d_{ij}. The market price will depend on the aggregate demand function for $j(D_j)$ and the aggregate supply Q_0.[1]

In a pure exchange economy, each individual is likely to be able to increase his utility by trading—buying and selling according to his utility function and subject to the constraint of his initial endowment of commodities. Suppose there are n individuals and m commodities. The quantities of each jth commodity initially held by each ith individual are data (given) and are denoted by q_{ij}^0, while the quantities finally consumed by each individual are denoted by q_{ij}. An individual's excess demand for j is $E_{ij} = q_{ij} - q_{ij}^0 = f(p_j)$. In Fig. 12.1, which depicts the ith individual's demand, i's excess demand is positive (he wants to buy) when market price falls below p_0, and negative (he wants to sell) when the market price rises above p_0. At p_0, market excess demand is zero and the market for commodity j is cleared. Each individual's excess demand for j need not be zero at the equilibrium price, but the sum of the individual excess demands for j is zero at the equilibrium price p_0. Under purely competitive conditions, an individual's decision to buy or sell will not affect the market price of commodities, and therefore the value of an individual's income can be measured by valuing the ith individual's initial commodity holdings ($\sum_{j=1}^{m} q_{ij}^0$) by the market price p_j of each of the m commodities; that

---

[1] There is a time lag before the first-order effects of an economic disturbance appear in particular markets; it takes even longer for the higher-order effects to appear in all markets. In reality, the working out of actions and reactions does not take place simultaneously. The production processes and market negotiations are time consuming; however, if the time horizon is long enough we can view the final outcome as the simultaneous solution of many equations, each representing a relevant economic relationship.

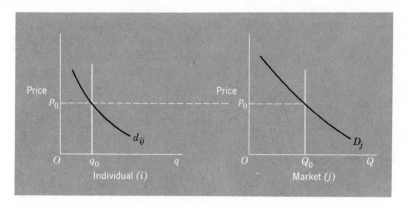

Fig. 12.1. Fixed stocks in market period.

is, j goes from 1 to m, which can be written $j = 1, \ldots, m$. The ith individual's income can then be expressed as $\sum_{j=1}^{m} p_j q_{ij}^{0}$.[2]

The variables in this pure exchange system are q_{ij}, which are the quantities consumed by each individual, and the prices p_j of each commodity. Prices are here understood to mean exchange rates or ratios and are expressed in terms of some one of the m commodities—say commodity 1. For convenience, let the price of commodity 1 equal unity ($p_1 = 1$). The price of each of the other $m - 1$ commodities is then expressed as the number of units of commodity 1 required to exchange for one unit of any other commodity. Commodity 1 is called the numéraire—it is our standard of value and unit of account.

For example, apparently the "primitive" Dodoth tribe in Uganda uses cattle as its numéraire or standard of value, at least with respect to wives. A young man of this tribe when he reaches a certain age typically begins exchanging cattle for wives. Let us say he exchanges 10 head of cattle ($q_1 = 10$) for 1 wife. The price of the wife (p_w) is then 10. (Ignoring divisibility problems this same exchange could be expressed as $\frac{1}{10}$ of a wife equals 1 head of cattle.) Whether or not cattle would serve as well as money in other systems is a question we shall not explore here. Money, of course, has other functions in addition to being a standard of value. In this primitive tribe, cattle serves most of the common functions of money. As the numéraire, cattle is the standard of value

[2] The notation used here will be found in J. M. Henderson and R. E. Quandt, *Microeconomic Theory, A Mathematical Approach,* New York: McGraw-Hill, 1958. For a more detailed analysis, see Chapters 5 and 6 of this text.

or unit of account in terms of which other goods are traded. It is also a medium of exchange, that is, it is itself acceptable as an exchange good. This is a necessary condition if the standard of value—the numéraire—is also to serve as money. It is finally a store of wealth or value.[3]

In the analysis of pure exchange, we have assumed some arbitrary distribution of the existing stock of m commodities among n individuals. In a more complete economic system encompassing production of new commodities, distribution is closely related to the process of production. Ownership and sale of the factors of production generate income; the individual with the most valuable factor endowment is usually the one to command the largest part of the total produce.

The value of the individual's initial commodity holdings constitutes the individual's budget constraint. He can trade all or part of his initial stock of commodities, but he cannot trade for more than the value of his initial endowment of commodities, his real income. Each ith individual is assumed to have some known ordinal utility function

$$U_i = U_i(q_{i1} \cdot \cdot \cdot \cdot q_{im})$$

where U_i—the ordinal utility index—is a function of the quantities of the m commodities consumed.

Our primary behavioral assumption is that each individual will pursue the objective of maximizing utility, subject to his budget constraint. An individual may originally possess more or less of a commodity than he desires; his excess demand for a single commodity $(q_{ij} - q_{ij}^0)$ may be positive or negative, depending on his utility function (given), his initial commodity endowment (given), and the m commodities' market prices (variables). The individual's budget constraint can be expressed as

$$\sum_{j=1}^{m} p_j(q_{ij} - q_{ij}^0) = \sum_{j=1}^{m} p_j E_{ij} = 0$$

[3] Elizabeth M. Thompson, "The Warrior Herdsmen," *New Yorker*, May issues, 1965. For this tribe, cattle was the major form of wealth and only sometimes served the other above mentioned functions of money. It is quite understandable that this tribe of herdsmen settled on cattle as their main store of value (form of wealth), and as the standard of value by which they measured the relative value of other things, and occasionally as a medium of exchange. Apart from its use in trade, cattle had great utility in their lives; they ate its meat after the cattle grew old and died, they used the milk to drink and to eat in the form of cheese, they used the excrement as flooring for their dwellings, and they used the urine as a cleansing agent. In most advanced economies money is not useful in and for itself.

The individual's excess demand for all m commodities must be zero. The individual's income equals the value of his original commodity endowment $\left(\sum\limits_{j=1}^{m} p_j q_{ij}^{0} \right)$. We assume, here, that his income equals the value of the commodities he purchases and consumes $\left(\sum\limits_{j=1}^{m} p_j q_{ij} \right)$—total consumption equals initial real income: $\sum\limits_{j=1}^{m} p_j q_{ij} = \sum\limits_{j=1}^{m} p_j q_{ij}^{0}$, and the value of his purchases equals the value of his sales.

To have done the best he could with what he had available—to have maximized utility subject to his budget constraint—the individual's marginal rate of substitution MRS (= ratio of marginal utilities) between any pair of commodities must equal the relative prices or exchange ratio:[4]

$$\text{MRS}_{j \, for \, j+1} = \frac{\text{MU}_j}{\text{MU}_{j+1}} = \frac{p_j}{p_{j+1}}$$

or

$$\frac{\text{MU}_j}{p_j} = \frac{\text{MU}_{j+1}}{p_{j+1}}$$

Each consumer allocates his income in such a manner that the additional satisfaction from the last dollar spent on each commodity is equal to $\text{MU}_1/(p_1 = 1)$ for all commodities purchased. Each individual's excess demand function for each of the m commodities, $q_{ij} - q_{ij}^{0}$ as a function of all prices, can be derived from this equilibrium condition and the budget constraint.

In a pure exchange "barter" economy, we are concerned with relative prices. The excess demand functions will not change if all prices change by the same proportion. In mathematical language, the excess demand functions are said to be homogeneous of degree zero in prices. Each individual would be indifferent to proportionate changes in absolute prices (the value of the numéraire) so long as the exchange ratios or relative prices remain constant.

---

[4] This condition was explained in Chapter 3. The mathematical derivation requires maximizing the Lagrangian function, which contains the utility function and the budget constraint. The necessary or first-order maximizing conditions require that the partial derivatives formed from the Lagrangian function equal zero. To ensure that the extremes are maxima, the second-order conditions must also be met.

In a perfectly competitive system a single price is set for each commodity market. The price of a given commodity is identical for each consumer, and a single consumer's buying and selling activities cannot affect the market price. To maximize utility, each individual will exchange commodities until the marginal rates of substitution between pairs of commodities equal the common price ratios between pairs of commodities. Now with the same relative prices or exchange ratios facing all individuals, we can conclude that the marginal rates of substitution between pairs of commodities will be equivalent to the common prevailing exchange ratios, and therefore the same for all individuals.

Equilibrium for the individual in a pure exchange economy means that at the equilibrium prices no further exchanges would result in additional utility. The individual excess demand functions for a particular commodity (j) can be summed over all n individuals to obtain the market

excess demand for commodity j: $E_j \equiv Q_j - Q_j{}^0 = \sum\limits_{i=1}^{n} (q_{ij} - q_{ij}{}^0)$, remem-

bering that each $q_{ij} - q_{ij}{}^0$ is a function of all commodity prices. If we derive the market excess demand functions in this manner for all m commodities, we would have m market excess demand functions: $E_j \equiv Q_j - Q_j{}^0$ ($j = 1, \ldots, m$), one for each commodity and each a function of all m commodity prices. When all markets are in equilibrium, each market excess demand function equals zero ($E_j = 0$). The quantity consumed equals the aggregate stock. Since each E_j is a function of all m commodity prices, a general equilibrium solution requires a simultaneous solution of the system of equations in terms of the m commodity prices.

Can it be demonstrated that there will be some set of prices that will satisfy this equilibrium condition? In our pure exchange economy there are now m market excess demand equations, one for each commodity, and m variables representing the prices of the m commodities. So there are m equations and m variables, but one of the m market excess demand equations is not independent of the remaining $m - 1$ equations.

Why are there only $m - 1$ independent equations? With given aggregate income and assuming that all commodities are consumed: $\sum\limits_{j=1}^{m} p_j Q_j{}^0 =$

$\sum\limits_{j=1}^{m} p_j Q_j$, which may be written $\sum\limits_{j=1}^{m} p_j (Q_j - Q_j{}^0) = 0$, and given the condition that in equilibrium excess demand in a market equals zero (our market clearing requirement), we can deduce that excess demand in the remaining market ($Q_m - Q_m{}^0$) must be in equilibrium if all other $m - 1$

markets are in equilibrium; that is, if $\sum_{j=1}^{m-1} p_j(Q_j - Q_j^0) = 0$.[5]

The demand for the remaining commodity is $Q_m = Q_m^0$, and one of the m market excess demand equations is redundant. In equilibrium, it is dependent on the other $m - 1$ equations.

With only m — 1 independent equations and m variables, we would not be able to solve for a unique set of m variables representing absolute prices—our system of equations would be underdetermined. By expressing the prices of all commodities relative to the arbitrarily assigned price of the numéraire commodity, Q_1, and letting $p_1 = 1$, we can usually solve the system of $m - 1$ excess demand functions for the $m - 1$ relative prices, $p_2/p_1, p_3/p_1, \ldots , p_m/p_1$.[6] The number of equations equals the number of unknowns, so the necessary condition for a determinate solution is satisfied. Substituting the equilibrium relative prices (market exchange ratios) into the individual excess demand function, we can solve for individual excess demands $q_{ij} - q_{ij}^0$.[7]

Pure Exchange—Two Persons and Two Commodities

An individual maximizes utility if the marginal rate of substitution (MRS) between pairs of commodities equals the ratio of commodity prices. The MRS is the slope of an indifference curve on which every point represents a combination of commodities that yields a given index of utility.

The equality of the marginal rate of substitution for each individual to the common price or exchange rate can be illustrated for two persons and two commodities using the Edgeworth Box diagram. Let $U_1(q_{11},q_{12})$ and $U_2(q_{21},q_{22})$ be indexes of ordinal utility for individuals 1 and 2.

[5] $\sum_{j=1}^{m} p_j(Q_j - Q_j^0) = 0$ and $\sum_{j=1}^{m-1} p_j(Q_j - Q_j^0) = 0$, so by subtracting we get $p_m(Q_m - Q_m^0) = 0$, then since all prices are positive, $Q_m - Q_m^0$ must be equal to zero.

[6] Since the excess demand functions are homogeneous of zero degree in price, dividing each adsolute price by a constant (p_1) will not affect the values of the market excess demands, $Q_j - Q_j^0$.

[7] Recall that the market excess demand functions were formed by summing the individual excess demand functions. Although mathematically correct, this aggregation process assumes independence among individuals. The individual excess demand functions were derived from the individual utility functions and budget constraint. The same results or solutions to this static equilibrium system could have been obtained without the intermediate step of summing the individual excess demand functions to form market excess demand functions.

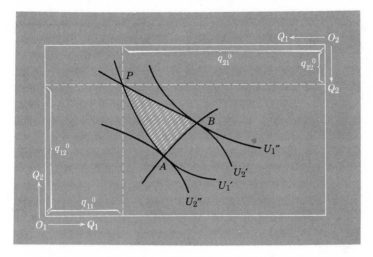

Fig. 12.2

They can be represented in the box diagram by 1's indifference curves convex to 1's origin (O_1) at the lower left corner, and by 2's indifference curves convex to 2's origin (O_2) at the upper right corner of the box.

The length of the box represents the total stock of Q_1 available and the height of the box represents the total stock of Q_2 available. Suppose individual 1 is initially allocated q_{11}^0 and q_{12}^0, while individual 2 is initially allocated q_{21}^0 and q_{22}^0. This initial allocation is represented by point P in the Edgeworth Box diagram in Fig. 12.2.

Recall that the individual's excess demand for each commodity $E_{ij} = q_{ij} - q_{ij}^0$ is a function of prices. In this case, for example, $(q_{11} - q_{11}^0) = f_1(p_1, p_2)$, and $(q_{12} - q_{12}^0) = f_2(p_1, p_2)$ are individual 1's excess demand functions for Q_1 and Q_2, respectively.

Since the excess demand functions are homogeneous of zero degree in prices, the excess demands are unaffected if expressed in terms of relative prices, p_2/p_1. If we let Q_1 be the numéraire commodity and divide both prices by the price of the numéraire (p_1), we shall find, as in the analysis of the general case, that one market excess demand equation is redundant, which leaves us with one market demand equation and one price variable, p_2/p_1.

The total initial stock of commodities is equivalent to real income. The initial allocation of commodities at point P is not an optimum allocation. If the individuals are free to trade or exchange they are likely to find exchange ratios or terms-of-trade which can take them closer to an optimum position. The use of the Edgeworth Box diagram illustrates nicely the gains from exchange and the sense in which the term optimum, used here, was first employed by Pareto.

If a market price ratio (p_1/p_2) existed, the individual in equilibrium would trade to the point of tangency between the price line and the indifference curve, where the slopes of each are equal:

$$\text{MRS}_{2 \text{ for } 1} = -\frac{\text{MU}_1}{\text{MU}_2} = -\frac{p_1}{p_2}$$

In equilibrium the individual's valuation ($\text{MRS}_{2 \text{ for } 1}$) concurs with the market valuation or terms-of-trade between commodities (p_1/p_2). At the prevailing exchange rate, the point of tangency will be the point of maximum utility (highest indifference curve) attainable by the individual given his budget constraint.

The indifference curves for both individuals are presented in the Edgeworth Box diagram; the locus of points where the indifference curves of one individual are tangent to those of the other is called a contract curve. At any point on the contract curve, the MRS is equal for both individuals. If the two individuals begin at some point (an initial commodity allocation) off the contract curve such as P in Fig. 12.2, a movement onto the contract curve can be mutually beneficial. The points on the contract curve, where each person's MRS is equal, are said to be Pareto-optimum, since once on the contract curve any further change can only benefit one person by harming the other. An exchange of commodities bringing both individuals from an initial point P, off the contract curve, to a point on the contract curve between points A and B will benefit at least one of the individuals without harming the other. Except at the extreme points, A and B, trading to the contract curve between A and B will be mutually beneficial. The points A and B are related to point P, since it is at P that the two indifference curves through points A and B converge. A move from P to any other point within the shaded area in Fig. 12.2 will benefit both parties. A distinction has been made between trading, which is mutually rewarding, and conflict—a change along the contract curve which benefits one at the other's expense. A skillful trader or negotiator will trade to an advantageous position along the contract curve. For any point off the contract curve, there exists some point on the curve that will benefit at least one of the persons without hurting the other. This is not to say that every point on the contract curve is an improvement over—or comparable with—every point off the contract curve.

Exactly where the two individuals will move to on the contract curve between A and B, or what combination of goods they finally consume, will depend on the relative price or terms-of-trade finally agreed upon. Relative price can be brought into the Edgeworth Box illustration by imagining price or budget lines of varying slopes passing though the initial commodity allocation point P. Each individual will want to vary his initial holdings, depending on whether his excess demand is positive or negative and on which price line applies, until each individual trades to a tangency position where the slope of the price line and slopes of each party's indifference curve are equal. The locus of points of tangency between the price lines and indifference curves is called the offer curve. In a perfect market, one price line applies to both individuals. The final equilibrium position will lie at some point on the contract curve where the individuals' indifference curves are tangent to each other and their slopes are equal to the slope of the common price line. Each individual will seek to be on his offer curve. The offer curves will intersect at some point on the contract curve if there is an equilibrium solution. At this point the market excess demand functions are cleared and the values of commodities bought and sold are equal. The existence of an equilibrium for two persons requires that the individuals know their preferences and are able to reach a single agreement on terms-of-trade that takes them to a point on the contract curve. Each person's excess demands, E_{ij}, can be derived from his utility function and budget constraint and expressed as a function of relative prices. $E_j = \sum_{i=1}^{n} E_{ij}$ is the market demand by all individuals for each commodity.

The market clearing requirement for the two person—two commodity case can be expressed as

$$E_1 = E_{11} + E_{21} = 0 \quad \text{and} \quad E_2 = E_{12} + E_{22} = 0$$

These market-clearing conditions permit us to express market excess demands for commodities 1 and 2, E_1 and E_2, as functions of the price ratio: these are relative prices. We need only one of these equations, say $E_1 = f(p_2/p_1) = 0$, to solve for the equilibrium market price ratio, p_2/p_1. Having determined the market terms-of-trade between the two commodities, it is a simple matter to substitute back into the individual excess demand expressions $(q_{ij} - q^0_{ij})$ to find the four individual equilibrium quantities: q_{11}, q_{12}, q_{21}, and q_{22}.

With tastes and initial commodity allocation (distribution of real income) given, any point on the contract curve is a Pareto-optimum position in the terms of welfare economics. Once a position on the contract curve is reached, no further trade will benefit either individual without harming the other. Further movements along a contract curve will result in conflict—a gain in utility to one individual can be secured only at a loss to the other. Policies that result in a gain to some at the expense of others required subjective judgments. All societies continually make such judgments, and hopefully we move in a direction that will result in net social benefit. Eschewing subjective interpersonal utility comparisons, the economist is qualified to make expert recommendations which move toward Pareto-optimum positions—adding to the utility of one or more individuals without causing a loss in utility to any. Within the rules or sanctions of the society, policy measures that benefit some and harm others (movements along a contract curve) are constantly being proposed and enacted. Implicit subjective weights are assigned to the aggregate gains or losses. Measures are exacted that reflect the values and objectives of the society's decision-makers and the nature of the political processes.

General Equilibrium—Production and Exchange

The analysis of pure exchange can be extended to include production of commodities, instead of assuming a fixed stock of m produced commodities as in the pure exchange case. In fact, we assume here zero initial stock of produced goods. In the pure exchange case wealth and income are identical. An individual's share depends on the initial distribution of final goods. With the introduction of production, we define commodities to include s primary factors as well as $m-s$ produced goods. Both primary factors and produced goods may be used as inputs in production and both may be consumed by households. Of course, not all primary factors or produced goods are desired for final consumption by households.

The individual's income is equal to the value of his initial supply of primary factors. It may be that the individual attaches utility to primary factors as he does to final goods. For example, time may be desired in the form of leisure (nonwork) instead of work. Land, which is owned, may be withheld in order to be used nonremuneratively by the owner (perhaps as a complementary good with leisure).

Little needs to be added to the preceding pure exchange analysis to describe consumer markets. The individual's income is assumed equal to the value of commodities purchased (some of these may be inputs). This is the individual's budget constraint. In terms of excess demands, similar budget constraints and utility functions apply. We may derive similar first-order conditions for maximizing individual utility; the consumer's marginal rates of substitution must equal the market price ratios for all pairs of commodities. From these conditions can be derived each consumer's excess demand for each of the m commodities as a function of all m commodity prices. The market demand is obtained by summing individual demands.

We now add technical knowledge in the form of a production function, which indicates the quantities of the m commodities (inputs) required to produce each final good:

$$\bar{q}_{hj} = f_{hj}(q^*_{hjk}) \qquad (k = 1, \ldots, m)$$

where q_{hj} is firm h's output in the jth industry. All kth inputs are starred. q^*_{hjk} represents the quantities of the m commodities used as inputs by firm h in the production of commodity j.

The firm is presumed to maximize profit; it attempts to maximize the gap between the value of the final good produced and the cost of the m commodities (both produced commodities and primary resources) required to produce it. For simplicity, let each firm produce a single good for sale in a single market.

The profit function π_{hj} of the hth firm in the jth industry is equal to price p_j times the firm's output $\bar{q}_{hj}$, or total revenue $p_j\bar{q}_{hj}$ minus input prices times input quantities, or total input costs $\displaystyle\sum_{k=1}^{m} p_k q^*_{hjk}$:

$$\pi_{hj} = p_j\bar{q}_{hj} - \sum_{k=1}^{m} p_k q^*_{hjk}$$

Since the firm only purchases inputs, the firm's excess demand for inputs, E^*_{hjk}, must equal q^*_{hjk}—the quantities of the kth input used by the hth firm in the jth industry. To maximize profit, the perfectly competitive firm must meet the following profit-maximizing condition: Each input is used up to the point where the value of the marginal product of the kth input equals the price of the input, $\text{VMP}_{hjk} = p_j\text{MP}_{hjk} = p_k$ ($k = 1, \ldots, m$). The solution of these m equations determines the firm's excess demand for inputs $E^*_{hjk} = q^*_{hjk}$.[8]

The excess demand for each input by the firm is a function of all prices. If there are N_j identical representative firms in the jth industry, the jth industry's excess demand for the kth input can be expressed as a function of all prices and the number of firms in the industry:

$$E_{jk}^* = E_{jk}^*(p_1, \ldots, p_m, N_j)$$

[8] This is the first-order condition derived by taking the partial derivatives of the profit function with respect to each input, and setting the partial derivatives equal to zero. The second-order condition for a maximum must be satisfied. It will be if diminishing marginal product holds for each input.

The firm's output (supply or negative excess demand) can be computed by substituting the firm's excess demands for its inputs E^*_{hjk} into its production function to yield the firm's output $\bar{E}_{hj}$ as a function of m prices. The industry's output $\bar{E}_j$ is obtained by multiplying $\bar{E}_{hj}$ by the number of firms N_j in the jth industry:

$$\bar{E}_j = \bar{E}_j(p_1, \ldots, p_m, N_j)$$

The aggregate excess demand for each of the m-s produced commodities includes the market demand by consumers, the demand by industries using the commodity as an input, and the negative excess demand or output of the commodity by the supplying industry. Only the first two components of demand apply in the case of the s primary factors.[9]

The equilibrium condition is that all markets be cleared. This means that the excess demand for all commodities must be zero. The quantity supplied by producing industries must equal the quantity demanded by final consumers and by industrial users.

In general equilibrium, the aggregate excess demand must be zero for every commodity in every market, whatever the time period. In the long-run, the number of firms in an industry is a variable. In long-run equilibrium, each firm's profit and the industry's profit must equal zero. Excess demand can be expressed as a function of m commodity prices and the number of firms in each of the m-s producing industries:

$$E_j(p_1, \ldots, p_m, N_{s+1}, \ldots, N_m) = 0 \qquad (j = 1, \ldots, m)$$

The long-run profit for each representative firm in each of the jth m-s producing industries is π_j, which is a function of the m commodity prices and equals zero in equilibrium:

$$\pi_j(p_1, \ldots, p_m) = 0 \qquad (j = s + 1, \ldots, m)[10]$$

As in the pure exchange case, one of the excess market demand equations is dependent on the others and thus is redundant. Since the excess demand functions are homogeneous of zero degree in price, and since in long-run equilibrium the representative firm's profit equals zero, one of the price variables can be eliminated by dividing through by the

[9] The s commodities which are primary factors of production are not actually produced by any firm but are supplied to firms by individual consumers (households). In such cases the number of firms equals zero since there are no firms producing these primary factors. Also the profit functions do not exist for these primary factors.

[10] In the short-run, the number of firms in each industry is a parameter, and each firm's profit need not be zero; in the short-run, profit is treated as a component of consumers' income.

price of the numéraire to express all prices relative to the price of the numéraire, p_1.

A long-run general equilibrium solution of the system of equations here involves $2m$-s-1 variables: m-1 relative prices and the number of firms in each of m-s producing industries. In long-run equilibrium, there are $2m$-s-1 independent equations representing the general equilibrium conditions: m-1 market excess demand equations and m-s profit functions for a representative firm in each of the m-s producing industries.[11]

Input-Output

Input-output analysis attempts to measure the higher-order effects within a framework of interindustry relationships. It is a simplified version of the production function equations of the general equilibrium system, but it is not an equilibrium model and there are no maximizing assumptions. The industrial sector rather than the firm is the basic unit. To make the model operational certain simplifying assumptions are made. Input is assumed a constant proportion of output at any output level—fixed production coefficients. The simplest of linear production functions is employed.

Prices are assumed fixed and no input substitution is allowed. This is in contrast to the Walrasian general equilibrium model where the system was solved for equilibrium prices and outputs. The input coefficients are estimated for the production functions relating inputs to outputs in each producing sector. These technical relationships are the crucial equations in the model.

Final demands by nonproducing sectors as well as information on available stocks of primary factors and sector capacities are data exogenous to this "open" model, in which the only unknowns are the

---

[11] Suppose money is introduced as a separate commodity. The excess demand for each commodity, including money, is a function of all m commodity prices. Under certain assumptions the quantity of money can determine the *absolute price level* in the "monetary sector." For example, let us assume individuals wish their money stocks to be a fixed proportion of the value of their commodity holdings. The absolute price level was left completely indeterminate in the above analysis of the "real" sector where only relative prices were pertinent to the analysis. If money is added as an additional commodity to the consumers' budget constraint, an equilibrium level of absolute prices can be achieved when the aggregate excess demands for each commodity and for money equal zero. If, in equilibrium, the amount of money individuals desire to hold is assumed equal to the initial stock, prices adjust accordingly. If all commodity markets are cleared, the money market must be cleared also.

sector outputs required to satisfy any given set of final demands (including demands by households, government, and the foreign sector).[12] The feasibility of the solution may be checked with information on resource availability and sector capacity. The model may also be used to see what final demands and sector output levels are consistent with maximum use of resources.

In exchange for the restrictive and simplified assumptions, the input-output model yields useful numerical answers. The accuracy of the solution is closely related to the estimates of the production coefficients from interindustry accounting flow data.[13]

The outputs of the producing sectors are the unknowns—the endogenous variables, whose values depend on the solution of the system of equations. The units of measure may be physical, but it is more convenient to use base year values ($'s at base year prices).

The fixed production coefficients a_{ij} apply to the producing sectors. The production relationships are assumed constant and independent of the levels of output. a_{ij} represents the amount of the various inputs Q_i required for each unit (constant $1) of output. The sum of a_{ij} for a given producing sector j (column vector) must equal unity: $\sum_{i=1}^{m+r} a_{ij} = 1$.

$$q_{ij} = a_{ij}q_j \qquad (j = 1, \ldots , m)$$

or

$$a_{ij} = \frac{q_{ij}}{q_j} \qquad (i = 1, \ldots , m + r)$$

q_j is the level of output of the producing sector Q_j. q_{ij} is the level of output in the input sector Q_i required to produce q_j. q_{ij} is the amount of Q_i delivered to industry j. The inputs Q_i include the outputs of the m endogenous producing sectors Q_j as well as the r factors of production, which can be assumed supplied by households (the exogenous sector). q_i is total output, which is distributed to all the producing sectors and to final demand. The final demands c_i are consumed by households or

---

[12] We are here concerned with the "open" model where final demands are given and assumed independent of the levels of output in the producing sector. Final demands are exogenous to the model and independent of the current period results. There are no exogenous sectors in the closed model, which is discussed at length in Wassily W. Leontief, *The Structure of the American Economy, 1919–1939*, 2d. ed., New York, Oxford University Press, 1951.

[13] The simplified production function assumptions are more likely to be reasonable approximations for long-run rather than short-run problems, and for cases not too far removed from the period in which the interindustry flow data were collected.

Table 12.1

Q_i \ Q_j	1 2 $\cdots$ m	c_i	q_i
1	$q_{11}\,q_{12}\ \cdots\ q_{1m}$	c_1	q_1
$\vdots$		$\vdots$	$\vdots$
m	$q_{m1}\,q_{m2}\ \cdots\ q_{mm}$	c_m	q_m
$m+1$			
$\vdots$			
$m+r$			
q_j	$q_1\ q_2\ \cdots\ q_m$		

government or other countries. The input-output flows are illustrated in Table 12.1.

The basic flow equation can be written

$$q_i = \sum_{j=1}^{m} q_{ij} + c_i = \sum_{j=1}^{m} a_{ij}q_j + c_i \qquad (i = 1,\ \ldots,m)$$

In the input-output flows above, the row output totals equal the column input totals ($q_i = q_j$ for $i = j$). The total (revenue) output demanded of a sector equals total (cost) inputs required to produce the output.

Once the sector boundaries have been decided and the flows recorded

Table 12.2 Three-Sector Example

	1. (Agr.)	2. (Mfr.)	(Final Demand)	
1. Agriculture	$ 4,000	$ 9,000	$7,000	$(20,000)
2. Manufacturing	6,000	15,000	9,000	(30,000)
3. Factor of production	10,000	6,000		
Σ	$20,000	$30,000		

Table 12.3

	1	2
1.	0.2	0.3
2.	0.3	0.5
3.	0.5	0.2
Σ	1.0	1.0

as in our three-sector model, the table of input coefficients can be computed:

$$\text{Input Coefficient } (a_{ij}) = \frac{\text{Input } (q_{ij})}{\text{Total Output } (q_j)}$$

For example, $a_{11} = \$4,000/\$20,000$. Under the constant proportionality assumption, the constant coefficient $a_{11} = 0.2$ means that for every \$ of agricultural output, 20 cents of its own output is required as an input, for example, grain to feed livestock. This relation holds independent of output.

If final demand for agriculture increased, there would be a proportionate increase required of each of the three input sectors including agriculture. This would increase the output requirement for each of the three sectors beyond the initial increase in final demand for sector 1. The indirect effects of the initial increase in final demand would continue until output in each sector is sufficient to meet the new set of final demands.

This abridged example can be written in equation form and solved. Initially, we leave out a_{31} and a_{32} since it is assumed there is no c_3—no final demand for factors of production. Following the solution for q_1 and q_2, we can easily derive the factor levels required:

$$q_1 = a_{11}q_1 + a_{12}q_2 + c_1; \qquad (1 - a_{11})\,q_1 - a_{12}q_2 = c_1$$
$$q_2 = a_{21}q_1 + a_{22}q_2 + c_2; \qquad -a_{21}q_1 + (1 - a_{22})q_2 = c_2$$

If $a_{11} = 0.2$, $a_{12} = 0.3$, $a_{21} = 0.3$, $a_{22} = 0.5$, $c_1 = \$7000$ and $c_2 = \$9000$, the required outputs to satisfy the final demands, c_1 and c_2, would be $q_1 = \$20,000$ and $q_2 = \$30,000$. These results are of course equal to our original q_i's from which the input coefficients were derived.

The factor requirements can now be derived, given $a_{31} = 0.5$ and $a_{32} = 0.2$, from $q_{31} = a_{31}q_1 = 0.5(\$20,000) = \$10,000$ and $q_{32} = a_{32}q_2 = 0.2(\$30,000) = \$6000$. The sector and factor requirements can be compared with available capacities to see if there are apparent bottlenecks.

13

Welfare Economics

Much of the new welfare economics is built upon Pareto's necessary condition for efficiency, discussed in Chapter 12. We looked at efficient exchange in the context of the gains from exchange, using the Edgeworth trading box. The Pareto-optimality condition for efficient exchange held everywhere along the contract curve. Recall that the contract curve was defined as the locus of positions from which no improvement in anyone's position was possible except at someone's expense. To decide which of two positions along the contract curve is superior would require interpersonal comparisons, which are not possible in terms of our ordinal utility measures. Pareto-efficiency, in general, means that no increase (improvement) in the value of one variable is possible without a decrease (deterioration) in the value of some other variable. This does not imply that all points off the contract curve are inferior or even comparable with the Pareto-efficient points on the contract curve. However, for every point off the contract curve—a point which by definition is not Pareto-efficient—there exists the possibility of gain to at least one without loss to any through exchange or by trading onto the contract curve. Once there, at a position that is Pareto-optimal—even though one or the other party may be very unhappy with this position on the contract curve—any move to another position harms someone. There is then a direct confrontation or conflict.

We shall explain Pareto-efficient possibilities and the marginal conditions for efficiency with the aid of Edgeworth box diagrams.[1] There are two inputs in inelastic (fixed) supply—land D and labor L, to be allocated between two outputs—apples A and nuts N, which are to be distributed between two persons, X and Y. We shall consider what is

[1] The analysis and the symbols follow closely those of the excellent article by F. M. Bator, "Simple Analytics of Welfare Maximization," *AER*, March 1957, Vol. XLVII, No. 1, pp. 22-59.

the "best" allocation of resources, and what is the "best" distribution of outputs among the two persons in our analysis. The values to be determined are:

Allocation of Resources	Distribution of Output
L_A—labor to apples	A_x—apples to X
L_N—labor to nuts	N_x—nuts to X
D_A—land to apples	A_y—apples to Y
D_N—land to nuts	N_y—nuts to Y

We assume certain fixed input-endowments; the stocks of labor and land are fixed and owned by persons X and Y (in amounts not yet specified). The production functions indicating the possibilities for transforming inputs into output—$A = F_A(L_A,D_A)$ and $N = F_N(L_N,D_N)$—are given and illustrated by the isoquants in Fig. 13.1a. Given, too, are the ordinal preference functions, representing the ordinal utility indices for each person, X and Y, as a function of the products to be consumed, A and N: $U_x = f_x(A_x,N_x)$ and $U_y = f_y(A_y,N_y)$. They are illustrated in the form of indifference curves in the Edgeworth trading box in Fig. 13.1b. Note that the ordinal index U_x cannot be compared with U_y. The production functions, the ordinal preference functions, and the initial input-endowments are all given in our analysis.[2]

Efficient Production

Let us first consider the most efficient use of resources in the production of apples and nuts. In the box diagram in Fig. 13.1a, we use the southwest corner (lower left) as the origin for apples and the northeast corner (upper right) as the origin for nuts. The dimensions of the box are the fixed supplies of labor L and land D.

The isoquants for apples are convex to O_A and those for nuts are convex to O_N. Each isoquant represents a fixed amount of apples $(A_1,A_2 \ldots)$ or of nuts $(N_1,N_2 \ldots)$ producible with varying combinations of labor and land. Points in the box represent amounts of inputs allocated to apples (L_A,D_A) with the remainder of the input supply at any point devoted to nuts (L_N,D_N). $L_A + L_N = L$ and $D_A + D_N = D$. By transferring some land from apple to nut production and some labor from nuts to apples, we may be able to increase the production of apples or nuts (or both) without decreasing the output of either. Such a transfer is possible except at points on the production-contract curve where the

---

[2] We assume the same convexities and other properties of isoquants and indifference curves as in the earlier chapters.

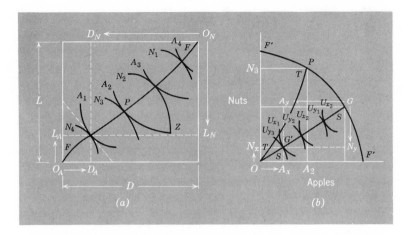

Fig. 13.1

apple isoquants are tangent to the nut isoquants. At the points of tangency of the convex isoquants, their slopes are equal: $\text{RTS}_{LD}{}^A = \text{RTS}_{LD}{}^N$. The production-contract curve is the locus of these points of tangency representing input allocations which are Pareto-optimum.

Points on the production-contract curve are Pareto-efficient in production in the same sense that points on the exchange-contract curve are Pareto-efficient. Trading onto the exchange-contract curve from a point off the curve improved the utility position of at least one of the parties without harming any. Here, a transfer or reallocation of resources from a point off the production-contract curve, say from Z to P in Fig. 13.1a—devoting less land to apples and more to nuts, but devoting more labor to apples and less to nuts—would cause no loss in production of apples (both P and Z are on the same apple isoquant, A_2) but would, in fact, increase the yield of nuts. The reallocation would take us from Z on the nut isoquant N_2 to P on the higher nut isoquant N_3. A transfer of resources taking us from Z to V would leave us on the same nut isoquant, N_2, but would bring us onto a higher apple isoquant, A_3. The apple yield would increase from A_2 to A_3.

A move from point Z off the contract curve to any point on the contract curve between P and V will increase the yield of both apples and nuts. Every point on the production-contract curve in Fig. 13.1a represents a Pareto-efficient use of resources in the production of apples and nuts. Everywhere along the production-contract curve the convex isoquants are tangent to each other, so that the slopes of the apple isoquants equal the slopes of the nut isoquants. This equality of the slopes of the apple and nut isoquants fulfills the marginal condition for production efficiency: equal rates of technical substitution (RTS) between inputs for all products using these inputs ($RTS_{DL}{}^A = RTS_{DL}{}^N$). Since the rate of technical substitution equals the ratio of marginal products of the inputs, this equality condition can be expressed in terms of the ratios of the marginal products:

$$\frac{MP_{DA}}{MP_{LA}} = \frac{MP_{DN}}{MP_{LN}}{}^3 \tag{13.1}$$

Each point on the production-contract curve FF can be mapped from input space (in Fig. 13.1*a*) into the output space of Fig. 13.1*b* to form the transformation curve, $F'F'$. Point P in Figs. 13.1*a* and 13.1*b* represents the same output of apples and nuts (A_2,N_3) and implies the same efficient allocation of the inputs between apples and nuts.

The transformation or production-possibility curve $F'F'$ in Fig. 13.1*b* is concave to the origin. Its slope is called the marginal rate of transformation (MRT) of apples into nuts—the number of nuts that can be produced by transferring or reallocating resources that were used to produce an apple from apples to nuts. The marginal rate of transformation is the marginal cost of apples at the margin in terms of the alternative product, nuts. It is the number of nuts foregone by releasing the resources necessary to produce an apple. The concavity reflects the increase in the marginal cost of apples relative to nuts, as more apples and fewer nuts are produced, and vice versa. Every point on the transformation curve represents that maximum attainable amount of one commodity for given amounts of the other, with given technology and resource base. If N_2 is given, A_3 is the maximum number of apples that can be produced. In general, $MRT_{NA}(= MC_A/MC_N)$ must be equal for all producers of these products to obtain the optimal degree of product specialization.

For each Pareto-efficient output combination point on the production-possibility curve $F'F'$ in Fig. 13.1*b*, we may construct another Edgeworth Box, within which we can reproduce the gains from exchange analysis of the previous chapter. The exchange-contract curve is the locus of the points of tangency of X's indifference curves $(U_{x1},U_{x2},U_{x3}, \ldots)$ convex to X's origin at the southwest (lower left) corner and Y's indifference curves $(U_{y1},U_{y2},U_{y3}, \ldots)$ convex to Y's

---

[3] It is also true that the marginal product of a single factor must be equal in all uses:

$$MP_{DA} = MP_{DN} \quad \text{and} \quad MP_{LA} = MP_{LN}$$

origin at the northeast (upper right) corner. Whatever the initial distribution of apples and nuts between persons X and Y, trade or exchange onto the contract curve (Pareto-optimal positions) will enable one or both persons to increase their utility without any loss in utility to the other. The marginal condition for efficiency in exchange is the equality of the marginal rates of substitution between nuts and apples for both person X and person Y:

$$\mathrm{MRS}_{NA}{}^{X} = \mathrm{MRS}_{NA}{}^{Y} \quad \text{or} \quad \frac{\mathrm{MU}_{Ax}}{\mathrm{MU}_{Nx}} = \frac{\mathrm{MU}_{Ay}}{\mathrm{MU}_{Ny}} \tag{13.2}$$

The contract curve SS representing the locus of points that are Pareto-efficient in exchange is one of an infinite number of such exchange-contract curves, each of which takes as its northeast corner any one of the infinite number of Pareto-efficient output combinations that lie on the production-possibility curve, such as points G or P in Fig. 13.1b. The exchange-contract curves such as SS or TT in Fig. 13.1b, which represent Pareto-optimum exchange positions for any given efficient output combination (with the indifference curves indicating some level of ordinal utility), can be mapped from output space into utility space, as in Fig. 13.2. $S'S'$ in Fig. 13.2 corresponds to the exchange-contract curve SS in Fig. 13.1b drawn with respect to output combination G. $T'T'$ represents Pareto-efficient combinations of utility that lie on the exchange-contract curve TT drawn with respect to the output combination P in Fig. 13.1b.

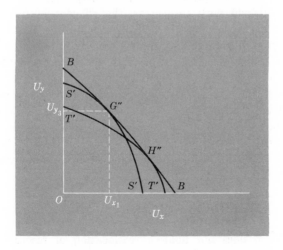

Fig. 13.2

Grand Utility-Possibility Frontier

For every efficient output combination on the production-possibility curve, a separate "utility-possibility frontier" may be drawn. Each point on a given utility-possibility frontier shows possible combinations of utility that are Pareto-optimal. Whatever the distribution of the produced commodities, at least one of the parties will benefit without loss to the other until the exchange-contract curve is reached. For every efficient combination of commodities produced, a separate exchange-contract curves can be drawn. Mapped in utility space, these exchange-contract curves become the utility-possibility curves. $S'S'$ and $T'T'$ in Fig. 13.2 are examples from an infinite number of such curves.

So far, we have assumed nothing at all about how outputs actually are distributed between persons X and Y, nor have we made any explicit assumption about each person's initial input-endowment. A third marginal efficiency condition enables us to choose a single optimal point on each exchange-contract curve, or on each utility-possibility curve in 13.2. The technical transformation possibilities are represented by the slope of the production-possibility curve—the marginal rate of transformation (MRT) between apples and nuts. The psychological transformation possibilities are represented by the rates of subjective indifference between apples and nuts—the marginal rates of substitution, which we know are equal for both persons along the exchange-contract curve where the second optimal marginal condition is satisfied.

Every point on the frontier of a particular utility-possibility curve such as $S'S'$, drawn with respect to the efficient output combination G—the northeast corner of the Edgeworth trading box—represents a Pareto-efficient utility combination attainable with output G. The utility combinations along this utility-possibility (exchange-contract) curve imply Pareto-efficient distributions of outputs.

There exists on every exchange-contract curve a common MRS ($\text{MRS}^x = \text{MRS}^y$) whose slope equals the MRT with respect to which the trading box is constructed. In Fig. 13.1b, the common MRS along the exchange-contract curve at G' equals the MRT at G on the production-possibility curve. The third efficiency condition states that the common MRS must equal the MRT:

$$\text{MRS}_{NA}{}^x = \text{MRS}_{NA}{}^y = \text{MRT}_{NA} \qquad (13.3)$$

If this condition does not hold, a reallocation of resources to permit product substitution may be desirable. Suppose that MRT is 4, so that 4 nuts can be produced at a cost of 1 apple, but MRS = 1, so that persons X and Y are indifferent between 1 apple and 1 nut. If we go ahead and reduce apple production by 1, 1 less apple will be consumed by, say, person X, but 1 nut can be substituted for the apple without any change in utility. The remaining 3 nuts to be distributed will increase U_x, U_y, or both. Only where the MRS (of consumers of apples and nuts) and the MRT (of producers of apples and nuts) are equal is it not possible through product substitution to increase X or Y's utility without any loss to either person.

A particular Pareto-efficient combination of utilities, $U_x U_y$, may be obtained for the various output combinations along the production-possibility curve. For each output combination there is an infinite number of Pareto-efficient $U_x U_y$ combinations: the utility-possibility curves plotted in utility space. However, not every point on a particular utility-possibility curve drawn with respect to a particular output combination is Pareto-efficient in the sense of satisfying the third efficiency condition, as stated in Eq. 13.3. We may ignore combinations of $U_x U_y$ that are not Pareto-efficient with respect to output substitution. We select only combinations of $U_x U_y$ that cannot be improved upon by product substitution brought about by a reallocation of inputs.

The grand utility-possibility frontier is the "envelope" of points on particular utility-possibility functions such that utility combinations which are efficient in exchange cannot be improved upon by output substitution. Associated with each output combination on the production-possibility curve, we find a point on the exchange-contract curve where the common MRS equals the MRT. In Fig. 13.2, G'' and H'' lie on the grand utility-possibility frontier, BB. BB, the grand utility-possibility frontier, includes points on each particular utility-possibility curve. All points on the grand frontier BB fulfill the third efficiency condition: MRS = MRT. BB is shown again in Fig. 13.3. At this stage in our analysis we can trace along line BB—the grand utility frontier—an infinite number of Pareto-efficient theoretical possibilities, given the resource base, production possibilities, and consumer preferences. Each point along BB represents a maximum attainable combination of utilities, $U_x U_y$. As we move downward to the right along BB, we move to positions which consumer X finds more preferable and consumer Y less preferable. Recall that consumer preferences are represented by ordinal indices, which do not permit interpersonal comparisons. We cannot say that $U_x = 100$ is better than or more satisfying to person X than $U_y = 400$ is to person Y.

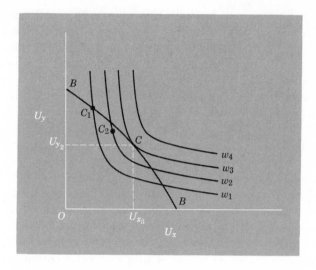

Fig. 13.3

Social Welfare Function

Only by "imposing" ethical judgments in the form of a Bergson-Samuelson social-welfare function[4] is it possible, in principle, to judge whether any one position along BB is superior to any other. In order to examine the consequences of changes in social and economic variables, new value judgments are introduced that may be permitted to supersede values inherent in the analysis up to this point. Each individual's utility is a function of a great many economic and social variables. A social welfare function can be viewed as a function of individual utilities with a certain distribution of weights explicitly assigned to the individual utilities, in accordance with the particular "ethic" involved. The evaluation of possible combinations of individual utilities rests on these extra-scientific ethical judgments. Everyone need not approve of the particular function being examined, nor of the method by which the particular function was determined.

The welfare contours of a Bergson-Samuelson social welfare function represent values, which may dominate the interests of individual consumers. It is quite possible that individuals may not agree to the same

[4] Abram Bergson, "A Reformulation of Certain Aspects of Welfare Economics," *QJE*, LII, 1938, pp. 310–334.

social-welfare function; they may accept or be forced to accept a unique social welfare function that does not represent their own interest.[5]

The problem of how the ethical judgments made explicit in a social welfare function are to be formulated is often set aside. It has been demonstrated that if a democratic social decision-making process meets certain reasonable (but rather restrictive) conditions, a group's majority choice (among alternatives) may be inconsistent (not transitive) with respect to individuals' ordinal choices. There is reason to doubt the ability of a group to formulate through democratic process a social welfare function that accurately reflects individual preferences.

It is impossible to form a unique community indifference function from individual indifference curves by aggregating individual ordinal preferences except in the highly unlikely case where individuals have identical tastes that remain identical with changes in income distribution.[6] Each society in fact makes decisions through political processes ranging from "perfect" democracy to "absolute" dictatorship, but these decisions require ethical judgments, which are implicit in all political decisions. The social welfare function makes these ethical judgments explicit.

In our example, each individual's utility is a function of his consumption of economic goods or services. Interpersonal judgments are made

[5] Professor Samuelson's description of a social welfare function makes this quite clear:
"Without inquiring into its origins, we take as a starting point for our discussion a function of all the economic magnitudes of a system which is supposed to characterize some ethical belief—that of a benevolent despot, or a complete egotist, or "all men of good will," a misanthrope, the state, race or group mind, God, etc. . . . We only require that the belief be such as to admit of an unequivocal answer as to whether one configuration of the economic system is "better" or "worse" than any other or "indifferent," and that these relationships are transitive; i.e., *A* better than *B, B* better than *C,* implies *A* better than *C,* etc. The function need only be ordinally defined, and it may or may not be convenient to work with (any) one cardinal index or indicator. There is no need to assume any particular curvature of the loci (in hyper-space) of indifference of this function. Utilizing one out of an infinity of possible indicators or cardinal indices, we may write this function in the form $W = W(Z_1, Z_2, \ldots)$, where the Z's represent all possible variables, many of them non-economic in character." Paul A. Samuelson, *Foundations of Economic Analysis,* New York: Atheneum, 1965, p. 221. The whole of Chapter VIII on Welfare Economics is highly recommended.

[6] The problem of forming a community indifference function from individual indifference curves is discussed in Paul A. Samuelson, "Social Indifference Curves," *Review of Economic Studies,* IX, pp. 89–110. See also Kenneth J. Arrow, *Social Choice and Individual Values,* New York: John Wiley and Sons, 1951. Also a critique by Julian H. Blau, "The Existence of Social Welfare Functions," *Econometrica,* Vol. 25, April 1957.

and certain distributions of goods and services among individuals are judged to be "socially" better than others. Certainly, a complete social welfare function would include many other variables in addition to private goods and services allocated to and consumed by individuals. We might include collective goods either as variables in a separate collective or community utility function or as additional variables in each individual's utility function. A collective (public) good can be defined as a good whose consumption by any one person does not diminish its consumption by any other person. Often the utility an individual may expect to derive from a collective good is not so much a function of the "amount consumed" as it is of the "total amount available to be consumed." Often this puts an impossible burden on prices, if an optimal rationing of private and public goods is to be achieved.

Many noneconomic variables, even the group decision process itself, might affect individual utilities and ultimately the social welfare as viewed as a weighted combination of individual utilities. The important "side relations" connecting economic values such as maximization and efficiency with noneconomic values such as peace and power could conceivably be considered within the framework of a complex social welfare function.

The importance of individual consumer preferences and of Pareto-efficiency in exchange and in production are values implicit in all points on the grand utility frontier BB. Points along the grand utility frontier satisfy the necessary conditions for welfare maximization. The social welfare function is represented by the indifference contours $(w_1, w_2, \ldots)$ in Fig. 13.3. They are numbered in ascending order from the origin. The point marked C_2 in Fig. 13.3 is not on the grand frontier BB. At point C_2 there is some allocative inefficiency, and yet point C_2 lines on a higher welfare contour (w_2) than does point C_1 (on w_1), even though C_1 lies on the grand frontier and does meet the marginal conditions that derive from the Pareto-efficiency criterion.

The constrained-bliss point, C in Fig. 13.3, is the highest Paretian welfare position attainable. (All attainable points are bounded by the grand utility-possibility frontier BB.) Points within the frontier such as point C_2—less than maximally attainable points—may be preferred to points such as point C_1 on the boundary BB. However, given the shape of the welfare contour, for any point not on the grand utility-frontier, there exists some preferred point on the frontier. The most preferred position on the grand utility-possibility frontier is the *constrained-bliss* point. Given the shapes of our welfare and grand utility functions, there is only one constrained-bliss point, C, which falls on the grand utility frontier. This unique point on the efficiency frontier determines that the output combination and its distribution will be Pareto-efficient.

"Best" Inputs, Outputs, and Commodity Distribution

If we can agree that maximum social welfare is achieved at the constrained-bliss point, C, where BB touches the highest welfare contour, we can then determine unique values for the optimal output combination that can be produced with a given resource base; in addition, we can determine the optimal distribution of output between persons X and Y and we can determine the optimal allocation of inputs between the outputs.

We know that each $U_x U_y$ point on the grand utility-possibility frontier, BB, corresponds to a particular output combination of the production-possibility curve, and implies a certain distribution of output within the Edgeworth trading box, whose northeast corner is on the production-possibility curve. C in Fig. 13.3 corresponds to C'' in the trading box in Fig. 13.4 with output combination C' (A_1, N_4) as its northeast corner. This "best" utility combination C'' $(U_{x3} U_{y2})$ determines the "best" combination of nuts and apples to be produced, C' (A_1, N_4), and the best distribution of nuts and apples between person X and person Y along the contract curve in that trading box. A_x, A_y, N_x, N_y are determined in that trading box (whose northeast corner is C') at C'', where the common slope (MRS) equals the slope (MRT) of the production-possibility curve at C'.

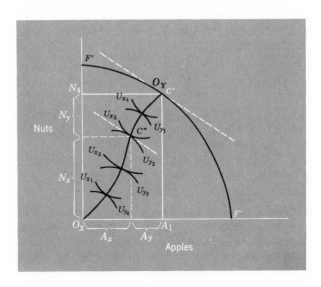

Fig. 13.4

The contract curve representing Pareto-efficient production possibilities in Fig. 13.1a determines the most efficient input allocation associated with the best output combination (A_1, N_4).

Shadow-price ratios can be imputed from the constrained-bliss point. The outputs, utilities, and inputs implied by the constrained-bliss point have been identified in the graphic analysis. In Fig. 13.1a, the optimal apples-nuts combination (A_1, N_4) on the production-contract curve satisfies the first marginal condition for maximum welfare—that the RTS of labor for land be identical in production of both apples and nuts. This common RTS$_{LD}$ is a constant in the solution of the welfare-maximizing problem. From our earlier analysis of production and cost, we know that under perfectly competitive factor market conditions the profit-maximizing producer will equate RTS$_{LD}$ ($= $ MP$_D$MP$_L$) with the ratio of input prices r/w, where r is the rental rate for land and w is the wage rate of labor. This is a least-cost condition for producing any commodity at any rate of output. The shadow-price ratio must be identical with the common RTS$_{LD}$ for producers of both apples and nuts along the production-contract curve, if production is to be efficient. In Fig. 13.1a, the dashed line tangent to isoquants A_1 and N_4 represents the shadow-price ratio r/w.

A similar shadow-price ratio can be imputed to the price of the goods consumed, if the optimal conditions for exchange and product substitution are to hold. At the constrained-bliss point, the MRT$_{NA}$ equals the common MRS$_{NA}$ for both persons X and Y. This common MRS$_{NA}$ is a constant in the welfare-maximizing solution. We know from our analysis of consumer behavior that in equilibrium the MRS$_{NA}$ ($= $ MU$_A$/MU$_N$) equals the price ratio P_A/P_N for each utility-maximizing consumer. This common MRS$_{NA}$ for both consumers can be located on the exchange-contract curve in Fig. 13.4. The dashed line through C'' can be taken as the constant price ratio in accord with which consumers allocate their income to maximize utility. This shadow-price ratio P_A/P_N equals the common slope of X and Y's indifference curves at the point of tangency along the exchange-contract curve where this MRS$_{NA}$ equals the MRT.

After identifying both the shadow-price ratio r/w (the dashed line in Fig. 13.1a) representing the imputed price ratio for the inputs and the shadow-price ratio P_A/P_N (the dotted line in Fig. 13.4) representing the imputed price ratio for outputs, we can determine algebraically the relationship between the input prices and output prices.

We know that under perfect competition, profit-maximizing producers hire labor up to the point where the value of the marginal product VMP equals the input price. Nut producers hire labor under perfect competition according to the following rule: VMP$_{LN}$ ($= $ MP$_{LN} \cdot P_N$) $= w$.

Apple producers hire labor to where $\text{VMP}_{LA}(= \text{MP}_{LA} \cdot P_A) = w$. Since there is a single input price for labor (w) throughout the market, $w = \text{VMP}_{LA} = \text{VMP}_{LN}$ or $w = \text{MP}_{LN} \cdot P_N = \text{MP}_{IA} \cdot P_A$. This is consistent with the profit-maximizing rule in the product market: $P_N = w/\text{MP}_{LN}$ ($= \text{MC}_N$) and $P_A = w/\text{MP}_{LA}$ ($= \text{MC}_A$). In terms of land, $r = \text{MP}_{DN}P_N = \text{MP}_{DA}P_A$, or $P_N = r/\text{MP}_{DN}(= \text{MC}_N)$ and $P_A = r/\text{MP}_{DA}$ ($= \text{MC}_A$). Since all of the marginal products are known, we can solve for any three prices in terms of the fourth (the numéraire). Suppose we let $w = 1$, $P_N = w = 1/\text{MP}_{LN}$ and $P_A = w = 1/\text{MP}_{LA}$. Once P_N and P_A are known (in terms of w), we can easily solve for r. We have demonstrated that the relation between input prices, r/w, and output prices, P_A/P_N, can be determined using the profit-maximizing rule.[7]

Perfect Competition and Maximum Welfare

Under perfect competition a single price prevails in each market. Input and output prices are taken as parameters and are common to all who operate in a given market. The common price is not affected by the independent action of any single individual. Each attempts to equate the relevant rate of substitution or transformation with the given price ratio. All utility-maximizing consumers in the market allocate their income by equating their marginal rates of substitution with the given price ratio for any pair of commodities: $\text{MRS}_{NA} = P_A/P_N$. (At least, this relationship holds true if they succeed in maximizing utility.) Since under perfect competition all consumers in the market face the same common price ratio for any two commodities, the MRS between any two commodities is identical for all consumers. Under perfect competition, the following relationship holds true in the two-person, two-commodity case: $\text{MRS}_{NA}{}^X = \text{MRS}_{NA}{}^Y = P_A/P_N$.

Pareto-efficient exchange can be achieved under conditions of perfect competition. The necessary conditions for optimal exchange—$\text{MRS}_{NA}{}^X = \text{MRS}_{NA}{}^Y$—is fulfilled under conditions of perfect competition, providing that there are no external economies or diseconomies.

[7] An alternative method of relating input and output prices is as follows: $\text{MRS}_{NA} = P_A/P_N$ and $\text{RTS}_{LD} = r/w$. These equilibrium conditions can be expressed $P_A = P_N \cdot \text{MRS}_{NA}$ and $r = w \cdot \text{RTS}_{LD}$. The former can be substituted into one of the profit-maximizing conditions for hiring inputs. For example, $w = \text{MP}_{LA}(P_A) = \text{MP}_{LA}(P_N \cdot \text{MRS}_{NA})$, which can then be substituted into $r = w \cdot \text{RTS}_{LD} = P_N \text{MP}_{LA} \text{MRS}_{NA} \text{RTS}_{LD}$. r can be solved in terms of P_N since MP, MRS, and RTS are known. By substituting, we can solve for the remaining prices in terms of the numéraire.

Producers, too, under perfectly competitive conditions face constant input and output prices. All producers minimize cost by equating the rate of technical substitution with the single input price ratio r/w. This would hold for the apple producers and nut producers in our illustrative two-commodity case. Under perfectly competitive conditions, inputs are used according to the marginal welfare condition: $\mathrm{RTS}_{LD}{}^A = \mathrm{RTS}_{LD}{}^N$, since both $\mathrm{RTS}_{LD}{}^A$ and $\mathrm{RTS}_{LD}{}^N$ are equated to the single input price ratio r/w.

Producers, maximizing profit under perfectly competitive conditions, equate marginal cost and output price for all commodities. In our two-commodity case, this means $P_A = \mathrm{MC}_A$ and $P_N = \mathrm{MC}_N$, so that $P_A/P_N = \mathrm{MC}_A/\mathrm{MC}_N$. Therefore, the third marginal welfare condition—$\mathrm{MRS}_{NA} = \mathrm{MRT}_{NA}$—holds under perfect competition since $\mathrm{MRS}_{NA} = P_A/P_N$ and $\mathrm{MRT}_{NA} = \mathrm{MC}_A/\mathrm{MC}_N = P_A/P_N$.[8]

All the necessary marginal conditions for optimal welfare are fulfilled under perfectly competitive conditions, where a single set of relative input prices and output prices confront all consumers and producers. A perfectly competitive economy meets the necessary conditions which derive from the Paretian welfare criterion. The necessary conditions bring us somewhere onto the grand utility frontier, where we are assured that resources are efficiently allocated and outputs are efficiently distributed.

The shadow-prices imbedded in the analysis are a set of constants, equal to the Pareto-efficient transformation and substitution rates and therefore consistent with the values implied by that point on the grand utility-possibility frontier which we have called the constrained-bliss point. These constants were identified as the price of apples P_A, the price of nuts P_N, the wage rate w, and rent for land r. Utility-maximizing consumers and profit-maximizing producers reacting independently, as under perfectly competitive market conditions, to this particular set of relative prices—the absolute price level is of no consequence—will reach the constrained-bliss output and input values: A_x, A_y, N_x, N_y, D_A, D_N, L_A, and L_N. This solution does not necessarily require the existence of perfectly competitive markets, but there is no assurance that any other system will bring us closer to a position of maximum welfare.

[8] Note that for MRS to always equal MRT, equality between price and marginal cost for all commodities is necessary. Constant proportionality between price and marginal cost is not sufficient if the MRS between a primary resource (leisure) and an output (bread) is to equal the MRT of the primary resource into the output. The marginal rate of transformation between a primary resource and output is actually the marginal product. If the rate at which the input (leisure) can be converted into the output (bread) is greater than the rate of substitution (representing the rate of indifference between bread and leisure), less leisure will be used for consumption purposes.

Externalities

External economies and diseconomies were considered earlier. The possibility of their presence in consumption and production raises an important qualification on the capacity of a perfectly competitive economy to meet the necessary Pareto conditions for maximum welfare. For example, the marginal rate of transformation of nuts to apples measures the opportunity cost of one output in terms of the other: $MRT_{NA} = MC_A/MC_N = P_A/P_N$. If there are external economies or diseconomies, the private marginal costs to which producers respond may not correspond to the social marginal costs. The lack of equality between social costs and social benefits is reflected in the discrepancy between the marginal rate of substitution and the "social" marginal rate of transformation. Elements of monopoly or other imperfections in markets may also result in failure to fulfill the necessary efficiency conditions.

Sufficient conditions for fulfilling marginal welfare conditions require convexity to the origin of indifference curves and concavity to the origin of production-possibility curves. Even then, unless relative shapes are of the proper order of magnitude, corner solutions (marginal inequalities) rather than tangency solutions (marginal equalities) may be necessary for maximum welfare. There may also be cases where the range of values of variables is institutionally bounded, prohibiting the fulfillment of marginal conditions.[9]

Optimal Income Distribution

Pareto-efficiency contributes very little to the question: What constitutes an optimal distribution of income or factor-endowment? If greater equality in the distribution of income (involving loss to some) enables the society to climb to a higher contour of the social welfare function, the optimum welfare position may not lie on the boundary of the grand

---

[9] External effects or externalities can be couched in the more recent language of *Direct Interaction,* focusing on the interdependencies (external to the price system) between economic groups and economic functions. Professor Bator suggests the following three categories of externalities which account for "divergence between private and social cost-benefit calculations." Each is considered separately as a "cause of failure of decentralized markets to sustain as optimal welfare solution: (1) Ownership Externalities (nonappropriability), (2) Technical Externalities (nonconvexity), and (3) Public Good Externalities." Francis M. Bator, "The Anatomy of Market Failure," QJE, 72, p. 363 (August 1958).

utility-possibility frontier, where all the Pareto-efficiency conditions are met.[10]

The constrained-bliss point implied a certain optimal distribution of apples and nuts to persons X and Y. But nothing in the analysis guaranteed that the shadow-prices, w, r, P_A, and P_N, imbedded in the analysis and implied by the constrained-bliss point, would enable persons X and Y to purchase the outputs A_x, N_x, A_y, N_y. Only accidentally would the initial factor-endowments of persons X and Y enable them to purchase the outputs in conformity with the constrained-bliss distribution. Does person X own enough land (D_x) and labor (L_x) to purchase A_x and N_x at the implied shadow-prices? Does $wL_x + rD_x = P_AA_x + P_NN_x$? And, similarly, does person Y own enough of each input to purchase A_y and N_y?

Only by coincidence will existing factor-endowments $(L_x + L_y = L$ and $D_x + D_y = D)$ be such that each person will have sufficient income (the value of his factor-endowment) to purchase the optimal outputs assigned to X and Y in the maximum welfare solution.

If the initial input-endowment is taken as given, there exists some Pareto-efficient position on the grand utility-possibility frontier that is consistent with the existing (arbitrary) input distribution, but it is not likely that it will be identical to the constrained-bliss point. In theory it is possible to "devise" income transfers that will permit the purchase of the socially optimal distribution of outputs determined by the constrained-bliss position, whatever the existing factor-endowments. Alternatively, the constrained-bliss position implies a certain set of factor-endowments that is consistent with the determined solution. The value of the factors owned by persons X and Y will then be just sufficient to enable them to purchase the outputs indicated at the constrained-bliss position.[11]

Compensation Principle

Prior to the introduction of the Bergson-Samuelson social-welfare function, as an ethic to be applied by the political body—a guide for judging the desirability of an infinite number of economically possible positions—economists gave serious consideration to the compensation principle. Many felt that Pareto-efficiency was inadequate as a guide to

[10] Where the social welfare function is not a monotonic function of individual utilities, a position of optimal social welfare may lie inside the grand frontier. There is no particular reason why the social welfare function *should be* based solely on individual consumer preferences.

[11] Throughout, we have assumed a fixed resource base—that L and D were zero-elastic with respect to input prices, individual preferences, and levels of welfare.

maximum welfare. The Pareto welfare criterion permits an infinite number of optimal positions, but even more serious, it poses an automatic veto to any policy that involves loss to someone—a movement along the contract curve. That most important political decisions violate the Pareto-efficiency conditions may be taken for granted. Hicks and Kaldor attempted to define a criterion by which positions, which were noncomparable in terms of Paretian optimality, could be compared.

Kaldor suggested that a policy proposal should be accepted, even if it did not lead to a Pareto-optimal position, providing that those who stood to benefit were able to bribe the losers into accepting the proposal. For example, if the winners expected to gain $3000 and the losers expected to lose $1000, a bribe of something over $1000 would more than compensate the losers and insure a net gain to those who expected to benefit directly.

Hicks proposed a different version of the compensation principle. In Kaldor's version, the loser, in effect, had to grant permission for the change. In Hicks' version, those who stand to gain can initiate the change without the permission of the loser, so the loser attempts to bribe the winner into not effecting the change. If the winner stands to win more than the loser stands to lose, the loser cannot profitably offer a sufficiently large bribe to prevent the change. For example, suppose the winner stands to win $3000 and the loser stands to lose $1000, then the loser cannot prevent the change. Neither Hicks' nor Kaldor's criterion required that the compensating payments need actually be made in order to judge whether one position was superior to another—their measures of welfare were, in this sense, independent of distribution.

Scitovsky suggested a double criterion. Both the Hicks and Kaldor criteria must be met before one position is deemed preferable to another: that winners can profitably bribe losers into accepting the change, and at the same time losers are unable to profitably bribe the potential winners into not effecting the change. In addition, the compensation agreed upon must actually be paid to the losers before such a move can be judged desirable. (In the absence of the actual payment, the losers might have profitably prevented the change.) In effect, if the compensation is considered as part of the change, and if the double criterion is met, the change becomes Pareto-efficient. Very little help is provided by this extreme version of the compensation principle in choosing among the infinite number of possible Pareto-efficient positions.

The social welfare function, which takes us outside the bounds of judgments based on individual preferences and Pareto-efficient allocation, seems to offer the most fruitful path for future efforts to define conditions for social-optimum and to suggest policies that contribute to maximum welfare.

Selected Bibliography

Introduction

Black, Duncan, "The Unity of Economic and Political Science," *Economic Journal*, **60**, 506–514 (September 1950).

Friedman, Milton, "The Methodology of Positive Economics," *Essays in Positive Economics*, Chicago: University of Chicago Press, 1953, 1–43.

Keynes, J. M., *The Scope and Method of Political Economy*, London: Macmillan, 1930, 4th ed.

Knight, F. H., *The Economic Organization*, New York: Kelley and Millman, 1951, 3–30.

Lange, O., "The Scope and Method of Economics," *Review of Economic Studies*, **13**, 19–32 (1945–1946).

Robbins, Lionel, *An Essay on the Nature and Significance of Economic Science*, New York: Macmillan, 1935, 2nd ed.

Ruggles, Richard, "Methodological Developments," *A Survey of Contemporary Economics*, B. F. Haley, ed, Vol. 2, Homewood, Ill.: Richard D. Irwin, 1952, 408–453.

Schumpeter, Joseph A., "Science and Ideology," *American Economic Review*, **39**, 345–519 (March 1949).

Wickstead, P. H., *The Commonsense of Political Economy*, London, 1933, Chaps. 1–4.

Demand and Utility and Consumer Choice

Alchian, A. A., "The Meaning of Utility Measurement," *American Economic Review*, **18**, 26–50 (March 1953).

Allen, R. G. D., "A Reconsideration of the Theory of Value II," *Economica*, N.S. 1, 196–219 (1934).

Arrow, Kenneth, *Social Choice and Individual Values*, New York: John Wiley and Sons, 1951.

Bailey, Martin J., "The Marshallian Demand Curve," *Journal of Political Economy*, **62**, 255–261 (1954).

276

Becker, Gary S., "Irrational Behavior and Economic Theory," *Journal of Political Economy*, **70**, 1–13 (February 1962).

Clark, J. M., "Realism and Relevance in the Theory of Demand," *Journal of Political Economy*, **54**, 342–353 (August 1946).

Clarkson, Geoffrey P. E., *The Theory of Consumer Demand: A Critical Appraisal*, Englewood Cliffs, N.J.: Prentice-Hall, 1963.

Duesenberry, J. S., *Income, Saving, and the Theory of Consumer Behavior*, Cambridge: Harvard University Press, 1949.

Ellsberg, D., "Classic and Current Notions of 'Measurable Utility,' " *Economic Journal*, **64**, 528–556 (September 1954).

Ferber, R., "Research in Household Behavior," *American Economic Review*, **52**, 19–63 (March 1962).

Friedman, Milton, "The Marshallian Demand Curve," *Journal of Political Economy*, **57**, 463–495 (1949).

Friedman, Milton, *A Theory of the Consumption Function*, New York: National Bureau of Economic Research, 1957.

Girshick, M. A., and Haavelmo, Trygve, "Statistical Analysis of the Demand for Food. Examples of Simultaneous Estimation of Structural Equations," in *Studies in Econometric Methods*, Cowles Commission Monograph No. 14, ed. William C. Hood and Tjalling C. Koopmans, New York: John Wiley and Sons, 1953.

Hicks, J. R. "A Reconsideration of the Theory of Value I," *Economica*, N.S. 1, 52–76 (1934).

Hicks, J. R., *A Revision of Demand Theory*, Oxford: Clarendon Press, 1956.

Hicks, J. R., *Value and Capital*, Oxford: Oxford University Press, 1946, 1–41, 305–311.

Houthakker, H. S., "Revealed Preference and the Utility Function," *Economica*, N.S. 17, 159–174 (1950).

Klein, Lawrence R., *An Introduction to Econometrics*, Englewood Cliffs, N.J.: Prentice-Hall, 1962, Chap. 4.

Knight, Frank H., "Realism and Relevance in the Theory of Demand," *Journal of Political Economy*, **52**, 289–318 (1944).

Lampman, Robert J., "Making Utility Predictions Verifiable," *Southern Economic Journal*, **22**, 360–366 (January 1956).

Lange, Oscar, "Complementarity and Interrelations of Shifts in Demand," *Review of Economic Studies*, **7**, 58–63 (1940–1941).

Leibenstein, Harvey, "Bandwagon, Snob and Veblen Effects in the Theory of Consumer's Demand," *Quarterly Journal of Economics*, **64**, 183–207 (May 1950).

Marschak, J., "Rational Behavior, Uncertain Prospects and Measurable Utility," *Econometrica*, **18**, 111–141 (April 1950).

Marshall, Alfred, *Principles of Economics,* 8th ed., New York: Macmillan, 1920, Book III, 92–137.

Mosak, Jacob L., "On the Interpretation of the Fundamental Equation of Value Theory," in *Studies in Mathematical Economics and Econometrics,* ed. by O. Lange, F. McIntyre, and T. O. Yntema, Chicago: The University of Chicago Press, 1942, 69–74.

Mosteller, F., and Nogee, P., "An Experimental Measurement of Utility," *Journal of Political Economy,* **59,** 371–404 (1951).

Oxenfeldt, A. R., "Consumer Knowledge, Its Measurement and Extent," *Review of Economics and Statistics,* **32,** 300–314 (November 1950).

Pfouts, R. W., "Prolegomena to the Testing of Utility Theory," *Southern Economic Journal,* **22,** 178–188 (October 1955).

Prais, S. J., and Houthakker, H. S., *The Analysis of Family Budgets,* Cambridge: Cambridge University Press, 1955.

Robertson, D. H., *Utility and All That and Other Essays,* London: Macmillan, 1952.

Samuelson, Paul A., "Consumption Theory in Terms of Revealed Preference," *Economica.* N.S. 15, 243–253 (1948).

Schultz, Henry, *The Theory and Measurement of Demand,* Chicago: University of Chicago Press, 1938, Chaps. 2–6.

Slutsky, E. E., "On the Theory of the Budget of the Consumer," *Giornale degli Economisti,* **51,** 1–26 (July 1915). Reprinted in *A.E.A. Readings in Price Theory,* Homewood, Ill.: Richard D. Irwin, 1952, 27–56.

Stigler, George J., "The Development of Utility Theory," *Journal of Political Economy,* **58,** 369–387 (1950).

Stigler, George J., "Notes on the History of the Giffen Paradox," *Journal of Political Economy,* **55,** 152–156 (April 1947).

Suits, Daniel B., "The Demand for New Automobiles in the U.S., 1929–1956," *Review of Economics and Statistics,* **40,** 273–280 (August 1958).

Wold, Herman O. A., with Jureen, Lars, *Demand Analysis,* New York: John Wiley and Sons, 1953.

Working, E., "What Do Statistical 'Demand Curves' Show?," *Quarterly Journal of Economics,* **41,** 212–235 (1927). Reprinted in *A.E.A. Readings in Price Theory,* Chicago: Richard D. Irwin, 1952.

Production

Borts, George H., and Mishan, E. J., "Exploring the 'Uneconomic Region' of the Profit Function," *Review of Economic Studies,* **29,** 300–312 (1962).

Bronfenbrenner, M., and Douglas, Paul H., "Cross-Section Studies in the Cobb-Douglas Function," *Journal of Political Economy,* **47,** 761–785 (December 1939).

Cassels, J. M., "On the Law of Variable Proportions," *Readings in the Theory of Income Distribution*, eds. W. Fellner and B. F. Haley, Philadelphia: Blakiston, 1946, 103–118.

Chamberlin, E. H., "Proportionality, Divisibility, and Economies of Scale," *Quarterly Journal of Economics*, **62** (February 1948).

Chenery, H. B., "Engineering Production Functions," *Quarterly Journal of Economics*, **63,** 507–531 (1948–1949).

Clark, J. M., "Diminishing Returns," *Encyclopaedia of the Social Sciences*, Vol. 5, New York: Macmillan, 144–146.

Cobb, C. W., and Douglas, P. H., "A Theory of Production," *American Economic Review Supplement*, **18,** 139–165 (1938).

Dorfman, Robert, *Applications of Linear Programming to the Theory of the Firm*, Berkeley: University of California Press, 1951.

Douglas, P. H., "Are There Laws of Production?," *American Economic Review* (March 1948).

Hicks, John R., *Value and Capital*, 2d ed., Oxford: University Press, 1946, 78–98.

Klein, Lawrence R., *An Introduction to Econometrics*, Englewood Cliffs, N.J.: Prentice-Hall, 1962, 83–111.

Knight, Frank H., *Risk, Uncertainty, and Profit*, Boston: Houghton Mifflin Co., 1921.

Machlup, Fritz, "On the Meaning of the Marginal Product," in *A.E.A. Readings in the Theory of Income Distribution*, Philadelphia: Blakiston, 1951.

Moore, F. T., "Economics of Scale—Some Statistical Evidence," *Quarterly Journal of Economics*, **73,** 232–245 (May 1959).

Robertson, D. H., "Those Empty Boxes," *Economic Journal*, **34,** 16–31 (March 1924).

Robinson, E. A. G., *The Structure of Competitive Industry*, London: Nisbet, 1935.

Robinson, Joan, "The Production Function," *Economic Journal*, **65,** 67–71 (1955).

Smith, V. L., *Investment and Production*, Cambridge, Mass.: Harvard University Press, 1961.

Solow, Robert M., "The Production Function and the Theory of Capital," *Review of Economic Studies*, **23,** 101–108 (1955–1956).

Solow, Robert M., "Substitution and Fixed Proportions on the Theory of Capital," *Review of Economic Studies*, **29,** 207–218 (1962).

Sraffa, Piero, "The Laws of Returns Under Competitive Conditions," *Economic Journal*, **36,** 535–550 (December 1926).

Stigler, George J., *Production and Distribution Theories*, New York: Macmillan, 1946.

Production and Cost

Alchian, A., "Costs and Outputs," in *The Allocation of Economic Resources,* Palo Alto, Calif.: Stanford University Press, 1959.

Bishop, R. L., "Cost Discontinuities, Declining Costs and Marginal Analysis," *American Economic Review,* **38,** 607–617 (1948).

Clark, J. M., *Studies in the Economics of Overhead Costs,* Chicago: University of Chicago Press, 1923.

Cobb, C. W., and Douglas, Paul H., "A Theory of Production," *American Economic Review Supplement,* **18,** 139–165 (1938).

Eiteman, W. J., "The Least Cost Point, Capacity and Marginal Analysis," *American Economic Review,* **38,** 899–904 (December 1948).

Ellis, H. S., and Fellner, W., "External Economies and Diseconomies," *American Economic Review,* **33,** 493–511 (September 1943).

Friedman, M., *Price Theory,* Chicago: Aldine, 1962, Chaps. 5, 6.

Haines, W. W., "Capacity Production and the Least Cost Point," *American Economic Review,* **38,** 617–624 (September 1948).

Hirshleifer, J., "The Firm's Cost Function: a Successful Reconstruction," *Journal of Business* (July 1962).

Johnston, J., *Statistical Cost Analysis,* New York: McGraw-Hill, 1960.

Klein, Lawrence R., *An Introduction to Econometrics,* Englewood Cliffs, N.J.: Prentice-Hall, 1962, 111–129.

Mayer, J. R., Ferguson, A. R., and Borts, G. H., "Statistical Cost Function," *American Economic Review, Supplement,* **48,** 209–238 (May 1958).

Moore, F. T., "Economies of Scale: Some Statistical Evidence," *Quarterly Journal of Economics,* **73,** 232–245 (May 1959).

Solow, Robert M., "Technical Change and the Aggregate Production Function," *Review of Economics and Statistics,* **39,** 312–320 (1957).

Staehle, Hans, "The Measurement of Statistical Cost Functions: An Appraisal of Some Recent Contributions," in *A.E.A. Readings in Price Theory,* eds. George J. Stigler and Kenneth E. Boulding, Homewood, Ill.: Richard D. Irwin, 1952, Chap. 13.

Viner, J., "Cost Curves and Supply Curves," reprinted in *A.E.A. Readings in Price Theory,* eds. G. J. Stigler and K. Boulding, Homewood, Ill.: Richard D. Irwin, 1952.

The Purely Competitive Market

Baumol, W. J., *Economic Dynamics,* 2d ed., New York: Macmillan, 1959.

Buchanan, N. S., "A Reconsideration of the Cobweb Theorem," *Journal of Political Economy,* **47,** 67–81 (February 1939).

Coase, Ronald, "The Problem of Social Cost," *Journal of Law and Economics,* **3** (1961).

Friedman Joan, and Foote, Richard J., *Computation Methods for Handling Systems of Simultaneous Equations,* Agricultural Handbook No. 94, U.S. Department of Agriculture.

Henderson, J. M., and Quandt, R. E., *Microeconomic Theory,* New York: McGraw-Hill, 1958.

Hicks, J. R., *Value and Capital,* 2d. ed., Oxford: Clarendon Press, 1946.

Knight, Frank H., *Risk, Uncertainty, and Profit,* Boston: Houghton Mifflin Co., 1921.

Koopmans, T. C., *Three Essays on the State of Economic Science,* New York: McGraw-Hill, 1957.

Koopmans, T. C., and Hood, W. C., "The Estimation of Simultaneous Linear Economic Relationships," in Hood and Koopmans, eds., *Studies in Econometric Method,* Cowles Commission Monograph No. 10, New York: John Wiley and Sons, 1953, 135–142.

Marshall, A., *Principles of Economics,* 8th ed., London: Macmillan, 1936, 5.

Robbins, Lionel, "The Representative Firm," *Economic Journal,* **38,** 387–404 (September 1938).

Stigler, George J., "Perfect Competition, Historically Contemplated," *Journal of Political Economy,* **65,** 1–17 (1957).

Walras, Leon, *Elements of Pure Economics,* trans. William Jaffe, Homewood, Ill.: Richard D. Irwin, 1954.

Wicksteed, P. H., *The Commonsense of Political Economy,* London: George Rutledge and Sons, 1934, 2, Bk. 3.

Wolfe, J. N., "The Representative Firm," *Economic Journal,* **64,** 337–349 (June 1954).

The Theory of the Firm

Alchian, A., "Uncertainty, Evolution, and Economic Theory," *Journal of Political Economy,* **58,** 211–221 (1950).

Baumol, William J., *Business Behavior, Value and Growth,* New York: Macmillan, 1959, Chaps. 6–8.

Baumol, William J., "The Theory of Expansion of the Firm," *American Economic Review,* **52** (December 1962).

Boulding, Kenneth E., "The Theory of the Firm in the Last Ten Years," *American Economic Review,* **32,** 791–802 (1942).

Cohen, Kalman, J., and Cyert, Richard M., *Theory of the Firm,* Englewood Cliffs, N.J.: Prentice-Hall, 1965.

Cooper, W. W., "A Proposal for Extending the Theory of the Firm," *Quarterly Journal of Economics,* **65,** 87–109 (February 1951).

Cooper, W. W., "Theory of the Firm: Some Suggestions for Revision," *American Economic Review*, **39**, 1204–1222 (1949).

Cyert, R. M. and March, J. G., *A Behavioral Theory of the Firm*, Englewood Cliffs, N.J.: Prentice-Hall, 1963.

Dorfman, Robert, *Application of Linear Programming to the Theory of the Firm*, Berkeley: University of California Press, 1951.

Gordon, Myron J., *The Investment, Financing, and Valuation of the Corporation*, Homewood, Ill.: Richard D. Irwin, 1962.

Greenhut, Melvin L., "A General Theory of Maximum Profit," *Southern Economic Journal*, **28**, 278–285 (1962).

Hall, R. L. and Hitch, C. J., "Price Theory and Business Behavior," *Oxford Economic Papers*, **2** (1939).

Lester, Richard A., "Shortcomings of Marginal Analysis for Wage-Employment Problems," *American Economic Review*, **36** (March 1946).

Machlup, Fritz, "Marginal Analysis and Empirical Research," *American Economic Review*, **36** (September 1946).

Mason, E. S., ed., *The Corporation in Modern Society*, Cambridge, Mass.: Harvard University Press, 1960.

Modigliani, F., and Miller, M. H., "The Cost of Capital, Corporation Finance and the Theory of Investment," *American Economic Review*, June 1958.

Nelson, J. R., ed. *Marginal Cost Pricing in Practice*, Englewood Cliffs, N.J.: Prentice-Hall, 1964.

Papandreou, A. G., "Some Basic Problems in the Theory of the Firm," in B. F. Haley, ed., *Survey of Contemporary Economics*, 2, Homewood, Ill.: Richard D. Irwin, 1952.

Scitovsky, Tibor, "A Note on Profit Maximization and Its Implications," *Review of Economic Studies*, **11** (1943). Reprinted in *A.E.A. Readings in Price Theory*, Homewood, Ill.: Richard D. Irwin, 1952.

Shillinglaw, G., "Profit Analysis for Abandonment Decisions," *Journal of Business*, **30**, 17–19 (January 1957).

Simon, Herbert A., *Models of Man*, New York: John Wiley and Sons, 1957, Chap. 14.

Simon, Herbert A., "New Developments in the Theory of the Firm," *A.E.A. Papers and Proceedings*, **52**, 1–15 (1962).

Simon, Herbert A., "Theories of Decision Making in Economics," *American Economic Review*, **49** (June 1959).

Solomon, Ezra, "Measuring a Company's Cost of Capital," *Journal of Business* (October 1955). Also in *The Management of Corporate Capital*, Ezra Solomon, ed., Glencoe, Ill.: Free Press.

Weston, J. F., "The Profit Concept and Theory: A Restatement," *Journal of Political Economy*, **62**, 152–170 (April 1954).

Wiles, P. J., "Empirical Research and Marginal Analysis," *Economic Journal*, **60**, 513–530 (September 1950).

Williamson, O. E., "Managerial Discretion and Business Behavior," *American Economic Review*, **53**, 1032–1057 (December 1963).

Monopoly

Adams, Walter and Gray, H. H., *Monopoly in America: The Government as Promotor*, New York: Macmillan, 1955.

Bain, Joe S., "A Note on Pricing in Monopoly and Oligopoly," *American Economic Review*, **39**, 448–467 (1949).

Clemens, E. W., "Price Discrimination and the Multi-Product Firm," *Review of Economic Studies*, **19**, 1–11 (1951–1952).

Harberger, Arnold C., "Monopoly and Resource Allocation," *American Economic Review*, **44**, 2 (May 1954).

Hicks, J. R., "Annual Survey of Economic Theory: The Theory of Monopoly," *Econometrica*, **3**, 1–20 (1935). Reprinted in *A.E.A. Readings in Price Theory*, G. J. Stigler and K. E. Boulding, eds., Chap. 18, Homewood, Ill: Richard D. Irwin, 1952.

Hotelling, Harold, "Stability in Competition," *Economic Journal*, **39**, 41–57 (1929). Reprinted in *A.E.A. Readings in Price Theory*, Chicago, Ill.: Richard D. Irwin, 1952.

Kaysen, Carl, *United States v. United States Shoe Machinery Company*, Cambridge, Mass.: Harvard University Press, 1956.

Machlup, Fritz, *The Political Economy of Monopoly*, Baltimore, Md.: Johns Hopkins Press, 1952.

Marshall, Alfred, *Industry and Trade*, London: Macmillan, 1932, Bk. 3.

Mason, E. S., *Economic Concentration and the Monopoly Problem*, Cambridge: Harvard University Press, 1957.

Pfouts, Ralph W., "The Theory of Cost and Production in the Multi-Product Firm," *Econometrica*, **29**, 650–658 (1961).

Robinson, Joan, *The Economics of Imperfect Competition*, London: Macmillan, 1933.

Ruggles, Nancy, "Recent Developments in the Theory of Marginal Cost Pricing," *Review of Economic Studies*, **17**, 107–126 (1949–1950).

Ruggles, Nancy, "The Welfare Basis of Marginal Cost Pricing," *Review of Economic Studies*, **17**, 29–46. 1949–1950.

Schwartzman, D., "The Effect of Monopoly on Price," *Journal of Political Economy*, **67**, 352–362 (August 1959).

Simkin, C. G. F., "Some Aspects and Generalizations of the Theory of Discrimination," *Review of Economic Studies*, **15**, 1–13 (1948–1949).

Stigler, George J., "The Statistics of Monopoly and Merger," *Journal of Political Economy*, **14**, 33–40 (February 1956).

Weiss, Leonard W., *Case Studies in American Industry*, New York: John Wiley and Sons, 1967.

Weiss, Leonard W., *Economics and American Industry,* New York: John Wiley and Sons, 1961.

Wilcox, Clair, *Competition and Monopoly in American Industry,* Temporary National Economic Committee, Monograph No. 21, Washington, D.C.: U.S. Government Printing Office, 1940, 121–132.

Imperfect Markets: Monopolistic Competition, Duopoly, Oligopoly

Archibald, G. C., "Chamberlin versus Chicago," *Review of Economic Studies,* **29,** 2 (1961–1962).

Bain, J. S., *Barriers to New Competition,* Cambridge, Mass.: Harvard University Press, 1956.

Bain, J. S., *Industrial Organization,* New York: John Wiley and Sons, 1959.

Baumol, William J., *Business Behavior, Value and Growth,* New York: Macmillan, 1959, Chaps. 3–8.

Baumol, William J., "On the Theory of Oligopoly," *Economica,* **25,** 187–198 (August 1958).

Bertrand, Joseph, "Theories Mathematique de la Richesse Sociale," *Journal des Savants* (Paris), 499–508 (1883).

Bishop, Robert L., "Duopoly: Collusion or Warfare?," *American Economic Review,* **50,** No. 1, 933–961 (December 1960).

Braff, Allan J., and Miller, Roger F., "Wage-Price Policies Under Public Pressure," *Southern Economic Journal,* **28,** No. 2 (October 1961).

Brems, H., "Employment, Prices and Monopolistic Competition," *Review of Economics and Statistics,* **34,** 314–325 (November 1952).

Brems, H., *Product Equilibrium in Monopolistic Competition,* Cambridge, Mass.: Harvard University Press, 1951.

Bronfenbrenner, M., "Imperfect Competition on a Long-Run Basis," *Journal of Business,* **23,** 81–93 (April 1950).

Chamberlin, Edward H., *The Theory of Monopolistic Competition,* 7th ed., Cambridge, Mass.: Harvard University Press, 1956.

Chamberlin, Edward H., *Toward a More General Theory of Value,* New York: Oxford University Press, 1957.

Cournot, A. A., *Reseaches into the Mathematical Principles of the Theory of Wealth* (1838), English trans. by N. T. Bacon, New York: Macmillan, 1897.

Dorfman, Robert, and Steiner, P. O., "Optimal Advertising and Optimal Quality," *American Economic Review,* **44,** 826–836 (1954).

Edgeworth, F. Y., *Papers Relating to Political Economy,* London: Macmillan, 1925.

Efroymson, Clarence, W., "A Note on Kinked Demand Curves," *American Economic Review,* **33,** 98–109 (March 1943).

Fellner, William, *Competition Among the Few*, New York: Alfred A. Knopf, 1949.

Ferguson, C. E., "Static Models of Average-Cost Pricing," *Southern Economic Journal*, **23**, 272–284 (1957).

Ferguson, C. E., and Pfouts, Ralph W., "Learning and Expectations in Dynamic Duopoly Behavior," *Behavioral Science*, **7**, 223–237 (1962).

Frisch, Ragnar, "Monopoly-Polypoly—The Concept of Force in the Economy," *International Economic Papers*, No. 1, 23–36 (1951).

Hahn, F. H., "Excess Capacity and Imperfect Competition," *Oxford Economic Papers*, **7**, No. 3, 229–240 (October 1955).

Harrod, R. F., *Economic Essays*, New York: Harcourt, Brace and Company, 1952.

Harsanyi, John C., "Approaches to the Bargaining Problem," *Econometrica*, **24** (April 1956).

Hotelling, Harold, "Stability in Competition," *Economic Journal*, **39**, 41–57 (March 1929).

Hurvicz, L., "The Theory of Economic Behavior," reprinted in *A.E.A. Readings in Price Theory*. Chicago, Ill.: Richard D. Irwin, 1952.

Isard, Walter, *Location and Space Economy: A General Theory Relating to Industrial Location, Market Areas, Land Use, and Urban Structures*, New York: John Wiley and Sons, 1956.

Joint Economic Committee, *93 Lots of Bids Involving Identical Bids Reported to the Department of Justice by the Federal Procurement Agencies in the Years 1955–1960*, 87th Congress, 1st Session, Washington D.C.: Government Printing Office, August 1961.

Kaplan, A. D. H., Dirlam, Joel B., and Lanzillotti, Robert F., *Pricing in Big Business: A Case Approach*, Washington, D.C.: The Brookings Institute, 1958.

Luce, R. D., and Raiffa, Howard, *Games and Decisions*, New York: John Wiley and Sons, 1957.

Machlup, Fritz, *The Economics of Sellers' Competition*, Baltimore, Md.: The Johns Hopkins Press, 1952.

Modigliani, Franco, "New Developments on the Oligopoly Front," *Journal of Political Economy*, **66** (June 1958).

Neumann, John von, and Morgenstern, Oskar, *Theory of Games and Economic Behavior*, Princeton, N.J.: Princeton University Press, 1953.

Patinkin, D., "Multiple-Plant Firms, Cartels, and Imperfect Competition," *Quarterly Journal of Economics*, **66**, 173–205 (February 1947).

Robinson, Joan, *The Economics of Imperfect Competition*, London: Macmillan, 1933.

Rothchild, K. W., "Price Theory and Oligopoly," *Economic Journal*, **57**, 299–320 (1947).

Schelling, T. C., *The Strategy of Conflict*, Cambridge, Mass.: Harvard University Press, 1960

Schelling, T. C., "The Strategy of Conflict: Prospectus for a Reorientation of Game Theory," *Journal of Conflict Resolution*, **2**, 203–264 (September 1958).

Session on "The Theory of Monopolistic Competition After Thirty Years," *American Economic Review, Papers and Proceedings*, **54**, No. 3, 28–57 (May 1964). Papers by Joe S. Bain, Robert L. Bishop, and William J. Baumol; discussants: Jesse W. Markham and Peter O. Steiner.

Shubik, Martin, "A Comparison of Treatments of a Duopoly Problem," *Econometrica*, **23**, 417–431 (1955).

Shubik, Martin, *Strategy and Market Structure*, New York: John Wiley and Sons, 1959.

Smithies, Arthur, "Equilibrium in Monopolistic Competition," *Quarterly Journal of Economics*, **55** (1940).

Smithies, Arthur, "Optimum Location in Spatial Competition," *Journal of Political Economy*, **49**, 423–439 (June 1941).

Smithies, Arthur, and Savage, L. J., "A Dynamic Problem in a Duopoly," *Econometrica*, **8**, 130–143 (1940).

Stackelberg, Heinrich von, *The Theory of the Market Economy*, New York: Oxford University Press, 1952, 194–204.

Stigler, George J., *Five Lectures on Economic Problems*, London: Longmans, Green & Co., 1959.

Stigler, George J., "The Kinky Oligopoly Demand Curve and Rigid Prices," *Journal of Political Economy*, **55** (October 1947).

Suppes, Patrick, and Carlsmith, J. Merrill, "Experimental Analysis of a Duopoly Situation from the Standpoint of Mathematical Learning Theory," *International Economic Review*, **3**, 60–78 (1962).

Sweezy, Paul, "Demand Under Conditions of Oligopoly," *Journal of Political Economy*, **47** (August 1939).

Triffen, Robert, *Monopolistic Competition and General Equilibrium Theory*, Cambridge, Mass.: Harvard University Press, 1941.

Williams, J. D., *The Compleat Strategyst, Being a Primer on the Theory of Games of Strategy*, New York: McGraw-Hill, 1954.

Zeuthen, F., *Problems of Monopoly and Economic Warfare*, London: Routledge, 1930, 62.

Income Distribution and Factor Markets

Boulding, K. E., "The Concept of Economic Surplus," *American Economic Review*, **35**, 851–869 (December 1945).

Bowen, W. G., *The Wage-Price Issue*, Princeton, N.J.: Princeton University Press, 1960.

Bronfenbrenner, M., "Potential Monopsony in Labor Markets," *Industrial Labor Relations Review*, 9, 577–588 (July 1956).

Bronfenbrenner, M., and Hicks, J. R., "Notes on the Elasticity of Derived Demand," *Oxford Economic Papers*, (October 1961) 254–261.

Cartter, A. M., *Theory of Wages and Employment*, Homewood, Ill.: Richard D. Irwin, 1959.

Clark, John Bates, *The Distribution of Wealth*, New York: Macmillan, 1902.

Davis, R. M., "The Current State of Profit Theory," *American Economic Review*, 40, 245–264 (June 1952).

Douglas, Paul, *The Theory of Wages*, New York: Macmillan, 1934.

Friedman, M., "Choice, Chance, and the Personal Distribution of Income," *Journal of Political Economy*, 61, 277–290 (1953).

Friedman, M., "Some Comments on the Significance of Labor Unions," in D. M. Wright, ed., *The Impact of the Union*, New York: Harcourt, Brace, 1956.

Hall, R. T., and Hitch, C. J., "Price Theory and Business Behavior," *Oxford Economic Papers*, 2 (1939).

Hicks, J. R., *The Theory of Wages*, New York: Macmillan, 1932.

Kaldor, Nicholas, "Alternative Theories of Distribution," *Review of Economic Studies*, 23, 2 (1955–1956).

Keirstead, B. S., *An Essay in the Theory of Profits and Income Distribution*, London: Basil Blackwell, 1953.

Kendrick, J. W., and Sato, Ryuzo, "Factor Prices, Productivity, and Growth," *American Economic Review*, 53, 974–1003 (1963).

Knight, F. H., *Risk, Uncertainty and Profit*, Boston: Houghton Mifflin, 1921.

Lester, Richard A., "Shortcomings of Marginal Analysis for Wage-Employment Problems," *American Economic Review*, 36 (March 1946).

Levinson, H. M., *Unionism, Wage Trends, and Income Distribution, 1914–1947*, Ann Arbor: University of Michigan Press, 1951.

Lewis, H. Gregg, *Unionism and Relative Wages in the United States: An Empirical Inquiry*, Chicago: University of Chicago Press, 1963.

Machlup, Fritz, "Marginal Analysis and Empirical Research," *American Economic Review*, 36 (September 1946).

Malthus, T. R., *An Essay on Population*, Everyman Library, No. 692, London: J. M. Dent & Sons, 1914.

Marshall, A., *Principles of Economics*, 8th ed., London: Macmillan, 1964, Bks. 4 and 6.

Mills, J. S., *Principles of Political Economy* (*1848*), London. Longmans, Green & Co., 1929.

Mishan, E. J., "Rent as a Measure of Welfare Change," *American Economic Review*, **49**, 386–395 (June 1959).

Reder, M. W., "Alternative Theories of Labor's Share," in *The Allocation of Economic Resources*, Essays in Honor of B. F. Haley, Stanford, Calif.: Stanford University Press, 1959.

Rees, A., *The Economics of Trade Unions*, Chicago: University of Chicago Press, 1962.

Ross, A. M., *Trade Union Wage Policy*, Berkeley: University of California Press, 1948.

Schumpeter, J., *Theory of Economic Development*, Cambridge, Mass.: Harvard University Press, 1934.

Schultz, G. P., and Myers, C. A., "Union Wage Decisions and Employment," *American Economic Review*, **40**, 362–380 (June 1950).

Solow, R. M., "A Skeptical Note on the Constancy of Relative Shares," *American Economic Review*, **48**, 618–631 (September 1958).

Stigler, G. J., *Production and Distribution Theories*, New York: Macmillan, 1941.

Weston, J. F., "The Profit Concept and Theory: A Restatement," *Journal of Political Economy*, **44**, 152–170 ((April 1954).

Worcester, Dean A., "A Reconsideration of the Theory of Rent," *American Economic Review*, **36**, 258–277 (June 1946).

General Equilibrium

Arrow, Kenneth J., and Debreu, Gerard, "Existence of an Equilibrium for a Competitive Economy," *Econometrica*, **22**, 265–290 (July 1954).

Dorfman, R., Samuelson, P., and Solow, R., *Linear Programming and Economic Analysis*, New York: McGraw-Hill, 1958.

Henderson, James M., and Quandt, Richard E., *Microeconomic Theory*, New York: McGraw-Hill, 1958.

Hicks, J. R., Value and Capital, Oxford: Oxford University Press, 1938.

Kuenne, R. E., *The Theory of General Equilibrium*, Princeton, N.J.: Princeton University Press, 1963.

Lange, O., "The Foundations of Welfare Economics." *Econometrica*, 1942.

Leontief, W. W., *The Structure of American Economy, 1919–1939*, 2d. ed., New York: Oxford University Press, 1951.

Newman, Peter, *The Theory of Exchange*, Englewood Cliffs, N.J.: Prentice-Hall, 1964.

Patinkin, Don, *Money, Interest and Prices*, 2d. ed., New York: Harper and Row, 1965.

Phelps-Brown, E. H., *The Framework of the Pricing System*, London: Chapman and Hall, 1936.

Samuelson, P. A., *Foundations of Economic Analysis*, Cambridge, Mass.: Harvard University Press, 1948.

Walras, L., *Elements of Pure Economics*, trans. by W. Jaffé, Homewood, Ill.: Richard D. Irwin, 1954.

Welfare Economics

Arrow, Kenneth, J., *Social Choice and Individual Values*, Cowles Commission Monograph No. 12, New York: John Wiley and Sons, 1951.

Bailey, M. J., "The Interpretation and Application of the Compensation Principle," *Economic Journal*, **64**, 39–52 (March 1954).

Bator, Francis M., "The Anatomy of Market Failure," *Quarterly Journal of Economics*, **72**, 351–379 (1958).

Bator, Francis M., "The Simple Analytics of Welfare Maximization," *American Economic Review*, **47**, 22–59 (March 1957).

Baumol, W. J., *Economic Theory and Operations Analysis*, 2d ed., Englewood Cliffs, N.J.: Prentice-Hall, 1965, Chap. 16.

Baumol, W. J., "External Economics and Second-Order Conditions," *American Economic Review*, **54**, 358–372 (1964).

Baumol, W. J., *Welfare Economics and the Theory of the State*, London: Longmans, 1952.

Bergson, Abram, *Essays in Normative Economics*, Cambridge, Mass.: Harvard University Press, 1965.

Bergson, Abram, "On the Concept of Social Welfare," *Quarterly Journal of Economics*, **68**, 233–252 (May 1954).

Davis, Otto A., and Whinston, Andrew, "Externalities, Welfare, and the Theory of Games," *Journal of Political Economy*, **70**, 241–262 (1962).

Graff, J. de V., *Theoretical Welfare Economics*, London: Cambridge University Press, 1957.

Henderson, A., "Consumer's Surplus and the Compensating Variation," *Review of Economic Studies*, **8**, 117–121 (1940–1941).

Henderson, James M., and Quandt, Richard E., *Microeconomic Theory*, New York: McGraw-Hill, 1958, 201–223.

Hicks, J. R., "The Foundations of Welfare Economics," *Economic Journal*, **49**, 696–712 (1939).

Kaldor, Nicholas, "Welfare Propositions in Economics and Interpersonal Comparisons of Utility," *Economic Journal*, **49**, 549–552 (September 1939).

Kenen, Peter B., "On the Geometry of Welfare Economics," *Quarterly Journal of Economics*, **71**, 426–447 (1957).

Knight, Frank H., "Some Fallacies in the Interpretation of Social Cost," in *A.E.A. Readings in Price Theory*, George J. Stigler and Kenneth E. Boulding, eds., Homewood, Ill.: Richard D. Irwin, 1952, Chap. 8.

Lange, Oskar, and Taylor, Fred M., *On the Economic Theory of Socialism*, Minneapolis: University of Minnesota Press, 1938.

Lerner, Abba P., *The Economics of Control*, New York: Macmillan, 1946.

Little, I. M. D., *A Critique of Welfare Economics*, 2d ed., Oxford: Oxford University Press, 1957.

Lipsey, R. G., and Lancaster, R. K., "The General Theory of Second Best," *Review of Economic Studies*, **24**, No. 63 (December 1956).

McKenzie, Lionel, "Ideal Output and the Interdependence of Firms," *Economic Journal*, **61**, 785–803 (1951).

Mishan, E. J., "A Survey of Welfare Economics, 1939–1959," *Economic Journal*, **70**, 197–265 (June 1960).

Pfouts, R. W., "A Critique of Some Recent Contributions to the Theory of Consumers' Surplus," *Southern Economic Journal*, **19**, 315–333 (1953).

Pigou, A. C., *The Economics of Welfare*, 4th ed., London: Macmillan, 1932.

Reder, Melvin, *Studies in the Theory of Welfare Economics*, New York: Columbia University Press, 1947.

Rothenberg, J., "Conditions for a Social Welfare Function," *Journal of Political Economy*, **61**, 388–405 (October 1953).

Rothenberg, J., *Measurement of Social Welfare*, Englewood Cliffs, N.J.: Prentice-Hall, 1961.

Rothenberg, J., "Welfare Comparisons and Changes in Taste," *American Economic Review*, 885–890 (December 1953).

Ruggles, Nancy, "The Welfare Basis of the Marginal Cost Pricing Principle *Review of Economic Studies*, **17**, 29–46 (1949–1950).

Samuelson, Paul A., *Foundations of Economic Analysis*, Cambridge, Mass.: Harvard University Press, 1948.

Samuelson, Paul A., "Social Indifference Curves," *Quarterly Journal of Economics*, **70**, 1–22 (1956).

Scitovsky, Tibor, "A Note on Welfare Propositions in Economics," *Review of Economic Studies*, **9**, 77–88 (1941–1942).

Scitovsky, Tibor, "The State of Welfare Economics," *American Economic Review*, **41**, 303 (June 1951).

Scitovsky, Tibor, *Welfare and Competition*, Homewood, Ill.: Richard D. Irwin, 1951.

Tinbergen, Jan, "Welfare Economics and Income Distribution," *American Economic Review*, Papers and Proceedings, **47**, Part 2, 490–503 (May 1957).

Vickrey, William, "Some Objections to Marginal-Cost Pricing," *Journal of Political Economy*, **56**, 218–238 (1948).

Wilson, Thomas, "The Inadequacy of the Theory of the Firm as a Branch of Welfare Economics," *Oxford Economic Papers*, **4**, 18–44 (February 1952).

Index